HOME Sweet HABITAT

PARTNERS IN THE KITCHEN

 **Habitat for Humanity**

This cookbook is a collection of our favorite recipes,
which are not necessarily original recipes.

All Biblical quotations are from the New International
King James Version.

Published by Habitat for Humanity International

Copyright© Habitat for Humanity International
121 Habitat Street
Americus, Georgia USA 31709-3498

Edited, Designed and Manufactured in the
United States of America by:
Favorite Recipes® Press
P.O. Box 305142
Nashville, Tennessee 37230
1-800-358-0560

Library of Congress Number: 95-61545
ISBN: 1-887921-00-1

Manufactured in the United States of America
First Printing: 1995   100,000 copies

Cover Art by Sally Stockbridge
Photograph on Back Cover by Julie A. Lopez

Contents

Foreword, 4

Nutritional Profiles, 6

Candy, Cookies, & Bars, 7   Crowd Pleasers, 129

Cakes & Frostings, 33   Light Delights, 157

Pies, Cobblers, & Puddings, 73   No-Bake Goodies, 175

Cheesecakes & Tortes, 105   Holiday Treats, 193

Ice Cream, Frozen Desserts, & Mousses, 115   International Favorites, 219

Index, 233

Order Information, 239

Foreword

LINDA FULLER
CO-FOUNDER
HABITAT FOR HUMANITY
INTERNATIONAL

The first *Partners in the Kitchen, From Our House to Yours* cookbook, sold more than 100,000 copies, producing $500,000 for building Habitat for Humanity houses. Most of these cookbooks were sold through fund-raising efforts by local Habitat affiliates and chapters across the United States and Canada.

Building on this phenomenal success, and at the suggestion of many of our Habitat partners, we have decided to develop *Partners in the Kitchen* into a series. This newest cookbook, *Home Sweet Habitat*, features desserts. As we did with the first cookbook, we sent an appeal to Habitat for Humanity affiliates, campus chapters and special friends of this ministry to solicit dessert recipes. I want to express my appreciation to everyone who took the time to share their favorites.

Again, as with the first cookbook, it was interesting to receive the recipes. First Lady Hillary Rodham Clinton sent us her favorite cookie recipe. Angela Lansbury delighted us with her recipe for "Jessica's Cheesecake." Paul Newman and Bob Hope sent us more of their great favorites. The most fun was having Gary Redenbacher explain how to *safely* use a propane torch to brown the top of his and his wife Renae's "Crème Brûlée." You will find all of these and so many more within these pages.

From letters and comments, I have made an interesting discovery about cookbooks. I have learned they are often purchased by people who don't really spend much time in the kitchen. People tell me they find collecting and reading cookbooks satisfying and relaxing in itself. Cookbooks also make great gifts for all occasions. So now you can give this one in addition to the first one.

Future *Partners in the Kitchen* cookbooks will feature salads, casseroles, breads, etc. A number of people have suggested an international cookbook because of our work all over the world. We want to do this as soon as we resolve the problems associated with indigenous ingredients, measurements and wide varieties of cooking methods.

Out of a concern for health and diet restrictions, I specifically requested a special section in this cookbook on *low-calorie* and *low-fat* desserts. Personally, I often try reducing sugar one-third to one-half in a recipe. (In most cases, this will not negatively impact the end result.) Serving size also can be an important factor to those who monitor calorie, fat or sugar intake.

I want to express profound appreciation once again to Mary Cummings and Debbie Van Mol at Favorite Recipes® Press who worked so hard to produce this second great Habitat cookbook. Gratitude also goes to the artist, Sally Stockbridge, for creating another attractive cover. And, finally, my compliments and appreciation to those on staff at Habitat for Humanity International who worked so diligently on this book, especially start-up work by Allan Donaldson and continued work by Joy Highnote and Virginia Minter.

As with *From Our House to Yours*, proceeds from the sale of *Home Sweet Habitat* are used to further the work of Habitat for Humanity. Thank you for supporting the work of Habitat through your purchase. We hope this cookbook will prove to be a blessing to all who use it—and to all who are fortunate enough to sample its recipes!

ENJOY!

Linda Fuller

"We hope this cookbook will prove to be a blessing to all who use it—and to all who are fortunate enough to sample its recipes!"

Nutritional Profiles

The editors have attempted to present these family recipes in a form that shows approximate nutritional values. Persons with dietary or health problems or whose diets require close monitoring should not rely solely on the nutritional information provided. They should consult their physicians or a registered dietitian for specific information.

Abbreviations for Nutritional Profile

Cal — Calories	Fiber — Dietary Fiber	Sod — Sodium
Prot — Protein	T Fat — Total Fat	g — grams
Carbo — Carbohydrates	Chol — Cholesterol	mg — milligrams

Nutritional information for these recipes is computed from information derived from many sources, including materials supplied by the United States Department of Agriculture, computer databanks, and journals in which the information is assumed to be in the public domain. However, many specialty items, new products, and processed foods may not be available from these sources or may vary from the average values used in these profiles. More information on new and/or specific products may be obtained by reading the nutrient labels. Unless otherwise specified, the nutritional profile of these recipes is based on all measurements being level.

- **Artificial sweeteners** vary in use and strength so should be used "to taste," using the recipe ingredients as a guideline. Sweeteners using aspartame (NutraSweet and Equal) should not be used as a sweetener in recipes involving prolonged heating, which reduces the sweet taste. For further information on the use of these sweeteners, refer to package.
- **Alcoholic ingredients** have been analyzed for the basic ingredients, although cooking causes the evaporation of alcohol, thus decreasing caloric content.
- **Buttermilk, sour cream**, and **yogurt** are the types available commercially.
- **Cake mixes** which are prepared using package directions include 3 eggs and 1/2 cup oil.
- **Cottage cheese** is cream-style with 4.2% creaming mixture. Dry curd cottage cheese has no creaming mixture.
- **Eggs** are all large. To avoid raw eggs that may carry salmonella, as in eggnog, use an equivalent amount of commercial egg substitute.
- **Flour** is unsifted all-purpose flour.
- **Garnishes**, serving suggestions, and other optional additions and variations are not included in the profile.
- **Margarine** and **butter** are regular, not whipped or presoftened.
- **Milk** is whole milk, 3.5% butterfat. Lowfat milk is 1% butterfat. Evaporated milk is whole milk with 60% of the water removed.
- **Oil** is any type of vegetable cooking oil. **Shortening** is hydrogenated vegetable shortening.
- **Salt** and other ingredients to taste as noted in the ingredients have not been included in the nutritional profile.
- If a choice of ingredients has been given, the nutritional profile reflects the first option. If a choice of amounts has been given, the nutritional profile reflects the greater amount.

Photograph at right by HFHI

CANDY, COOKIES, & BARS

"Moreover there are workmen with you in abundance:
hewers and workers of stone and timber, and all types
of skillful men for every kind of work."

-1 Chronicles 22:15

Almond Roca

Yield: 32 servings

**1¹/₂ (7-ounce) Hershey bars
  with almonds, grated
2 cups butter**

2 cups sugar

Sprinkle ¹/₂ of the grated chocolate onto greased baking sheet. Melt butter in heavy saucepan over medium-high heat. Add sugar. Bring to a boil, stirring constantly. Cook to 250 to 268 degrees on a candy thermometer, hard-ball stage; mixture may separate and come back together during cooking. Pour sugar mixture over grated chocolate, spreading quickly. Sprinkle with remaining grated chocolate, spreading as chocolate melts. Let stand until cool. Break into bite-size pieces. May sprinkle slivered, sliced or whole almonds over grated chocolate before sugar mixture is added.

Approx Per Serving: Cal 199; Prot 1 g; Carbo 17 g; T Fat 15 g; 64% Calories from Fat; Chol 33 mg; Fiber 1 g; Sod 124 mg

Debra Hobson, HFH of Missoula, Stevensville, MT

Incredible Caramels

Yield: 36 servings

**2 cups butter
2 cups sugar
1³/₄ cups light corn syrup**

**1 cup half-and-half
1 cup whipping cream**

Coat sides and bottom of 9x9 or 7x11-inch metal pan with 1 to 2 tablespoons of the butter. Combine remaining butter, sugar, corn syrup and half-and-half in saucepan; mix well. Bring to a boil. Add whipping cream gradually, continuing to boil and stirring constantly. Cook for 45 minutes or to 244 to 245 degrees on candy thermometer, firm-ball stage. Spoon into prepared pan. Chill for 8 hours. Loosen around edges with knife; invert onto hard surface. Let stand until room temperature. Cut into squares; wrap individually. May add 1 cup pecan or walnut pieces at end of cooking time.

Photo by HFHI

Approx Per Serving: Cal 210; Prot <1 g; Carbo 24 g; T Fat 13 g; 56% Calories from Fat; Chol 39 mg; Fiber 0 g; Sod 129 mg

Jean Clappison, Polk HFH, Independence, OR

Chocolate Marshmallow Church Windows

Yield: 36 servings

1/2 cup margarine
2 cups semisweet chocolate
  chips
1 cup chopped pecans

1 (10-ounce) package colored
  miniature marshmallows
Shredded coconut to taste

Melt margarine and chocolate chips in saucepan over medium heat, stirring until smooth. Let stand to cool. Add pecans and marshmallows, mixing well. Shape into 2 logs. Sprinkle coconut over waxed paper. Roll logs in coconut. Wrap in foil. Freeze until firm. Cut into thin slices.

Approx Per Serving: Cal 115; Prot 1 g; Carbo 13 g; T Fat 8 g;
55% Calories from Fat; Chol 0 mg; Fiber 1 g; Sod 35 mg

Carolyn S. Bishop, HFH of Whitley County, Columbia City, IN

Fudge Delight

Yield: 18 servings

4 cups sugar
1 cup butter
1 (12-ounce) can evaporated
  milk
24 large marshmallows

1 tablespoon vanilla extract
13 ounces milk chocolate
12 ounces semisweet chocolate
2 ounces bittersweet chocolate

Combine sugar, butter and evaporated milk in saucepan. Bring to a boil over medium heat; reduce heat. Simmer, covered, for 5 minutes. Remove from heat. Add marshmallows and vanilla; mix well. Stir in chocolates. Spoon onto buttered baking sheet. Chill for 8 hours. Cut into squares. May add 1 cup chopped walnuts with chocolates.

Approx Per Serving: Cal 531; Prot 4 g; Carbo 80 g; T Fat 25 g;
40% Calories from Fat; Chol 38 mg; Fiber 2 g; Sod 148 mg

Marge Coneset, Uptown HFH, Chicago, IL

Lemon Fudge

Yield: 64 servings

2 (4-ounce) packages lemon
  pudding and pie filling mix
1/2 cup milk

1/2 cup butter or margarine
1 (1-pound) package
  confectioners' sugar

Bring pudding and pie filling mix, milk and butter to a boil in saucepan, stirring constantly. Remove from heat. Add confectioners' sugar, stirring until blended. Spoon into buttered 8x8-inch dish. Chill until firm. Cut into squares.

Approx Per Serving: Cal 54; Prot <1 g; Carbo 10 g; T Fat 2 g;
25% Calories from Fat; Chol 4 mg; Fiber 0 g; Sod 34 mg

Nellie C. Neuffer, Oregon Trail HFH, Hermiston, OR

Habitat for Humanity works in partnership with God and people everywhere to develop communities with God's people in need by building and renovating houses so that there are decent houses in decent communities in which people can live and grow into all that God intended.

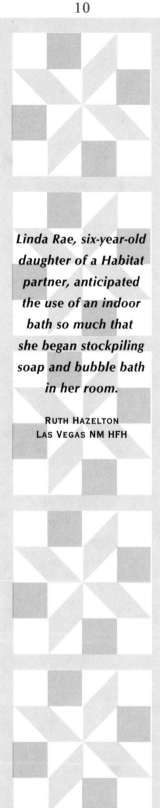

Smith College Fudge

Yield: 25 servings

1/4 cup butter
1 cup packed brown sugar
1 cup sugar
1/2 cup cream
1/4 cup dark corn syrup

2 (1-ounce) squares baking
   chocolate
1/2 teaspoon vanilla extract
1/2 cup chopped walnuts

Melt butter in saucepan over low heat. Add brown sugar, sugar, cream and corn syrup, mixing well. Increase the heat. Bring to a boil and boil for 2 1/2 minutes. Stir in chocolate. Cook to 234 to 240 degrees on candy thermometer, soft-ball stage. Beat until creamy. Add vanilla and walnuts, stirring until mixed. Spoon into greased 8x8-inch square dish. Let stand until cool. May substitute evaporated milk for cream.

Approx Per Serving: Cal 127; Prot 1 g; Carbo 19 g; T Fat 6 g; 42% Calories from Fat; Chol 12 mg; Fiber <1 g; Sod 29 mg

Ruth Hazelton, Las Vegas NM HFH, Las Vegas, NM

Microwave Peanut Brittle

Yield: 16 servings

1 cup sugar
1/2 cup light corn syrup
1 cup roasted salted peanuts

1 teaspoon butter
1 teaspoon vanilla extract
1 teaspoon baking soda

Combine sugar and corn syrup in microwave-safe 1 1/2-quart dish; mix well. Microwave on High for 4 minutes. Stir in peanuts. Microwave for 3 to 5 minutes or until light brown. Add butter and vanilla, stirring until blended. Microwave for 1 to 2 minutes longer or until hot. Add baking soda, stirring until light and foamy. Pour onto lightly greased baking sheet or ungreased nonstick baking sheet. Cool for 30 to 60 minutes. Break into pieces. Store in airtight container.

Approx Per Serving: Cal 132; Prot 2 g; Carbo 22 g; T Fat 5 g; 30% Calories from Fat; Chol 1 mg; Fiber 1 g; Sod 105 mg

Bill Cansfield, Tri-Cities Area HFH Inc., Grand Haven, MI

Amy Grant's Iced Pecan Halves

Yield: 4 servings

Amy Grant's mother Gloria has been making this since Amy was one month old. Every year Gloria and Burton would hand out this candy to their special friends and still continue this tradition.

1 cup pecan halves
1/2 cup sugar
2 tablespoons melted butter or margarine

1/2 teaspoon vanilla extract
3/4 teaspoon salt

Combine pecans, sugar and butter in heavy skillet. Cook over medium heat for 15 minutes or until pecans are crisp and sugar is golden brown, stirring constantly. Remove from heat. Stir in vanilla. Spread mixture on foil; sprinkle with salt. Let stand for 5 minutes; break into small clusters. Do not double recipe.

Approx Per Serving: Cal 328; Prot 2 g; Carbo 30 g; T Fat 24 g; 63% Calories from Fat; Chol 16 mg; Fiber 2 g; Sod 459 mg

Amy Grant, Nashville, TN

Best-Ever Pralines

Yield: 32 servings

2 cups sugar
1/2 teaspoon baking soda
2 cups milk, heated

1/8 teaspoon salt
2 cups pecan pieces
1 teaspoon vanilla extract

Combine sugar, baking soda, milk, salt, pecans and vanilla in saucepan; mix well. Cook to 234 to 240 degrees on candy thermometer, soft-ball stage. Remove from heat; place saucepan in larger pan filled with cold water. Beat just until beginning to set. Drop by tablespoonfuls onto waxed paper. Let stand until firm.

Approx Per Serving: Cal 107; Prot 1 g; Carbo 15 g; T Fat 6 g; 44% Calories from Fat; Chol 2 mg; Fiber <1 g; Sod 29 mg

Wilhelmina McNamara, Pensacola HFH, Pensacola, FL

When Millard came to our house, he had to stoop in order to avoid bumping his head. This brought tears to my eyes, because as I told the guests at dinner that evening, he reminded me so vividly of President Lincoln coming to free the slaves—but he was helping free people from poverty in housing.

WILHELMINA MCNAMARA
PENSACOLA HFH

Super Pralines

Yield: 30 servings

1 cup packed light brown sugar
1 cup sugar
1 cup evaporated milk

2 cups whole pecans
2 teaspoons vanilla extract
1/4 cup margarine

Combine brown sugar, sugar, evaporated milk and pecans in heavy 2-quart saucepan. Cook over medium-high heat for 20 to 25 minutes or to 234 to 240 degrees on candy thermometer, soft-ball stage. Remove from heat. Add vanilla and margarine, beating until cooled and thickened. Drop by tablespoonfuls onto waxed paper. Let stand until firm. Wrap individually in plastic wrap. Store in airtight container.

Approx Per Serving: Cal 121; Prot 1 g; Carbo 15 g; T Fat 7 g; 50% Calories from Fat; Chol 2 mg; Fiber <1 g; Sod 29 mg

Dani McAneny, Warren County HFH, Vicksburg, MS

Apple Cookies

Yield: 36 servings

2 cups sifted flour
1/2 teaspoon salt
1 teaspoon baking soda
1 teaspoon each ground
cinnamon and cloves
1/2 teaspoon ground nutmeg
1/2 cup butter, softened
1 1/3 cups packed brown sugar
1 egg

2 to 4 tablespoons milk
1 cup chopped walnuts
1 cup chopped unpeeled apple
2 1/2 tablespoons boiling water
1 teaspoon butter
1/2 teaspoon vanilla extract
1 1/2 cups sifted confectioners'
sugar

Sift flour, salt, baking soda and spices into bowl. Cream 1/2 cup butter, brown sugar and egg in mixer bowl; stir into dry ingredients. Add milk, mixing until mixture is of the consistency of cookie dough. Stir in walnuts and apple. Drop by teaspoonfuls onto greased cookie sheet. Bake at 375 degrees for 10 minutes. Remove to wire rack to cool. Combine boiling water, 1 teaspoon butter and vanilla in mixer bowl; mix well. Add confectioners' sugar. Beat for 2 to 3 minutes or until of spreading consistency. Spread over cookies.

Approx Per Serving: Cal 115; Prot 1 g; Carbo 17 g; T Fat 5 g; 38% Calories from Fat; Chol 13 mg; Fiber <1 g; Sod 85 mg

Ed Reid, Dane County HFH, Madison, WI

A group of us were sanding pasted joints. When lunch time came, we did not have facilities to wash up. So we clapped our hands and dug in. The plaster dust didn't show on the white icing and didn't stop the apple cookies from being delicious.

ED REID
DANE COUNTY HFH

Black Hearts (Spice Cookies)

Yield: 24 servings

1 cup butter, softened
1 cup sugar
1 egg
2 cups flour
2 tablespoons baking cocoa

1 teaspoon ground cloves
1¹/₂ teaspoons cinnamon
1 cup finely ground pecans
1 teaspoon vanilla extract

Cream butter and sugar in mixer bowl. Add egg, beating until blended. Add mixture of flour, baking cocoa, cloves and cinnamon; mix well. Stir in pecans and vanilla. Chill for up to 8 hours or until dough is firm enough to roll. Roll ¹/₈ inch thick on lightly floured surface. Cut with heart-shaped cookie cutter. Place on ungreased cookie sheet. Bake at 375 degrees for 5 to 7 minutes or until light brown. May chill or freeze dough until ready to bake.

Approx Per Serving: Cal 169; Prot 2 g; Carbo 17 g; T Fat 11 g; 56% Calories from Fat; Chol 30 mg; Fiber 1 g; Sod 81 mg

Kathy Watkins, Warren County HFH, Front Royal, VA

Different Brownie Cookies

Yield: 120 servings

2 (22-ounce) packages fudge
  brownie mix
1 (2-layer) package lemon
  supreme cake mix

³/₄ cup egg substitute
³/₄ cup vegetable oil
1 cup water
1¹/₂ cups chopped walnuts

Combine brownie and cake mixes in bowl; mix well. Combine egg substitute, oil and water in bowl, stirring until blended. Pour over cake mix, stirring until smooth. May make stiffer dough by adding 2 to 3 tablespoons flour. Stir in walnuts. Drop by rounded teaspoonfuls 2 inches apart on buttered cookie sheet. Bake at 350 degrees for 10 to 12 minutes or until cookies test done. Remove to wire rack to cool. Store completely cooled cookies in covered container.

Approx Per Serving: Cal 74; Prot 1 g; Carbo 10 g; T Fat 3 g; 41% Calories from Fat; Chol <1 mg; Fiber <1 g; Sod 65 mg

Elizabeth L. Dunford, Southwest Volusia HFH, Orange City, FL

Halfway through our work camp in Lake County Michigan, we were out of money and couldn't complete our work. Should we pack up and go home? As we discussed what to do, in walked the pastor from our home church. "I've brought some monetary gifts from our congregation," he said. Miracles happen!

BILL CANSFIELD
TRI-CITIES AREA HFH INC.

Caramel Cookies

Yield: 24 servings

1 (14-ounce) package light caramels
2/3 cup evaporated milk
1 (2-layer) package German chocolate cake mix

1 cup chopped walnuts
3/4 cup melted margarine
1 cup chocolate chips

Combine caramels and 1/3 cup of the evaporated milk in double boiler. Cook over hot water until smooth, stirring constantly. Combine cake mix, walnuts, margarine and remaining evaporated milk in bowl, stirring until batter forms a ball. Press 1/2 of the dough into greased 9x13-inch baking pan. Bake at 350 degrees for 6 minutes. Sprinkle with chocolate chips; drizzle with caramel mixture. Crumble remaining dough over prepared layers. Bake for 15 to 18 minutes longer or until edges pull from sides of pan. Let stand until cool. Cut into squares.

Approx Per Serving: Cal 279; Prot 3 g; Carbo 36 g; T Fat 15 g; 46% Calories from Fat; Chol 3 mg; Fiber 1 g; Sod 316 mg

Mona Bauer, Oconee County HFH, Salem, SC

Chocolate Chip Cookies

Yield: 15 servings

1/2 cup margarine, softened
1 egg
1/2 teaspoon vanilla extract
1/2 cup sugar
1/4 cup packed brown sugar

1 1/4 cups flour
1/2 teaspoon baking soda
1/2 teaspoon salt
1/2 cup chocolate chips

Combine margarine, egg and vanilla in mixer bowl; mix well. Add sugar and brown sugar, beating until blended. Add sifted mixture of flour, baking soda and salt gradually; mix well. Stir in chocolate chips. Drop by teaspoonfuls onto greased cookie sheet. Bake at 400 degrees for 8 to 10 minutes or until light brown. Remove to wire rack to cool.

Approx Per Serving: Cal 161; Prot 2 g; Carbo 21 g; T Fat 8 g; 44% Calories from Fat; Chol 14 mg; Fiber 1 g; Sod 176 mg

JoAnn Hayward, Burlington County HFH, Mt. Holly, NJ

Love the Lord your God with all your heart and with all your soul, and with all your mind. This is the first and greatest commandment. And the second is like it: Love your neighbor as yourself. All the Law and the Prophets hang on these two commandments.

MATTHEW 22:36–40

Hillary Clinton's Chocolate Chip Cookies

Yield: 18 servings

1¹/₂ cups flour
1 teaspoon salt
1 teaspoon baking soda
1 cup shortening
1 cup packed light brown sugar
¹/₂ cup sugar

1 teaspoon vanilla extract
2 eggs
2 cups rolled oats
2 cups semisweet
  chocolate chips

Photo by Kimberly Prenda

HILLARY RODHAM CLINTON

Combine flour, salt and baking soda in bowl. Cream shortening, brown sugar, sugar and vanilla in mixer bowl. Add eggs, beating until light and fluffy. Beat in flour mixture and oats gradually. Stir in chocolate chips. Drop by rounded teaspoonfuls onto greased cookie sheets. Bake at 350 degrees for 8 to 10 minutes or until golden brown. Cool on cookie sheets on wire rack for 2 minutes. Remove cookies to wire rack to cool completely.

Approx Per Serving: Cal 331; Prot 4 g; Carbo 41 g; T Fat 18 g; 47% Calories from Fat; Chol 24 mg; Fiber 2 g; Sod 178 mg

Hillary Rodham Clinton, The White House, Washington, DC

Take-a-Break Chocolate Chip Cookies

Yield: 48 servings

These cookies are just right for mid-morning breaks at your favorite Habitat work site, providing lots of quick energy renewal. They are especially popular with block layers and building framers and less so with painters. Drywall mudders should not eat them until their hands are clean.

³/₄ cup packed brown sugar
¹/₂ cup sugar
¹/₂ cup butter or margarine,
  softened
¹/₂ cup shortening
1¹/₂ teaspoons vanilla extract

1 egg
1³/₄ cups flour
1 teaspoon baking soda
¹/₂ teaspoon salt
³/₄ cup chocolate chips, or to
  taste

Combine brown sugar, sugar, butter, shortening, vanilla and egg in mixer bowl; mix well. Add flour, baking soda and salt, beating until blended. Stir in chocolate chips. Drop by rounded teaspoonfuls onto greased cookie sheet. Bake at 375 degrees for 10 to 12 minutes or until light to medium brown. May freeze for future use.

Approx Per Serving: Cal 85; Prot 1 g; Carbo 10 g; T Fat 5 g; 51% Calories from Fat; Chol 10 mg; Fiber <1 g; Sod 62 mg

J. William Gavett, Flower City HFH, Pittsford, NY

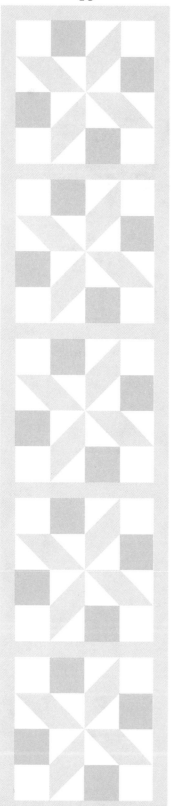

Cocoa Cheese Sandwich Cookies

Yield: 30 servings

2 cups flour
1/2 teaspoon salt
3/4 cup sugar
1/3 cup baking cocoa
3/4 cup butter or margarine, softened
1 egg
1 teaspoon vanilla extract

30 pecan halves
1 tablespoon cream
3 tablespoons butter or margarine, softened
3 ounces cream cheese, softened
2 cups confectioners' sugar
1/4 teaspoon salt

Combine flour, 1/2 teaspoon salt, sugar, baking cocoa, 3/4 cup butter, egg and vanilla in mixer bowl. Beat at low speed until blended, scraping bowl occasionally. Divide dough into 2 portions. Shape each portion into a log. Wrap in waxed paper. Chill for 2 hours or longer. Cut into 1/8-inch thick slices. Place on ungreased cookie sheet. Top half the slices with pecan halves. Bake at 350 degrees for 8 to 10 minutes or until cookies test done. Beat cream, 3 tablespoons butter, cream cheese, confectioners' sugar and 1/4 teaspoon salt in mixer bowl until of spreading consistency. Spread plain cookies with cream cheese mixture. Top with pecan-topped cookies.

Approx Per Serving: Cal 160; Prot 2 g; Carbo 20 g; T Fat 9 g; 47% Calories from Fat; Chol 26 mg; Fiber 1 g; Sod 123 mg

Richard James, Cumberland County HFH, Burkesville, KY

Coconut Chocolate Chip Tea Cakes

Yield: 48 servings

1 cup unsalted butter
1/2 cup confectioners' sugar
1 teaspoon vanilla extract
2 1/4 cups sifted flour
1/4 teaspoon salt

1 cup shredded coconut
1 cup semisweet chocolate chips
1 cup shredded coconut
Confectioners' sugar to taste

Cream butter in mixer bowl until light. Add confectioners' sugar; beat until light and fluffy. Add vanilla, flour, salt and 1 cup coconut, beating well after each addition. Stir in chocolate chips. Shape into balls; roll in 1 cup coconut. Place 1 inch apart on ungreased baking sheet. Bake at 350 degrees for 8 to 10 minutes or until edges turn golden brown. Dust warm cookies with confectioners' sugar. Remove to wire rack to cool.

Approx Per Serving: Cal 95; Prot 1 g; Carbo 10 g; T Fat 6 g; 58% Calories from Fat; Chol 10 mg; Fiber 1 g; Sod 22 mg

Raeann Spencer, Central Oklahoma HFH, Oklahoma City, OK

Cookie-Jar Specials

Yield: 48 servings

3 egg whites
1/2 teaspoon salt
1 1/2 cups sugar

1/2 teaspoon vanilla extract
1 1/2 cups shredded coconut
3 cups cornflakes

Combine egg whites and salt in mixer bowl; beat until stiff, but not dry. Add sugar gradually, beating after each addition until stiff peaks form. Beat in vanilla. Fold in coconut and cornflakes. Drop by teaspoonfuls onto greased cookie sheet. Bake at 325 degrees for 20 to 25 minutes or until light brown. Remove to wire rack immediately.

Approx Per Serving: Cal 46; Prot <1 g; Carbo 9 g; T Fat 1 g; 20% Calories from Fat; Chol 0 mg; Fiber <1 g; Sod 49 mg

Linda Richards, Southwest Iowa HFH, Shenandoah, IA

Cowboy Cookies

Yield: 60 servings

1 cup sugar
1 cup packed brown sugar
1 cup margarine or butter, softened
2 eggs
1 teaspoon vanilla extract

2 cups flour
1 1/2 teaspoons baking soda
1 teaspoon baking powder
1/2 teaspoon salt
2 cups rolled oats
1 cup semisweet chocolate chips

Cream sugar, brown sugar and margarine in mixer bowl until light and fluffy. Beat in eggs and vanilla. Add sifted mixture of flour, baking soda, baking powder and salt; mix well. Add oats and chocolate chips, mixing well after each addition. Drop by teaspoonfuls onto greased cookie sheet. Bake at 350 degrees for 10 to 15 minutes or until light brown. Remove to wire rack to cool.

Approx Per Serving: Cal 93; Prot 1 g; Carbo 13 g; T Fat 4 g; 40% Calories from Fat; Chol 7 mg; Fiber 1 g; Sod 83 mg

Cheryl Jackson Baker, Blount County HFH, Maryville, TN

Cream Cheese Cookies

Yield: 48 servings

1 cup butter, softened
1/2 cup sugar
3 ounces cream cheese, softened

1 1/2 cups flour
1/8 teaspoon salt
1 teaspoon vanilla extract
1/3 cup finely chopped walnuts

Cream butter, sugar and cream cheese in mixer bowl until light and fluffy. Stir in flour, salt, vanilla and walnuts. Shape into 1-inch balls. Place on ungreased cookie sheet; flatten with fork. Bake at 350 degrees for 10 to 15 minutes or until light brown. Remove to wire rack to cool.

Approx Per Serving: Cal 68; Prot 1 g; Carbo 5 g; T Fat 5 g; 65% Calories from Fat; Chol 12 mg; Fiber <1 g; Sod 50 mg

Patricia Lemieux, Pinellas HFH, St. Petersburg, FL

I am part of the family selection committee and have cherished seeing the faces of the families when we tell them they are selected.

LINDA RICHARDS
SOUTHWEST IOWA HFH

Gobs

Yield: 30 servings

These chocolate sandwich cookies are a popular tradition in my home-town of Johnstown, Pennsylvania. They are great to take to picnics and bake sales.

1 cup shortening	**3 cups flour**
2 eggs	**1 cup milk**
2 cups sugar	**1/4 cup flour**
1 cup sour milk	**1/2 cup shortening**
1/2 cup water	**1/2 cup butter or margarine,**
1 cup baking cocoa	**softened**
2 teaspoons baking soda	**1 cup sugar**
2 teaspoons vanilla extract	

Combine 1 cup shortening, eggs and 2 cups sugar in mixer bowl; beat until light and fluffy. Add sour milk, water, baking cocoa, baking soda, vanilla and 3 cups flour, mixing well. Drop by rounded teaspoonfuls onto lightly greased cookie sheet, allowing space for cookies to spread. Bake at 400 degrees for 10 minutes. Remove to wire rack to cool. Combine milk and 1/4 cup flour in saucepan. Bring to a boil, stirring until mixture pulls from side of pan. Let stand until cool. Combine 1/2 cup shortening, 1/2 cup butter and 1 cup sugar in bowl; beat until light and fluffy. Stir into flour mixture, beating until smooth. Spread half the cookies with sugar mixture; top with remaining cookies. Wrap individually in waxed paper. May combine 1 tablespoon vinegar with enough milk to measure 1 cup, let stand for 5 minutes and use as a substitute for sour milk.

Approx Per Serving: Cal 266; Prot 3 g; Carbo 33 g; T Fat 15 g; 48% Calories from Fat; Chol 25 mg; Fiber 1g; Sod 99 mg

Sally Matts, HFH/St. Joseph County IN, South Bend, IN

Granola Cereal Cookies

Yield: 36 servings

1/2 cup shortening	**1 1/4 cups flour**
1 cup packed brown sugar	**1/2 teaspoon baking soda**
1 egg	**1/4 teaspoon salt**
1 teaspoon vanilla extract	**2 cups granola cereal**
3 tablespoons milk	

Combine shortening, brown sugar, egg, vanilla and milk in mixer bowl. Add flour, baking soda and salt. Stir in granola; mix well. Drop by teaspoonfuls onto greased cookie sheet. Bake at 350 degrees for 10 to 12 minutes or until light brown. Remove to wire rack to cool.

Approx Per Serving: Cal 91; Prot 1 g; Carbo 13 g; T Fat 4 g; 40% Calories from Fat; Chol 6 mg; Fiber 1 g; Sod 44 mg

Lin Logan, Pinellas HFH, St. Petersburg, FL

Guess-Again Cookies

Yield: 40 servings

1 cup margarine, softened
1/2 cup sugar
1 teaspoon vanilla extract
1/2 cup crushed potato chips
1/2 cup chopped pecans
2 cups flour

Cream margarine, sugar and vanilla in mixer bowl until light and fluffy. Stir in potato chips, pecans and flour. Drop by teaspoonfuls 2 inches apart onto ungreased cookie sheet. Flatten with glass greased and dipped in additional sugar. Bake at 350 degrees for 10 minutes. Remove to wire rack to cool.

Approx Per Serving: Cal 87; Prot 1 g; Carbo 8 g; T Fat 6 g; 60% Calories from Fat; Chol 0 mg; Fiber <1 g; Sod 58 mg

Teresa Cook, HFH of Venice FL, Venice, FL

Lemon Cookies

Yield: 30 servings

2 tablespoons fresh lemon juice
1 egg
1 (2-layer) package lemon cake mix
4 1/2 ounces whipped topping
1 cup confectioners' sugar

Combine lemon juice and egg in mixer bowl; blend well. Stir in cake mix and whipped topping; beat until smooth and creamy. Chill for 8 hours. Shape with flour-coated hands into balls; roll in confectioners' sugar. Bake at 325 degrees for 8 minutes or until cookies are light brown. Remove to wire rack to cool.

Approx Per Serving: Cal 103; Prot 1 g; Carbo 19 g; T Fat 3 g; 24% Calories from Fat; Chol 7 mg; Fiber <1 g; Sod 110 mg

Louella Thut, Wayne County Wooster HFH, Orrville, OH

Photo by Tally Lancaster

Oatmeal Cookies

Yield: 36 servings

3/4 cup shortening
1 cup packed brown sugar
1/2 cup sugar
1 egg
1/4 cup water
1 teaspoon vanilla extract

1 cup flour
1/2 teaspoon salt
1/2 teaspoon baking soda
3 cups rolled oats
1 cup shredded coconut

Cream shortening, brown sugar and sugar in mixer bowl until light and fluffy. Add egg, water and vanilla; mix well. Stir mixture of flour, salt and baking soda into creamed mixture. Add oats and coconut; mix well. Drop by teaspoonfuls onto greased cookie sheet. Bake at 350 degrees for 12 to 15 minutes or until light brown. Remove to wire rack to cool.

Approx Per Serving: Cal 118; Prot 2 g; Carbo 16 g; T Fat 6 g; 42% Calories from Fat; Chol 6 mg; Fiber 1 g; Sod 46 mg

Arthur Woodward, Flower City HFH/Rochester, Rochester, NY

Snickerdoodles

Yield: 60 servings

1 cup shortening
1 1/2 cups sugar
2 eggs
2 2/3 cups sifted flour
2 teaspoons cream of tartar

1 teaspoon baking soda
1/4 teaspoon salt
3 tablespoons sugar
3 tablespoons cinnamon

Cream shortening, 1 1/2 cups sugar and eggs in mixer bowl until light and fluffy. Stir in sifted mixture of flour, cream of tartar, baking soda and salt. Shape into 1-inch balls. Roll in mixture of 3 tablespoons sugar and cinnamon. Place 2 inches apart on ungreased cookie sheet. Bake at 400 degrees for 8 to 10 minutes or until light brown. Remove to wire rack to cool.

Approx Per Serving: Cal 74; Prot 1 g; Carbo 10 g; T Fat 4 g; 44% Calories from Fat; Chol 7 mg; Fiber <1 g; Sod 25 mg

Betty S. Snyder, Milledgeville/Baldwin County HFH, Milledgeville, GA

Sugar Cookies

Yield: 60 servings

1 cup shortening
1¹/₂ cups sugar
3 eggs
¹/₂ teaspoon salt

1 teaspoon vanilla extract
1 teaspoon baking soda
4¹/₂ cups flour

Cream shortening and sugar in mixer bowl until light and fluffy. Add eggs 1 at a time, beating well after each addition. Stir in salt and vanilla. Add mixture of baking soda and ¹/₂ cup of the flour; mix well. Stir in remaining flour until blended. Roll on lightly floured surface; cut with cookie cutter. Bake at 350 degrees for 8 to 10 minutes or until light brown. Remove to wire rack to cool. Frost or decorate as desired.

Approx Per Serving: Cal 87; Prot 1 g; Carbo 12 g; T Fat 4 g; 39% Calories from Fat; Chol 11 mg; Fiber <1 g; Sod 35 mg

Joyce Boeck, Southwest Iowa HFH, Shenandoah, IA

Texas Crunch Cookies

Yield: 60 servings

1 cup sugar
1 cup confectioners' sugar
1 cup margarine or butter,
   softened
1 cup vegetable oil
2 eggs
1 teaspoon almond extract
3¹/₂ cups all-purpose flour

1 cup whole wheat flour
1 teaspoon baking soda
1 teaspoon salt
1 teaspoon cream of tartar
2 cups chopped almonds
1 cup almond brickle chips
2 cups sugar

Combine sugar, confectioners' sugar, margarine and oil in mixer bowl. Beat until smooth. Add eggs and almond flavoring; mix well. Add all-purpose flour, whole wheat flour, baking soda, salt and cream of tartar gradually, mixing well after each addition. Stir in almonds and almond brickle chips. Shape into balls; roll in 2 cups sugar. Place on ungreased cookie sheet. Flatten with fork dipped in sugar, making crisscross pattern. Bake at 350 degrees for 10 to 12 minutes or until light brown. Remove to wire rack to cool. May substitute pecans for almonds.

Approx Per Serving: Cal 189; Prot 2 g; Carbo 22 g; T Fat 11 g; 49% Calories from Fat; Chol 8 mg; Fiber 1 g; Sod 111 mg

Marlene Tobias, Black Hills Area HFH, Rapid City, SD

It's impossible to stop the enthusiasm, the sense of civic responsibility and duty, and even religious zeal that comes with the Habitat workers. The truth is they touch lives in profound ways far beyond the bricks and mortar associated with building the houses.

**HENRY CISNEROS
U.S. SECRETARY OF HOUSING
AND URBAN DEVELOPMENT**

Brownies
Yield: 36 servings

4 ounces unsweetened
  chocolate
1 cup butter or margarine,
  softened
2 cups sugar
4 eggs

1/2 teaspoon salt
1 teaspoon vanilla extract
1 cup flour
1 cup chopped walnuts
1 cup chocolate chips

Melt chocolate with butter in saucepan over low heat, stirring until smooth. Combine with sugar in mixer bowl, mixing well. Add eggs 1 at a time, beating well after each addition. Beat in salt, vanilla and flour. Stir in walnuts and chocolate chips. Spoon into greased 9x13-inch baking pan. Bake at 325 degrees for 30 to 35 minutes or until brownies test done. Let stand until cool. Cut into squares. May substitute pecans for walnuts.

Approx Per Serving: Cal 169; Prot 2 g; Carbo 18 g; T Fat 11 g; 55% Calories from Fat; Chol 37 mg; Fiber 1 g; Sod 90 mg

Mary K. Sasser, Tryon, NC

Butterscotch Brownies
Yield: 18 servings

1/2 cup margarine
2 cups packed light brown sugar
2 eggs
1 1/2 cups flour

2 teaspoons baking powder
1 teaspoon salt
1 teaspoon vanilla extract

Melt margarine in saucepan over low heat. Stir in brown sugar. Let stand until cool. Stir in eggs, flour, baking powder, salt and vanilla. Spoon into greased 9x9-inch baking pan. Bake at 350 degrees for 30 minutes. Let stand until cool. Cut into squares.

Approx Per Serving: Cal 168; Prot 2 g; Carbo 28 g; T Fat 6 g; 30% Calories from Fat; Chol 24 mg; Fiber <1 g; Sod 230 mg

Catherine N. Lohmann, Androscoggin County HFH, Auburn, ME

Favorite Brownies

Yield: 20 servings

4 eggs
2 cups sugar
^{2}/$_3$ cup vegetable oil
4 (1-ounce) squares
    unsweetened chocolate,
    melted

2 teaspoons vanilla extract
1^1/$_3$ cups flour
1 teaspoon baking powder
^{1}/$_2$ teaspoon salt
1 cup chopped walnuts

Beat eggs in mixer bowl until frothy. Add sugar gradually, beating after each addition until blended. Stir in oil, chocolate and vanilla. Add mixture of flour, baking powder and salt, stirring until blended. Mix in walnuts. Spread batter in buttered 9x13-inch baking pan. Bake at 350 degrees for 25 to 30 minutes or until brownies test done. Let stand until cool. Cut into 2-inch squares.

Approx Per Serving: Cal 255; Prot 4 g; Carbo 29 g; T Fat 15 g; 51% Calories from Fat; Chol 42 mg; Fiber 1 g; Sod 84 mg

Margaret L. Porter, Somerset County HFH, Markleton, PA

Frosted Brownies

Yield: 36 servings

^{1}/$_4$ cup baking cocoa
^{1}/$_2$ cup butter or margarine
4 eggs
^{1}/$_4$ teaspoon salt
2 cups sugar, sifted
1 teaspoon vanilla extract
1 cup flour

1 cup walnuts
4 ounces cream cheese,
    softened
1 teaspoon (rounded) margarine
1 cup confectioners' sugar
^{1}/$_4$ cup baking cocoa

Combine ^{1}/$_4$ cup baking cocoa and butter in saucepan. Cook until butter melts, stirring constantly. Let stand until cool. Beat eggs and salt in mixer bowl until frothy. Add sugar gradually, beating until light and creamy. Fold in cocoa mixture. Add vanilla and flour, beating until smooth. Stir in walnuts. Spoon into greased 9x13-inch baking pan. Bake at 325 degrees for 30 minutes. Remove from oven. Let stand until cool. Beat cream cheese, margarine, confectioners' sugar and ^{1}/$_4$ cup baking cocoa in mixer bowl until of spreading consistency. Spread over brownies. Cut into squares. May substitute pecans for walnuts.

Approx Per Serving: Cal 136; Prot 2 g; Carbo 18 g; T Fat 7 g; 42% Calories from Fat; Chol 34 mg; Fiber 1 g; Sod 59 mg

June Boyd, HFH of Marion Ohio, Marion, OH

Old-Fashioned Brownies   *Yield: 12 servings*

1 cup sugar
2 eggs
1/3 cup butter, softened
2 (1-ounce) squares
  unsweetened chocolate,
  melted

2/3 cup flour
1/2 teaspoon baking powder
1/4 teaspoon salt

Combine sugar, eggs, butter and chocolate in mixer bowl; beat until creamy. Add flour, baking powder and salt; mix well. Spoon into greased 8x8-inch baking pan. Bake at 350 degrees for 30 to 35 minutes or until brownies test done. May substitute liquid chocolate for chocolate squares. May add 1/2 cup chopped nuts to batter.

Approx Per Serving: Cal 172; Prot 2 g; Carbo 23 g; T Fat 9 g; 43% Calories from Fat; Chol 49 mg; Fiber 1 g; Sod 122 mg

Janet Faggioli, Norristown HFH, Wallingford, PA

Simply Delicious Brownies   *Yield: 12 servings*

2 (1-ounce) squares
  unsweetened chocolate
1/2 cup butter
1 cup sugar
2 eggs, beaten

1/2 teaspoon vanilla extract
1/4 cup flour
1/4 teaspoon salt
1 cup coarsely chopped walnuts

Combine chocolate and butter in microwave-safe bowl. Microwave for 1 minute or until smooth; mix well. Stir in sugar. Add eggs and vanilla, mixing well. Stir in flour, salt and walnuts. Spoon into buttered 8x8-inch baking pan. Bake at 325 degrees for 40 to 45 minutes or until brownies test done. Do not overcook; brownies should be soft. Cut into 12 squares while warm.

Approx Per Serving: Cal 243; Prot 3 g; Carbo 22 g; T Fat 17 g; 61% Calories from Fat; Chol 56 mg; Fiber 1 g; Sod 135 mg

Pearl Greenbank, West Plains Area HFH, Mountain View, MO

Cheesecake Bars

Yield: 28 servings

1/2 cup margarine, softened
1 egg
1 (2-layer) package yellow cake
  mix
8 ounces cream cheese,
  softened

2 eggs
1 (1-pound) package
  confectioners' sugar

Combine margarine, 1 egg and cake mix in mixer bowl; mix well. Pat into greased 10x13-inch baking pan. Beat cream cheese in mixer bowl until smooth. Beat in 2 eggs until blended. Add confectioners' sugar, mixing well. Spoon over mixture in prepared pan. Bake at 350 degrees for 45 minutes or until golden brown. Let stand until cool. Cut into bars.

Approx Per Serving: Cal 207; Prot 2 g; Carbo 31 g; T Fat 9 g; 38% Calories from Fat; Chol 32 mg; Fiber <1 g; Sod 189 mg

Donna Heffner, Appalachia HFH, Knoxville, TN

Chocolate Cherry Bars

Yield: 36 servings

1 (2-layer) package devil's food
  cake mix
1 (21-ounce) can cherry pie
  filling
1 teaspoon almond extract

2 eggs, beaten
1 cup sugar
1/3 cup milk
5 tablespoons margarine
1 cup chocolate chips

Combine cake mix, pie filling, almond extract and eggs in bowl; mix well. Spoon into greased jelly roll pan or 9x13-inch baking pan. Bake at 350 degrees for 20 to 30 minutes or until wooden pick inserted in center comes out clean. Bring sugar, milk and margarine to a boil in saucepan. Boil for 1 minute, stirring constantly. Remove from heat. Add chocolate chips, stirring until smooth. Pour over warm baked layer. Let stand until cool. Cut into bars.

Approx Per Serving: Cal 144; Prot 2 g; Carbo 25 g; T Fat 5 g; 29% Calories from Fat; Chol 12 mg; Fiber <1 g; Sod 149 mg

Marjorie Daniels, HFH of Greater Akron, Hudson, OH

Our granddaughter, Leanne Roncolato, asked her Sunday school class of eight-year-olds to collect pennies to help people in need. They got eight dollars worth of pennies which were presented to her grandfather, Bob Daniels, Akron HFH president, to use in building a Habitat home.

**MARJORIE DANIELS
HFH OF GREATER AKRON**

Chocolate Fruit Cookie Bars

Yield: 36 servings

1¼ cups flour
1 cup sugar
1 teaspoon salt
1½ teaspoons baking powder
3 eggs, beaten
½ teaspoon almond extract

1 cup chocolate chips
½ cup chopped dates or raisins
½ cup chopped maraschino cherries
1 cup pecans

Combine flour, sugar, salt and baking powder in bowl; mix well. Stir in eggs and almond flavoring. Add chocolate chips, dates, cherries and pecans; mix well. Spread evenly in greased 9x13-inch baking pan. Bake at 350 degrees for 30 to 35 minutes or until edges pull from sides of pan. Let stand until cool. Cut into bars. May substitute raisins for dates and walnuts for pecans. Store in tightly covered container.

Approx Per Serving: Cal 100; Prot 1 g; Carbo 16 g; T Fat 4 g; 35% Calories from Fat; Chol 18 mg; Fiber 1 g; Sod 79 mg

Mary Alice Henkel, Staunton/Augusta/Waynesboro HFH
Waynesboro, VA

Chocolate Peanut Butter Surprise Bars

Yield: 36 servings

1 tablespoon butter or margarine
¾ cup light corn syrup
¾ cup packed light brown sugar

¾ cup smooth or crunchy peanut butter
1 cup semisweet chocolate chips
6 cups crisp rice cereal

Coat side and bottom of 9x13-inch baking pan with butter. Combine corn syrup and brown sugar in heavy saucepan. Cook over medium heat until bubbly, stirring frequently. Remove from heat. Add peanut butter and chocolate chips, stirring until smooth. Stir in cereal. Spoon into prepared baking pan with buttered spoon. Pat down with waxed paper or dampened hands. Let stand for 1 hour or until cool. Cut into bars. Store at room temperature in covered container.

Approx Per Serving: Cal 108; Prot 2 g; Carbo 17 g; T Fat 4 g; 34% Calories from Fat; Chol 1 mg; Fiber 1 g; Sod 95 mg

Betty A. Bettin, HFH of Oshkosh Inc., Kewaskum, WI

Chocolate Pecan Bars

Yield: 48 servings

1³/₄ cups flour
¹/₃ cup packed brown sugar
³/₄ cup butter, softened
1 cup packed brown sugar
4 eggs, lightly beaten

1 cup light corn syrup
3 tablespoons melted butter
1 teaspoon vanilla extract
2 cups chopped pecans
1 cup semisweet chocolate chips

Combine flour and ¹/₃ cup brown sugar in bowl; mix well. Cut in ³/₄ cup butter with pastry blender or knife until crumbly. Press in bottom of greased 9x13-inch baking pan. Bake at 350 degrees for 15 to 17 minutes or until golden brown. Combine 1 cup brown sugar, eggs, corn syrup, 3 tablespoons butter and vanilla in bowl, mixing well. Stir in pecans. Pour over baked layer. Bake at 350 degrees for 40 to 45 minutes or until set. Remove from oven. Sprinkle with chocolate chips. Let stand for 5 minutes or until chocolate is softened; spread evenly over top. Let stand until cool. Cut into bars. May freeze in airtight container for up to 1 month. Thaw at room temperature before serving.

Approx Per Serving: Cal 143; Prot 2 g; Carbo 17 g; T Fat 8 g; 51% Calories from Fat; Chol 27 mg; Fiber 1 g; Sod 53 mg

Donna Long Wilson, HFH of Somerset/Pulaski County, Somerset, KY

Chocolate Streusel Bars

Yield: 24 servings

1¹/₃ cups flour
1 cup sugar
¹/₄ cup baking cocoa
¹/₂ cup butter
1 egg

1 (14-ounce) can sweetened
  condensed milk
2 cups chocolate chips
1 cup chopped pecans

Combine flour, sugar and baking cocoa in bowl; mix well. Cut in butter until crumbly. Add egg, mixing well. Reserve 1¹/₂ cups crumb mixture. Press remaining crumb mixture into greased 9x13-inch baking pan. Bake at 350 degrees for 10 minutes. Combine condensed milk and 1 cup of the chocolate chips in microwave-safe bowl. Microwave on High for 1 to 1¹/₂ minutes or until smooth. Pour over baked layer. Sprinkle mixture of pecans, remaining chocolate chips and reserved crumb mixture over top. Bake at 350 degrees for 25 to 30 minutes or until center is almost set. Let stand until cool. Cut into bars. Serve with ice cream.

Approx Per Serving: Cal 250; Prot 3 g; Carbo 33 g; T Fat 13 g; 45% Calories from Fat; Chol 25 mg; Fiber 2 g; Sod 65 mg

Mary Gorny, Maumee Valley HFH, Toledo, OH

Chewy Cream Cheese Bars

Yield: 24 servings

1 (2-layer) package yellow cake mix
1 egg
¹/₂ cup margarine, softened
1 cup coarsely chopped pecans

8 ounces cream cheese, softened
2 eggs
1 teaspoon vanilla extract
3¹/₂ cups confectioners' sugar

Combine cake mix, 1 egg, margarine and pecans in bowl; mix well. Press into greased 9x13-inch baking pan. Combine cream cheese, 2 eggs, vanilla and confectioners' sugar in mixer bowl; beat until blended. Spread over prepared layer. Bake at 350 degrees for 45 to 50 minutes or until wooden pick inserted in center comes out clean. Let stand until cool. Cut into bars.

Approx Per Serving: Cal 269; Prot 3 g; Carbo 35 g; T Fat 14 g; 44% Calories from Fat; Chol 37 mg; Fiber 1 g; Sod 220 mg

Bonnie Kinschner, Maumee Valley HFH, Toledo, OH

Date Nut Bars

Yield: 20 servings

³/₄ cup flour
³/₄ cup sugar
¹/₄ teaspoon baking powder
¹/₈ teaspoon salt
¹/₂ cup vegetable oil

2 eggs
1 teaspoon vanilla extract
1 cup chopped dates
1 cup chopped pecans

Combine flour, sugar, baking powder, salt, vegetable oil, eggs, vanilla, dates and pecans in order listed in bowl; mix well. Spoon into lightly greased 8x8-inch baking pan. Bake at 350 degrees for 35 minutes or until light brown. Let stand until cool. Cut into bars. May double recipe. May add ³/₄ cup shredded or flaked coconut.

Approx Per Serving: Cal 166; Prot 2 g; Carbo 19 g; T Fat 10 g; 53% Calories from Fat; Chol 21 mg; Fiber 1 g; Sod 24 mg

Janet Lawrence, Coachella Valley HFH, Indio, CA

While building our affiliate's second house in Desert Hot Springs, California, my six-year-old granddaughter often accompanied our group of volunteers. We would set up her playhouse a distance from the construction site and go about our work. A neighbor's dog, attracted to the site by the activity, made off with one of her stuffed animals. The canine kidnapper was persuaded to relinquish the hostage when offered one of these Date Nut Bars.

JANET LAWRENCE
COACHELLA VALLEY HFH

Date and Nut Squares

Yield: 30 servings

¹/₄ cup shortening
¹/₂ cup sifted flour
¹/₄ teaspoon baking powder
¹/₄ teaspoon salt
1 cup chopped dates

1 cup black walnuts
2 eggs, beaten
1 cup sugar
3 teaspoons wine

Melt shortening in saucepan. Let stand until cool. Combine sifted mixture of flour, baking powder and salt with dates and walnuts in bowl, tossing to coat. Combine eggs, shortening and sugar in bowl; mix well. Stir in flour mixture. Spoon into greased 9x9-inch baking pan. Bake at 350 degrees for 30 minutes. Remove from oven. Sprinkle with wine. Let stand until cool. Cut into 1-inch squares.

Approx Per Serving: Cal 123; Prot 2 g; Carbo 6 g; T Fat 11 g; 74% Calories from Fat; Chol 31 mg; Fiber 1 g; Sod 88 mg

Rosalie C. Vickers, Staunton/Augusta HFH, Staunton, VA

Fruit Squares

Yield: 30 servings

1 cup butter or margarine,
  softened
2 cups sugar
3 cups flour

4 eggs
1¹/₂ teaspoons vanilla extract
1 (21-ounce) can raspberry or
  cherry pie filling

Cream butter and sugar in mixer bowl until light and fluffy. Add flour, eggs and vanilla, beating until stiff dough forms. Spread ³/₄ of the dough in greased 9x13- or 11x15-inch baking pan. Spread pie filling evenly over dough. Sprinkle remaining dough over top. Bake at 375 degrees for 25 minutes or until edges pull from sides of pan. Let stand until cool. Cut into squares. May shape extra dough into ropes and form lattice over pie filling.

Approx Per Serving: Cal 185; Prot 2 g; Carbo 29 g; T Fat 7 g; 34% Calories from Fat; Chol 45 mg; Fiber <1 g; Sod 82 mg

Mary A. Crook, Syracuse HFH, Syracuse, NY

Fudge Squares

Yield: 12 servings

6 tablespoons butter
3 (1-ounce) squares chocolate
3 eggs, beaten
1¹/₂ cups sugar

1 cup flour
¹/₈ teaspoon salt
1 cup chopped walnuts
1 teaspoon vanilla extract

Combine butter and chocolate in saucepan. Cook over low heat until melted, stirring constantly. Stir in eggs and sugar. Add mixture of flour, salt and walnuts, mixing until blended. Add vanilla; mix well. Spoon into greased 8x8-inch square baking pan. Bake at 350 degrees for 25 to 30 minutes or until edges pull from sides of pan. Let stand until cool. Cut into squares.

Approx Per Serving: Cal 305; Prot 5 g; Carbo 37 g; T Fat 17 g; 48% Calories from Fat; Chol 69 mg; Fiber 2 g; Sod 99 mg

Janet Thomas, HFH of Washington County MD, Hagerstown, MD

Ho-Ho Bars

Yield: 32 servings

1 (2-layer) package chocolate
　cake mix
¹/₂ cup margarine
¹/₂ cup shortening
1 cup sugar
3 tablespoons flour
1 teaspoon vanilla extract

²/₃ cup milk
¹/₂ cup margarine
³/₄ cup baking cocoa
1 teaspoon vanilla extract
³/₄ cup confectioners' sugar
2¹/₂ tablespoons hot water

Prepare cake mix using package directions. Spoon batter into greased and floured 12x18-inch baking pan. Bake at 350 degrees for 15 minutes. Let stand until cool. Combine ¹/₂ cup margarine, shortening, sugar, flour and 1 teaspoon vanilla in mixer bowl; mix well. Add milk gradually, beating for 10 to 15 minutes or until fluffy. Spread over baked layer. Chill for 4 hours or longer. Combine ¹/₂ cup margarine and baking cocoa in saucepan. Cook until smooth, stirring constantly. Cool slightly. Stir in 1 teaspoon vanilla, confectioners' sugar and hot water, beating until smooth. Spread over chilled layers. Chill for 30 minutes or longer. Cut into bars.

Approx Per Serving: Cal 204; Prot 2 g; Carbo 24 g; T Fat 12 g; 52% Calories from Fat; Chol 15 mg; Fiber 1 g; Sod 217 mg

Suzanne Malone, Crawford County HFH, Meadville, PA

Peanut Butter Swirls

Yield: 24 servings

1/2 cup crunchy peanut butter
1/3 cup butter
2 teaspoons vanilla extract
2 eggs
3/4 cup packed brown sugar

3/4 cup sugar
1 teaspoon baking powder
1/4 teaspoon salt
1 cup flour
2 cups chocolate chips

Combine peanut butter, butter, vanilla, eggs, brown sugar and sugar in mixer bowl, beating until creamy. Add mixture of baking powder, salt and flour; mix well. Spread in greased 9x13-inch baking pan. Sprinkle with chocolate chips. Bake at 350 degrees for 5 minutes. Remove from oven. Swirl knife through mixture to marbleize. Bake for 25 minutes longer. Let stand until cool. Cut into squares.

Approx Per Serving: Cal 192; Prot 3 g; Carbo 26 g; T Fat 10 g; 43% Calories from Fat; Chol 25 mg; Fiber 1 g; Sod 97 mg

Debbie Konkol, HFH of Dane County, Madison, WI

Seven-Layer Bars

Yield: 15 servings

1/2 cup margarine or butter
1 cup graham cracker crumbs
1 cup flaked coconut
1 cup chocolate chips

1 cup butterscotch chips
1 (14-ounce) can sweetened
   condensed milk
1 cup finely chopped pecans

Melt margarine in 9x13-inch baking pan. Press graham cracker crumbs into margarine. Layer coconut, chocolate chips and butterscotch chips in order listed over graham cracker crumbs. Drizzle with condensed milk; sprinkle with pecans. Bake at 350 degrees for 25 to 30 minutes or until golden brown. Let stand until cool. Cut into bars.

Approx Per Serving: Cal 362; Prot 4 g; Carbo 39 g; T Fat 23 g; 54% Calories from Fat; Chol 9 mg; Fiber 2 g; Sod 167 mg

Connie Hicks, Hertford County HFH, Murfreesboro, NC

A successful Habitat project is led by a spirit of servanthood. It involves persons from all the various segments of the community in all aspects of the project and establishes an equal partnership among the members of the community of need and the community of support.

Frosty Strawberry Squares

Yield: 18 servings

1 cup flour
1/4 cup packed brown sugar
1/2 cup chopped pecans
1/2 cup melted margarine
2 egg whites
1 cup sugar

1 (10-ounce) package frozen
   sliced strawberries, partially
   thawed
2 tablespoons lemon juice
1 cup whipped cream

Combine flour, brown sugar, pecans and margarine in bowl, mixing until crumbly. Pat into greased 9x13-inch baking pan. Bake at 350 degrees for 20 minutes. Beat egg whites in mixer bowl until soft peaks form. Add sugar gradually, beating until stiff peaks form. Stir in strawberries and lemon juice. Fold in whipped cream. Sprinkle 1/2 of the baked crumb mixture over bottom of 9x13-inch baking pan. Spread with strawberry mixture. Sprinkle with remaining crumb mixture. Freeze for 6 hours or longer. Cut into 2- or 3-inch squares.

Approx Per Serving: Cal 185; Prot 2 g; Carbo 24 g; T Fat 10 g; 46% Calories from Fat; Chol 9 mg; Fiber 1 g; Sod 70 mg

Reba Ragsdale, Bryan/College Station HFH, Bryan, TX

Tipper Gore's Tennessee Treats

Yield: 24 servings

2 cups packed dark brown sugar
2 eggs
2 egg whites
2 tablespoons honey
1 teaspoon baking powder
1/4 cup boiling water
2 cups flour

1/2 teaspoon cinnamon
1/8 teaspoon allspice
1/8 teaspoon ground cloves
1/2 teaspoon salt
1/2 cup raisins
1/2 cup chopped dates
1/2 cup walnut pieces

TIPPER GORE

Photo by Kimberly Prenda

Combine brown sugar, eggs and egg whites in bowl; mix well. Stir in honey. Add mixture of baking powder and boiling water; mix well. Add mixture of flour, cinnamon, allspice, cloves and salt, stirring until smooth. Stir in raisins, dates and walnuts. Spoon into greased 8x12-inch baking pan. Bake at 350 degrees for 30 to 40 minutes or until wooden pick inserted in center comes out clean. Cut into squares while warm.

Approx Per Serving: Cal 143; Prot 2 g; Carbo 30 g; T Fat 2 g; 13% Calories from Fat; Chol 18 mg; Fiber 1 g; Sod 70 mg

Tipper Gore, Old Executive Office Building, Washington, DC

Photograph at right by Dennis E. Meola

CAKES & FROSTINGS

"How sweet are Your words to my taste,

sweeter than honey to my mouth!"

-Psalm 119:103

Ambrosia Cake

Yield: 15 servings

1 (2-layer) package yellow cake mix
1 (11-ounce) can mandarin oranges
1/2 cup vegetable oil
1/2 cup water

2 eggs
1 (20-ounce) can crushed pineapple
1 (4-ounce) package vanilla instant pudding mix
8 ounces whipped topping

Combine cake mix, mandarin oranges, oil, water and eggs in mixer bowl. Beat until combined, scraping bowl occasionally. Spoon into nonstick 9x13-inch cake pan. Bake at 350 degrees for 30 minutes. Let stand until cool. Combine pineapple, pudding mix and whipped topping in bowl, stirring until thickened. Spread over cake. Chill until serving time.

Approx Per Serving: Cal 349; Prot 4 g; Carbo 47 g; T Fat 17 g; 43% Calories from Fat; Chol 33 mg; Fiber 1 g; Sod 345 mg

Joan Hanson, Will County HFH, Joliet, IL

Apple Cake

Yield: 15 servings

1 cup salad oil
2 cups sugar
3 eggs
2 cups self-rising flour
3 cups chopped Golden Delicious apples

1 teaspoon vanilla extract
1 cup chopped pecans or walnuts
1/2 cup raisins
1 teaspoon cinnamon
1 teaspoon nutmeg

Beat oil, sugar and eggs in mixer bowl until smooth. Add flour; mix well. Stir in apples, vanilla, pecans, raisins, cinnamon and nutmeg. Spoon into greased and floured 9x13-inch cake pan. Bake at 350 degrees for 45 minutes or until cake tests done.

Approx Per Serving: Cal 390; Prot 4 g; Carbo 49 g; T Fat 21 g; 48% Calories from Fat; Chol 42 mg; Fiber 2 g; Sod 225 mg

Mary Margaret Whelan, Meade County HFH, Vine Grove, KY

Apple Nut Cake

Yield: 15 servings

4 cups chopped apples
2 cups sugar
2 eggs, lightly beaten
1/2 cup vegetable oil
2 cups flour
2 teaspoons baking soda
1 teaspoon salt
1 teaspoon cinnamon
2 teaspoons vanilla extract
1 cup chopped pecans

Combine apples and sugar in bowl; mix well. Let stand for several minutes. Combine eggs and oil in bowl; mix well. Stir in flour, baking soda, salt, cinnamon and vanilla. Add apple mixture and pecans; mix well. Spoon into greased and floured 9x13-inch cake pan. Bake at 350 degrees for 1 hour. Serve warm or cold with vanilla ice cream or whipped topping.

Approx Per Serving: Cal 310; Prot 3 g; Carbo 46 g; T Fat 14 g; 38% Calories from Fat; Chol 28 mg; Fiber 2 g; Sod 261 mg

Kathy Kramer, Alliance Area HFH, Alliance, OH

Frosted Apple Cake

Yield: 15 servings

2 eggs
2 cups sugar
1/2 cup vegetable oil
2 cups flour
2 teaspoons baking soda
1/4 teaspoon salt
2 teaspoons cinnamon
1 teaspoon vanilla extract
4 cups chopped apples
1 cup walnut pieces
1 1/2 cups confectioners' sugar
6 ounces cream cheese, softened
3 tablespoons butter or margarine, softened
Vanilla extract to taste
1/3 cup (or less) milk

Beat eggs, sugar and oil in mixer bowl until smooth. Add flour, baking soda, salt and cinnamon; mix well. Stir in 1 teaspoon vanilla, apples and walnuts. Spoon into nonstick 9x13-inch cake pan. Bake at 350 degrees for 45 minutes. Let stand until cool. Combine confectioners' sugar, cream cheese, butter and vanilla in mixer bowl. Beat until smooth, adding milk as needed for desired consistency. Spread frosting evenly over cake.

Approx Per Serving: Cal 415; Prot 5 g; Carbo 58 g; T Fat 19 g; 41% Calories from Fat; Chol 47 mg; Fiber 1 g; Sod 212 mg

Dorothy and Bud Texter, Barry County HFH, Delton, MI

Delicious Apple Pie Cake   *Yield: 16 servings*

2¹/₂ cups sliced peeled apples
2 tablespoons sugar
2 teaspoons cinnamon
3 cups flour
2¹/₂ cups sugar
¹/₂ teaspoon salt

1 tablespoon baking powder
3 tablespoons orange juice
4 eggs, beaten
1 cup vegetable oil
2¹/₂ teaspoons vanilla extract

Toss apples, 2 tablespoons sugar and cinnamon in bowl. Sift flour, 2¹/₂ cups sugar, salt and baking powder into bowl; mix well. Stir in orange juice, eggs, oil and vanilla until blended. Layer batter and apple mixture alternately in greased and floured 10-inch tube pan until all ingredients are used, ending with batter; do not allow apples to touch side of pan. Bake at 350 degrees for 1³/₄ hours.

Approx Per Serving: Cal 363; Prot 4 g; Carbo 54 g; T Fat 15 g; 37% Calories from Fat; Chol 53 mg; Fiber 1 g; Sod 145 mg

Mrs. Clayton O. Griffin, Staunton-Augusta HFH, Churchville, VA

Cocoa Apple Cake   *Yield: 16 servings*

1 cup butter, softened
2 cups sugar
3 eggs
¹/₂ cup water
2¹/₂ cups flour
2 tablespoons (rounded) baking
   cocoa
1 tablespoon baking soda

1 teaspoon cinnamon
1 teaspoon allspice
¹/₄ teaspoon salt
1 cup chopped pecans
¹/₂ cup chocolate chips
2 apples, chopped or grated
1 tablespoon vanilla extract

Cream butter and sugar in mixer bowl until light and fluffy. Add eggs and water, beating until smooth. Add flour, baking cocoa, baking soda, cinnamon, allspice and salt; mix well. Fold in pecans, chocolate chips, apples and vanilla. Spoon into greased and floured 10-inch tube pan or bundt pan. Bake at 325 degrees for 60 to 70 minutes or until cake tests done. Cool in pan. Invert onto serving platter.

Approx Per Serving: Cal 372; Prot 4 g; Carbo 48 g; T Fat 19 g; 46% Calories from Fat; Chol 71 mg; Fiber 2 g; Sod 318 mg

Ann Schutt, HFH of Nacogdoches, Nacogdoches, TX

Knobby Apple Cake
Yield: 18 servings

2 cups sugar
6 tablespoons shortening
2 eggs, beaten
2 cups flour
2 teaspoons baking soda
1 teaspoon salt

1 teaspoon cinnamon
1 teaspoon nutmeg
2 teaspoons vanilla extract
1/2 cup chopped walnuts
6 cups chopped apples

Beat sugar and shortening in mixer bowl until smooth. Add eggs, beating until light and fluffy. Add mixture of flour, baking soda, salt, cinnamon and nutmeg; mix well. Stir in vanilla and walnuts. Fold in apples. Spread in greased and floured 9x13-inch cake pan. Bake at 350 degrees for 55 minutes. Serve with whipped topping.

Approx Per Serving: Cal 228; Prot 3 g; Carbo 40 g; T Fat 7 g; 28% Calories from Fat; Chol 24 mg; Fiber 1 g; Sod 217 mg

Carol Filo, Calcasieu Area HFH, Moss Bluff, LA

Quick Apple Cake
Yield: 16 servings

2 eggs, beaten
2 cups chopped apples
1/2 cup corn oil
2 cups sugar
2 cups flour

2 teaspoons baking soda
2 teaspoons cinnamon
1/2 teaspoon salt

Combine eggs and apples in bowl; mix well. Stir in corn oil. Add mixture of sugar, flour, baking soda, cinnamon and salt; mix well. Spoon into greased bundt pan. Bake at 350 degrees for 1 hour. Serve warm with whipped cream.

Approx Per Serving: Cal 232; Prot 2 g; Carbo 39 g; T Fat 8 g; 29% Calories from Fat; Chol 27 mg; Fiber 1 g; Sod 178 mg

Carol Verploegh, Mesilla Valley HFH, Mesilla Park, NM

Photo by Julie A. Lopez

Rich Apple Cake
Yield: 9 servings

1 cup sugar	$1/8$ teaspoon salt
$1/4$ cup butter, softened	$1/2$ cup chopped pecans
1 egg	2 medium apples, peeled, grated
1 cup flour	$1/2$ cup packed brown sugar
1 teaspoon baking soda	$1/2$ cup sugar
$1/2$ teaspoon nutmeg	$1/2$ cup butter
$1/2$ teaspoon cinnamon	$1/2$ cup milk
$1/2$ teaspoon ground cloves	$1/2$ teaspoon vanilla extract

Beat 1 cup sugar and $1/4$ cup butter in mixer bowl until light and fluffy. Add egg; mix well. Add mixture of flour, baking soda, nutmeg, cinnamon, cloves and salt; mix well. Stir in pecans and apples. Spoon into greased 8x8-inch cake pan. Bake at 325 degrees for 30 minutes. Bring brown sugar, $1/2$ cup sugar, $1/2$ cup butter and milk to a boil in saucepan, stirring constantly. Remove from heat. Stir in vanilla. Cool slightly. Slice cake; drizzle with warm butter sauce.

Approx Per Serving: Cal 430; Prot 3 g; Carbo 60 g; T Fat 21 g; 43% Calories from Fat; Chol 67 mg; Fiber 1 g; Sod 295 mg

Jenny Hansen, Bay de Noc HFH, Gladstone, MI

Roman Apple Cake
Yield: 15 servings

1 cup shortening	2 eggs
2 cups sugar	8 apples, peeled, chopped
3 cups flour	$1/4$ cup melted margarine
2 teaspoons baking soda	2 tablespoons flour
2 tablespoons vanilla extract	$1/2$ cup sugar
2 teaspoons cinnamon	$1/2$ cup packed brown sugar
$1/2$ teaspoon salt	1 cup chopped pecans

Beat shortening and 2 cups sugar in mixer bowl until light and fluffy. Add 3 cups flour, baking soda, vanilla, cinnamon, salt and eggs; mix well. Stir in apples. Spoon into greased 9x13-inch cake pan. Combine margarine, 2 tablespoons flour, $1/2$ cup sugar, brown sugar and pecans in bowl; mix well. Spoon over prepared layer. Bake at 350 degrees for 45 minutes. Do not use Delicious apples.

Approx Per Serving: Cal 502; Prot 4 g; Carbo 71 g; T Fat 23 g; 41% Calories from Fat; Chol 28 mg; Fiber 3 g; Sod 228 mg

Maureen Taylor, HFH of South Dutchess, Hopewell Junction, NY

Winesap Apple Cake
Yield: 16 servings

2 cups sugar
1¹/₂ cups vegetable oil
3 eggs
3 cups flour
1 teaspoon salt
1 teaspoon baking soda

1 teaspoon vanilla extract
3 cups chopped Winesap apples
1 cup chopped pecans
1 cup packed brown sugar
¹/₂ cup margarine
¹/₂ cup orange juice

Beat sugar, oil and eggs in mixer bowl until light and fluffy. Add sifted mixture of flour, salt and baking soda gradually, mixing well after each addition. Add vanilla; mix well. Stir in apples and pecans. Spoon into greased and floured 10-inch tube pan or 2 loaf pans. Bake at 350 degrees for 1 hour or until cake or loaves test done. Invert onto serving platter. Bring brown sugar, margarine and orange juice to a boil in saucepan. Boil for 2¹/₂ minutes, stirring frequently. Pour over hot cake.

Approx Per Serving: Cal 537; Prot 4 g; Carbo 60 g; T Fat 32 g; 53% Calories from Fat; Chol 40 mg; Fiber 2 g; Sod 269 mg

Katherine Martin, Greenwood Area HFH, Greenwood, SC

Applesauce Cake
Yield: 12 servings

1 teaspoon baking soda
¹/₂ cup warm water
Salt to taste
2 cups flour
1 cup packed light brown sugar
¹/₄ cup butter, softened
1 teaspoon cinnamon

¹/₂ teaspoon ground cloves
¹/₈ teaspoon nutmeg
1 cup applesauce
1 cup confectioners' sugar
1 tablespoon butter, softened
2 tablespoons water

Dissolve baking soda in warm water in bowl. Stir in salt and flour. Cream brown sugar, ¹/₄ cup butter, cinnamon, cloves and nutmeg in mixer bowl until light and fluffy. Beat in flour mixture and applesauce until blended. Spoon into nonstick loaf pan. Bake at 350 degrees for 50 minutes. Beat confectioners' sugar, 1 tablespoons butter and water in mixer bowl until of spreading consistency. Spread over cake. May add 1 cup golden raisins or currants to batter.

Approx Per Serving: Cal 230; Prot 2 g; Carbo 45 g; T Fat 5 g; 19% Calories from Fat; Chol 13 mg; Fiber 1 g; Sod 124 mg

Patricia Chafin, Morgan County HFH, Brush, CO

Granny's Applesauce Cake

Yield: 16 servings

1¹/₂ cups raisins
1 cup chopped dates
1 cup chopped pecans
2 cups flour
2 teaspoons baking soda
1 teaspoon cinnamon

¹/₂ teaspoon nutmeg
¹/₂ teaspoon ground cloves
1 cup margarine, softened
1¹/₂ cups sugar
3 eggs
1 (12-ounce) can applesauce

Line bottom of 10-inch tube pan with parchment paper; grease and flour side and bottom. Combine raisins, dates and pecans in bowl; mix well. Add sifted mixture of flour, baking soda, cinnamon, nutmeg and cloves; mix well. Cream margarine and sugar in mixer bowl until light and fluffy. Add eggs 1 at a time, beating well after each addition. Add flour mixture alternately with applesauce, mixing after each addition. Spoon into prepared pan. Bake at 325 degrees for 1¹/₄ hours or until cake tests done. Loosen cake from side of pan with sharp knife. Cool in pan for 2 minutes. Invert onto wire rack to cool completely.

Approx Per Serving: Cal 388; Prot 4 g; Carbo 57 g; T Fat 18 g; 39% Calories from Fat; Chol 40 mg; Fiber 3 g; Sod 252 mg

Clayton O. Griffin, Staunton-Augusta HFH, Churchville, VA

Apricot Cake

Yield: 16 servings

¹/₂ cup finely chopped pecans
¹/₄ cup sifted cake flour
³/₄ cup chopped dried apricots
¹/₂ cup chopped pecans
1¹/₂ cups sugar
8 ounces cream cheese, softened
1 cup margarine, softened

1¹/₂ teaspoons vanilla extract
2 cups sifted cake flour
1¹/₂ teaspoons baking powder
4 eggs
1¹/₂ cups sifted confectioners' sugar
2 tablespoons orange juice
1 teaspoon grated orange rind

Grease side and bottom of 10-inch tube pan; sprinkle with ¹/₂ cup finely chopped pecans. Combine ¹/₄ cup cake flour, apricots and ¹/₂ cup chopped pecans in bowl; mix well. Cream sugar, cream cheese, margarine and vanilla in mixer bowl until light and fluffy. Add sifted mixture of 2 cups cake flour and baking powder gradually, mixing well after each addition. Fold in apricot mixture. Spoon batter into prepared pan. Bake at 325 degrees for 1 hour and 20 minutes. Cool in pan for 5 minutes. Invert onto wire rack to cool completely. Arrange on cake plate. Drizzle with mixture of confectioners' sugar, orange juice and orange rind. Garnish with additional apricots and pecans.

Approx Per Serving: Cal 408; Prot 5 g; Carbo 48 g; T Fat 23 g; 49% Calories from Fat; Chol 69 mg; Fiber 2 g; Sod 224 mg

Ken Pickwell, Niagara Area HFH, Niagara Falls, NY

Basic Layer Cake

Yield: 12 servings

³/₄ cup butter, softened
2 cups sugar
4 eggs
2 cups flour, sifted

1 cup self-rising flour, sifted
1 cup milk
1 teaspoon vanilla extract

Combine butter and sugar in mixer bowl. Beat at high speed for 15 minutes or until light and fluffy, scraping bowl occasionally; reduce speed to medium. Add eggs 1 at a time, beating well after each addition; reduce speed to low. Add mixture of the flours ¹/₃ cup at a time alternately with milk, beating well after each addition. Stir in vanilla. Spoon into 4 nonstick 9-inch cake pans. Bake at 350 degrees for 25 to 30 minutes or until layers pull from sides of pans. Let stand until cool. Spread your favorite frosting between layers and over top and side of cake.

Approx Per Serving: Cal 381; Prot 6 g; Carbo 58 g; T Fat 14 g; 33% Calories from Fat; Chol 104 mg; Fiber 1 g; Sod 281 mg

Annie H. Bradwell, Jackson County HFH, Greenwood, FL

Bishop's Cake

Yield: 16 servings

1 cup unsalted butter, softened
2 cups sugar
2 cups unbleached flour, sifted

1 tablespoon fresh lemon juice
1 teaspoon vanilla extract
5 eggs

Cream butter and sugar in mixer bowl until light and fluffy. Add flour, stirring just until moistened. Add lemon juice and vanilla; mix well. Add eggs 1 at a time, mixing well after each addition. Spoon batter into greased and floured bundt pan. Bake at 350 degrees for 30 minutes; cover with foil. Bake for 45 minutes longer or until cake tests done. Cool in pan for 10 minutes. Remove to wire rack to cool completely.

Approx Per Serving: Cal 272; Prot 4 g; Carbo 36 g; T Fat 13 g; 43% Calories from Fat; Chol 97 mg; Fiber <1 g; Sod 22 mg

Mary K. Henson, Arkansas Valley HFH, Fort Smith, AR

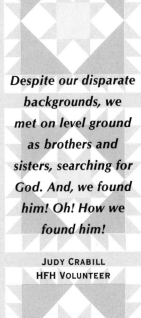

Despite our disparate backgrounds, we met on level ground as brothers and sisters, searching for God. And, we found him! Oh! How we found him!

JUDY CRABILL
HFH VOLUNTEER

Bonbon Cake

Yield: 12 servings

1 (2-layer) package yellow cake
   mix
2 eggs
$1/3$ cup vegetable oil
1 cup water

3 tablespoons orange juice
1 (8-ounce) jar apricot preserves
$1^{1}/3$ cups chocolate chips
2 tablespoons milk

Combine cake mix, eggs, oil and water in mixer bowl. Prepare and bake using package directions for 9x13-inch cake pan. Cool in pan. Cut cake into two $6^{1}/2$x9-inch portions; trim rounded top of each portion. Invert 1 portion onto serving plate; sprinkle with $1/2$ of the orange juice. Spread evenly with apricot preserves. Arrange the remaining cake portion over the preserves; sprinkle with remaining orange juice. Combine chocolate chips and milk in saucepan. Cook over low heat until smooth, stirring gently. Spread top and sides of cake with chocolate mixture. Let stand until cool. Store in refrigerator for up to 1 week.

Approx Per Serving: Cal 389; Prot 4 g; Carbo 58 g; T Fat 18 g; 39% Calories from Fat; Chol 37 mg; Fiber 2 g; Sod 301 mg

Nelida A. Amador, HFH of Lackawanna County, Scranton, PA

Candy Bar Cake

Yield: 16 servings

6 (2-ounce) Milky Way candy
   bars, chopped
$1/2$ cup butter or margarine
$1/2$ cup sugar
$1/2$ cup butter or margarine,
   softened

4 eggs
$2^{1}/2$ cups flour
$1/2$ teaspoon baking soda
$1^{1}/4$ cups buttermilk
1 teaspoon vanilla extract
1 cup chopped pecans

Combine candy bars and $1/2$ cup butter in saucepan. Cook over low heat until smooth, stirring constantly. Beat sugar and $1/2$ cup softened butter in mixer bowl until light and fluffy. Add eggs 1 at a time, beating well after each addition. Add mixture of flour and baking soda alternately with buttermilk, stirring until smooth. Stir in candy mixture until blended. Add vanilla and pecans; mix well. Spoon into greased and floured bundt pan. Bake at 350 degrees for 1 hour and 20 minutes or until cake tests done. Cool in pan on wire rack for 10 minutes. Loosen cake from side of pan with sharp knife. Remove to wire rack to cool completely. May substitute 13 fun-size Milky Way candy bars for six 2-ounce candy bars.

Approx Per Serving: Cal 362; Prot 6 g; Carbo 39 g; T Fat 21 g; 52% Calories from Fat; Chol 89 mg; Fiber 1 g; Sod 230 mg

Linda Hayes, Lebanon Area HFH, Lebanon, OR

Caramel Chocolate Cake

Yield: 15 servings

1 (2-layer) package German
chocolate cake mix
1 (14-ounce) can sweetened
condensed milk
1 (17-ounce) jar
butterscotch-caramel ice
cream topping
12 ounces whipped topping
3 Heath candy bars, crushed

Prepare and bake cake mix using package directions for 9x13-inch cake pan. Cool slightly. Pierce cake at 1-inch intervals with wooden spoon handle. Pour condensed milk over cake; spread evenly with ice cream topping. Chill for 1 hour or longer. Spread with whipped topping; sprinkle with crushed candy bars. Chill until serving time.

Approx Per Serving: Cal 487; Prot 6 g; Carbo 73 g; T Fat 20 g;
37% Calories from Fat; Chol 58 mg; Fiber <1 g; Sod 505 mg

Norma Thaler, Barry County HFH, Freeport, MI
JoAnn Wolfe, HFH of St. Joseph County South Bend IN, Granger, IN

Carrot Cake

Yield: 16 servings

1 cup vegetable oil
2 cups sugar
3 eggs
2 cups flour
1 teaspoon baking soda
1/2 teaspoon salt
1 teaspoon cinnamon
1 cup chopped walnuts
1 cup drained crushed
pineapple
2 cups grated carrots
8 ounces cream cheese,
softened
1/4 cup margarine, softened
1/2 (1-pound) package
confectioners' sugar
1/2 teaspoon vanilla extract
1/2 cup flaked coconut

Cream oil, sugar and eggs in mixer bowl until smooth. Add mixture of flour, baking soda, salt and cinnamon gradually, mixing well after each addition. Fold in walnuts, pineapple and carrots. Spoon into greased and floured 9x13-inch cake pan or 3 round 9-inch cake pans. Bake at 350 degrees for 45 minutes. Let stand until cool. Beat cream cheese and margarine in mixer bowl until light and fluffy. Add confectioners' sugar and vanilla, beating until of spreading consistency. Stir in coconut. Spread evenly over cake.

Approx Per Serving: Cal 491; Prot 5 g; Carbo 57 g; T Fat 28 g;
50% Calories from Fat; Chol 55 mg; Fiber 2 g; Sod 212 mg

Mary Ellen Amundsen, Americus HFH, Spokane, WA

If anyone has material possessions and sees his brother in need but has no pity on him, how can the love of God be in him? Dear children, let us not love with words or tongue but with actions and truth.

1 JOHN 3: 17–18

Carrot Cake with Cream Cheese Frosting

Yield: 16 servings

3/4 cup vegetable oil
1 cup packed brown sugar
1 cup sugar
4 eggs, lightly beaten
2 teaspoons vanilla extract
2 cups flour
1 teaspoon salt
2 teaspoons baking soda
2 teaspoons baking powder
2 teaspoons cinnamon
3 cups grated carrots
1/2 cup chopped walnuts
1/3 cup chopped dates
1 cup drained crushed
  pineapple
1 cup flaked coconut
4 ounces cream cheese,
  softened
1/2 cup margarine, softened
2 cups confectioners' sugar,
  sifted
1 tablespoon lemon juice

Beat oil, brown sugar and sugar in mixer bowl until smooth. Add eggs and vanilla; mix well. Add mixture of flour, salt, baking soda, baking powder and cinnamon; mix well. Stir in carrots, walnuts, dates, pineapple and coconut. Spoon into greased bundt pan. Bake at 350 degrees for 1 hour. Cool in pan for 10 minutes. Invert onto wire rack to cool completely. Arrange cake on serving platter. Beat cream cheese and margarine in mixer bowl until smooth. Add confectioners' sugar and lemon juice gradually, beating until of spreading consistency. Spread over top and side of cake.

Approx Per Serving: Cal 464; Prot 5 g; Carbo 61 g; T Fat 24 g; 45% Calories from Fat; Chol 61 mg; Fiber 2 g; Sod 394 mg

Barb Wozniak, HFH of Buffalo, Amherst, NY

Divine Carrot Cake

Yield: 12 servings

1/2 cup vegetable oil
1 cup packed brown sugar
3/4 cup sugar
2 cups flour
2 teaspoons baking soda
2 teaspoons cinnamon
1 teaspoon salt
1/4 teaspoon ground cloves
1 teaspoon vanilla extract
1/2 (6-ounce) can frozen orange
  juice concentrate, thawed
4 eggs
2 cups shredded carrots
1 cup chopped walnuts
1/2 cup raisins

Beat oil, brown sugar, sugar, flour, baking soda, cinnamon, salt, cloves, vanilla, orange juice concentrate and eggs in mixer bowl for 4 minutes, scraping bowl occasionally. Fold in carrots, walnuts and raisins. Spoon into 2 greased and floured 9-inch cake pans. Bake at 350 degrees for 55 to 60 minutes or until layers test done. Cool in pans on wire rack for 10 minutes. Invert onto wire rack to cool completely. Frost with cream cheese frosting or sprinkle with confectioners' sugar.

Approx Per Serving: Cal 390; Prot 6 g; Carbo 55 g; T Fat 17 g; 39% Calories from Fat; Chol 71 mg; Fiber 2 g; Sod 350 mg

Carol Cunningham

Fabulous Carrot Cake

Yield: 16 servings

3 cups sifted flour
2 teaspoons baking soda
2 teaspoons baking powder
1 teaspoon salt
2 teaspoons cinnamon
1 cup safflower or vegetable oil
2 cups sugar
4 eggs
3 cups grated carrots
1/2 cup chopped walnuts
1/2 cup raisins

Sift flour, baking soda, baking powder, salt and cinnamon into bowl; mix well. Add oil; mix well. Stir in sugar until blended. Add eggs 1 at a time, stirring well after each addition. Fold in carrots. Beat with wooden spoon 200 strokes or beat with mixer at low speed for several minutes. Stir in walnuts and raisins. Spoon into ungreased tube or bundt pan. Bake at 350 degrees for 45 to 60 minutes or until cake pulls from side of pan and top springs back when lightly touched. Cool in pan on wire rack. Store, tightly wrapped, for up to 2 weeks.

Approx Per Serving: Cal 363; Prot 5 g; Carbo 49 g; T Fat 18 g; 43% Calories from Fat; Chol 53 mg; Fiber 2 g; Sod 302 mg

Joan Battaglin, Southeastern Steuben County HFH, Corning, NY

Carrot Zucchini Cake

Yield: 36 servings

8 eggs
4 cups sugar
1 1/3 cups vegetable oil
5 cups flour
4 teaspoons baking soda
4 teaspoons baking powder
4 teaspoons cinnamon
2 teaspoons cloves
2 teaspoons allspice
2 teaspoons ginger
1 teaspoon nutmeg
2 teaspoons salt
4 cups shredded carrots
4 cups shredded zucchini
2 cups chopped walnuts
8 ounces cream cheese, softened
1/2 cup butter, softened
1 (1-pound) package confectioners' sugar
2 teaspoons vanilla extract

Beat eggs and sugar in mixer bowl until smooth. Add oil, beating until blended. Add mixture of flour, baking soda, baking powder, cinnamon, cloves, allspice, ginger, nutmeg and salt; mix well. Stir in carrots, zucchini and chopped walnuts. Spoon into greased 11x17-inch cake pan. Bake at 350 degrees for 50 minutes or until cake tests done. Let stand until cool. Beat cream cheese and butter in mixer bowl until light and fluffy. Add confectioners' sugar and vanilla, beating until of spreading consistency. Spread over cake. May serve unfrosted with cream or vanilla sauce.

Approx Per Serving: Cal 383; Prot 5 g; Carbo 52 g; T Fat 18 g; 42% Calories from Fat; Chol 61 mg; Fiber 2 g; Sod 311 mg

Paulette M. House, Rogue Valley HFH, Medford, OR

Millard Fuller, speaking at a Northeast Region Conference in Hartford, Connecticut said, and I paraphrase, "Acting in faith does not mean doing foolish things . . . but, I think we should get as close to foolishness as we possibly can." I have used that line many times to get myself and our board to move forward with less than certainty, and the money and the volunteers do seem to follow.

**BOB BATTAGLIN
SOUTHEASTERN STEUBEN
COUNTY HFH**

Celebration Cake

Yield: 12 servings

**1 cup pecan pieces
1 cup flaked coconut
1 cup semisweet chocolate chips
1 (2-layer) German chocolate
    cake mix**

**1/2 cup margarine
8 ounces cream cheese
1 (1-pound) package
    confectioners' sugar, sifted**

Sprinkle pecans in bottom of buttered 9x13-inch cake pan. Sprinkle coconut and chocolate chips in order listed over pecans. Prepare cake mix using package directions. Spread over prepared layers. Combine margarine and cream cheese in saucepan. Cook over low heat until smooth, stirring constantly. Remove from heat. Add confectioners' sugar, stirring until smooth. Spoon over prepared layers; do not spread. Bake at 350 degrees for 50 to 60 minutes or until cake tests done. Cool in pan.

Approx Per Serving: Cal 703; Prot 6 g; Carbo 87 g; T Fat 39 g; 49% Calories from Fat; Chol 76 mg; Fiber 2 g; Sod 568 mg

Lynn Merrill, HFH Atlanta, Atlanta, GA

Moist Chocolate Cake

Yield: 15 servings

**3 cups flour
2 cups sugar
1/2 cup baking cocoa
1 teaspoon salt
2 teaspoons baking soda
2 teaspoons vinegar
2 cups cold water
2 teaspoons vanilla extract
2/3 cup vegetable oil
2 (1-ounce) squares
    unsweetened chocolate,
    melted**

**6 tablespoons butter, softened
1 (1-pound) package
    confectioners' sugar
1 to 2 tablespoons corn syrup
1 teaspoon vanilla extract
1/4 cup (or more) milk or
    evaporated milk**

Combine flour, sugar, baking cocoa, salt and baking soda in bowl; mix well. Stir in vinegar, water, 2 teaspoons vanilla and oil until blended. Spoon into ungreased 9x12-inch cake pan. Bake at 350 degrees for 30 minutes or until cake tests done. Cool in pan on wire rack. Beat chocolate and butter in mixer bowl until smooth. Add confectioners' sugar, corn syrup and 1 teaspoon vanilla; mix well. Beat in enough milk to make of spreading consistency. Spread over cake.

Approx Per Serving: Cal 475; Prot 4 g; Carbo 81 g; T Fat 17 g; 31% Calories from Fat; Chol 13 mg; Fiber 2 g; Sod 306 mg

Mrs. Jack Kemp, Washington, DC

Chocolate Chip Cake

Yield: 16 servings

1 (4-ounce) package vanilla
   instant pudding mix
1 (2-layer) package yellow cake
   mix
4 eggs

1 1/2 cups milk
1/2 cup vegetable oil
4 ounces German's sweet
   chocolate, coarsely grated
1 cup chocolate chips

Combine pudding mix, cake mix, eggs, milk and oil in mixer bowl. Beat for 5 minutes, scraping bowl occasionally. Fold in grated sweet chocolate. Spoon into greased and floured bundt pan. Press chocolate chips into cake batter. Bake in moderate oven for 45 to 55 minutes or until cake tests done.

Approx Per Serving: Cal 343; Prot 4 g; Carbo 44 g; T Fat 18 g; 46% Calories from Fat; Chol 57 mg; Fiber 1 g; Sod 340 mg

Eve A. Earnest, HFH Atlanta, Atlanta, GA

Chocolate Sheet Cake

Yield: 15 servings

2 cups flour
2 cups sugar
1/2 cup margarine
1/4 cup baking cocoa
1 cup water
1/2 cup vegetable oil
1/2 cup buttermilk
1/2 teaspoon baking soda
2 eggs, lightly beaten

1 teaspoon vanilla extract
1/2 cup margarine
6 tablespoons buttermilk
3 tablespoons baking cocoa
1 (1-pound) package
   confectioners' sugar
1 cup chopped pecans
1 tablespoon vanilla extract

Combine flour and sugar in bowl. Bring 1/2 cup margarine, 1/4 cup baking cocoa, water and oil to a boil in saucepan, stirring occasionally. Pour over sugar mixture; mix well. Stir in mixture of 1/2 cup buttermilk and baking soda. Add eggs and 1 teaspoon vanilla; mix well. Spoon into nonstick 9x13-inch cake pan. Bake at 350 degrees for 30 minutes. Bring 1/2 cup margarine, 6 tablespoons buttermilk and 3 tablespoons baking cocoa to a boil in saucepan, stirring frequently. Remove from heat. Add confectioners' sugar, stirring until of spreading consistency. Stir in pecans and 1 tablespoon vanilla. Spoon over hot cake. Let stand until cool. Cut into squares.

Approx Per Serving: Cal 533; Prot 4 g; Carbo 73 g; T Fat 26 g; 43% Calories from Fat; Chol 29 mg; Fiber 2 g; Sod 195 mg

Nancy Porter, Haywood HFH, Waynesville, NC

White Chocolate Cake
Yield: 12 servings

1 cup butter, softened
2 cups sugar
4 ounces white chocolate, melted, slightly cooled
4 egg yolks
2¹/₂ cups cake flour
1 teaspoon baking powder
1 cup buttermilk
4 egg whites, stiffly beaten
1 cup chopped pecans
1 teaspoon vanilla extract
1 cup flaked coconut
2 cups sugar
1 cup margarine
1 (5-ounce) can evaporated milk
1 teaspoon vanilla extract

Cream butter and 2 cups sugar in mixer bowl until light and fluffy. Add white chocolate; mix well. Add egg yolks 1 at a time, beating well after each addition. Add sifted mixture of cake flour and baking powder alternately with buttermilk, beating well after each addition. Fold in egg whites, pecans, 1 teaspoon vanilla and coconut. Spoon into nonstick 9x13-inch cake pan or two 9-inch cake pans. Bake at 350 degrees for 40 to 45 minutes or until cake tests done. Let stand until cool. Combine 2 cups sugar, margarine and evaporated milk in saucepan. Cook to soft-ball stage, stirring frequently. Remove from heat. Add vanilla, beating until of spreading consistency. Spread over cake.

Approx Per Serving: Cal 805; Prot 7 g; Carbo 92 g; T Fat 48 g; 52% Calories from Fat; Chol 119 mg; Fiber 2 g; Sod 502 mg

Patricia O'Connor, Bowling Green/Warren County HFH
Bowling Green, KY

Coca-Cola Cake
Yield: 15 servings

2 cups sugar
2 cups flour
¹/₂ cup butter
¹/₂ cup vegetable oil
1 (12-ounce) can Coca-Cola
3 tablespoons baking cocoa
¹/₂ cup buttermilk
1 teaspoon baking soda
1 teaspoon vanilla extract
2 eggs, beaten
¹/₂ cup butter
3 tablespoons baking cocoa
1 (1-pound) package confectioners' sugar
1 teaspoon vanilla extract
1 cup chopped pecans

Combine sugar and flour in bowl; mix well. Bring ¹/₂ cup butter, oil, 1 cup of the Coca-Cola and 3 tablespoons baking cocoa to a boil in saucepan, stirring occasionally. Pour over the sugar mixture; mix well. Stir in mixture of buttermilk and baking soda. Add 1 teaspoon vanilla and eggs; mix well. Spoon into nonstick 9x13-inch cake pan. Bake at 350 degrees for 30 minutes. Bring ¹/₂ cup butter, 3 tablespoons baking cocoa and remaining Coca-Cola to a boil in saucepan, stirring occasionally. Remove from heat. Add confectioners' sugar and 1 teaspoon vanilla, stirring until of spreading consistency. Fold in pecans. Spread over cake.

Approx Per Serving: Cal 535; Prot 4 g; Carbo 75 g; T Fat 26 g; 43% Calories from Fat; Chol 62 mg; Fiber 2 g; Sod 199 mg

Elsie Hiatt, Ventura County CA HFH, Mannford, OK

Coke Cake

Yield: 24 servings

1 cup pecan pieces
2 tablespoons melted butter
2 cups flour
2 cups sugar
1 cup margarine
3 tablespoons baking cocoa
1 cup Coca-Cola
1/2 cup buttermilk
2 eggs
1 teaspoon vanilla
1 teaspoon baking soda
1 1/2 cups miniature marshmallows
1/2 cup margarine
3 tablespoons baking cocoa
6 tablespoons Coca-Cola
1 (1-pound) package confectioners' sugar

Combine pecans and butter in baking pan. Bake at 350 degrees for 15 minutes or until brown. Combine flour and sugar in bowl; mix well. Bring 1 cup margarine, 3 tablespoons baking cocoa and 1 cup Coca-Cola to a boil in saucepan, stirring occasionally. Pour over flour mixture; mix well. Stir in buttermilk, eggs, vanilla, baking soda and marshmallows. Spoon into nonstick sheet cake pan. Bake at 350 degrees for 30 minutes. Bring 1/2 cup margarine, 3 tablespoons baking cocoa and 6 tablespoons Coca-Cola to a boil in saucepan, stirring occasionally. Remove from heat. Add confectioners' sugar, beating until of spreading consistency. Stir in pecans. Spread over hot cake.

Approx Per Serving: Cal 346; Prot 3 g; Carbo 49 g; T Fat 17 g; 42% Calories from Fat; Chol 20 mg; Fiber 1 g; Sod 191 mg

Caren S. Whittier, HFH of Horry County, Myrtle Beach, SC

Cola Cake

Yield: 15 servings

2 cups flour
2 cups sugar
1/2 cup margarine
2 tablespoons baking cocoa
1 cup Coca-Cola
1 1/2 cups miniature marshmallows
1 teaspoon vanilla extract
1 cup sour cream
2 eggs, beaten
1 teaspoon baking soda
1/2 cup margarine
3 tablespoons baking cocoa
5 to 6 tablespoons Coca-Cola
1 (1-pound) package confectioners' sugar

Combine flour and sugar in mixer bowl; mix well. Combine margarine, 2 tablespoons baking cocoa, 1 cup Coca-Cola and marshmallows in saucepan. Cook over low heat until marshmallows melt, stirring frequently. Pour over flour mixture, beating until blended. Add vanilla, sour cream, eggs and baking soda in order listed, beating well after each addition. Spoon into nonstick 9x11-inch cake pan. Bake at 375 degrees for 1 hour or until cake begins to pull from sides of pan. Bring 1/2 cup margarine, 3 tablespoons baking cocoa and 5 to 6 tablespoons Coca-Cola to a boil in saucepan. Remove from heat. Add confectioners' sugar, beating until of spreading consistency. Spread over hot cake.

Approx Per Serving: Cal 461; Prot 4 g; Carbo 77 g; T Fat 17 g; 31% Calories from Fat; Chol 35 mg; Fiber 1 g; Sod 219 mg

Molly Sue Waidner, Bay de Noc HFH, Gladstone, MI

Coconut Cake

Yield: 16 servings

2 cups flour
1 1/2 teaspoons baking powder
1 teaspoon salt
1 cup shortening
2 cups sugar
5 eggs
1 cup buttermilk

1 1/2 teaspoons coconut extract
1 (7-ounce) package flaked
   coconut
1 cup confectioners' sugar
1/2 cup hot water
1 teaspoon coconut extract

Combine flour, baking powder and salt in bowl; mix well. Cream shortening and sugar in mixer bowl until light and fluffy. Add eggs; mix well. Add 1/2 of the flour mixture; mix well. Add mixture of buttermilk and 1 1/2 teaspoons coconut flavoring; mix well. Mix in remaining flour mixture until blended. Fold in coconut. Spoon into greased and floured bundt pan. Bake at 350 degrees for 1 hour. Let stand until pan is cool to the touch. Invert cake onto serving platter. Drizzle with mixture of confectioners' sugar, hot water and 1 teaspoon coconut flavoring.

Approx Per Serving: Cal 384; Prot 4 g; Carbo 51 g; T Fat 19 g; 43% Calories from Fat; Chol 67 mg; Fiber 2 g; Sod 203 mg

Libby Doubler, HFHI, Church Relations, Murfreesboro, TN

Cream of Coconut Cake

Yield: 15 servings

1 (2-layer) package white cake
   mix
1/4 cup vegetable oil
2 eggs
1 cup sour cream
1 (16-ounce) can cream of
   coconut

8 ounces cream cheese,
   softened
1 (1-pound) package
   confectioners' sugar
2 tablespoons milk
1 teaspoon vanilla extract
1 to 2 cups shredded coconut

Combine cake mix, oil and eggs in bowl; mix well. Stir in sour cream and cream of coconut until blended. Spoon into greased and floured 9x13-inch cake pan. Bake at 350 degrees for 30 to 35 minutes or until cake tests done. Let stand until cool. Beat cream cheese, confectioners' sugar, milk and vanilla in mixer bowl until of spreading consistency. Spread over cake; sprinkle with coconut.

Approx Per Serving: Cal 513; Prot 5 g; Carbo 65 g; T Fat 28 g; 47% Calories from Fat; Chol 52 mg; Fiber 2 g; Sod 325 mg

Pat Lemieux, West Plains Area HFH, West Plains, MO

Date Nut Loaf

Yield: 25 servings

2 pounds pitted dates, chopped
1 pound shelled English
   walnuts, broken
1 cup sugar
1 cup flour
1/2 teaspoon salt

2 teaspoons (heaping) baking
   powder
4 egg yolks
1 teaspoon vanilla extract
4 egg whites, stiffly beaten

Grease tube pan; line with waxed paper. Combine dates and walnuts in bowl; mix well. Sift mixture of sugar, flour, salt and baking powder over date mixture; mix well. Beat egg yolks in mixer bowl until lemon colored. Fold into date mixture. Add vanilla; mix well. Fold in egg whites. Spoon into prepared pan. Bake at 325 degrees for 1 hour.

Approx Per Serving: Cal 278; Prot 5 g; Carbo 42 g; T Fat 12 g; 37% Calories from Fat; Chol 34 mg; Fiber 4 g; Sod 82 mg

Brenda J. Harmon, My New Kentucky Home HFH, Lebanon, KY

Fruit Cocktail Cake

Yield: 15 servings

2 eggs, lightly beaten
1 1/2 cups sugar
1 (14-ounce) can fruit cocktail,
   puréed
2 cups flour
2 tablespoons baking soda

1/2 teaspoon salt
3/4 cup sugar
1/2 cup cream
1/2 cup butter
1 teaspoon vanilla extract

Combine eggs, 1 1/2 cups sugar and fruit cocktail in bowl; mix well. Stir in mixture of flour, baking soda and salt. Spoon into greased 9x13-inch cake pan. Bake at 350 degrees for 45 minutes. Bring 3/4 cup sugar, cream and butter to a boil in saucepan. Boil for 2 minutes, stirring occasionally. Stir in vanilla. Pour over hot cake. Serve warm with whipped cream or ice cream. Store in refrigerator for several days. May sprinkle prepared layer with 1/2 cup chopped nuts and 1/2 cup flaked coconut before baking.

Approx Per Serving: Cal 288; Prot 3 g; Carbo 48 g; T Fat 10 g; 31% Calories from Fat; Chol 56 mg; Fiber 1 g; Sod 476 mg

D. S. Simpson, Oconee County HFH, Salem, SC

God used us, Chet, Cathy, River City HFH, HFHI, the churches and the businesses that sponsored the homes. We were privileged to be able to be a small part of it. The Hartleys came to Tennessee and brought in the 1995 New Year with us. What wonderful friends, and what a wonderful ministry Habitat is!

LIBBY DOUBLER
HFHI, CHURCH RELATIONS

Funny Cake

Yield: 24 servings

3 cups flour
2 cups sugar
6 tablespoons baking cocoa
1 teaspoon salt
2 teaspoons baking powder

2 teaspoons vanilla extract
2 tablespoons vinegar
1/2 cup melted butter or margarine
2 cups cold water

Combine flour, sugar, baking cocoa, salt and baking powder in bowl; mix well. Sprinkle into ungreased 9x13-inch cake pan. Make 3 wells in dry ingredients. Pour vanilla, vinegar and melted butter in separate wells. Pour 2 cups cold water over top; mix well. Bake at 350 degrees for 30 minutes.

Approx Per Serving: Cal 159; Prot 2 g; Carbo 29 g; T Fat 4 g; 23% Calories from Fat; Chol 10 mg; Fiber 1 g; Sod 156 mg

Isabel Laney, Southwest Volusia HFH, Deltona, FL

Hummingbird Cake

Yield: 12 servings

3 cups flour
2 cups sugar
1 teaspoon baking soda
1 teaspoon salt
1 teaspoon cinnamon
3 eggs, beaten
1 cup vegetable oil
1 1/2 teaspoons vanilla extract
1 (8-ounce) can crushed pineapple

2 cups mashed bananas
1 cup chopped pecans
8 ounces cream cheese, softened
1/2 cup margarine, softened
1 (1-pound) package confectioners' sugar
1 teaspoon vanilla extract

Combine flour, sugar, baking soda, salt and cinnamon in bowl; mix well. Add eggs and oil, stirring just until moistened. Stir in 1 1/2 teaspoons vanilla, undrained pineapple, bananas and pecans. Spoon into 3 non-stick round cake pans. Bake at 350 degrees for 25 to 30 minutes or until layers test done. Let stand until cool. Beat cream cheese and margarine in mixer bowl until light and fluffy. Add confectioners' sugar and 1 teaspoon vanilla, beating until of spreading consistency. Spread between layers and over top and side of cake. May bake in 9x13-inch cake pan.

Approx Per Serving: Cal 818; Prot 8 g; Carbo 110 g; T Fat 41 g; 44% Calories from Fat; Chol 74 mg; Fiber 2 g; Sod 409 mg

Bertha Thaler, Barry County HFH, Freeport, MI

Busy Day Jam Cake

Yield: 12 servings

1 (2-layer) package spice cake
   mix
1 (4-ounce) package vanilla
   instant pudding mix
1¼ cups blackberry jam
¾ cup water
¼ cup vegetable oil
4 eggs
1 cup raisins
1 cup chopped black walnuts
2 tablespoons flour

Combine cake mix, pudding mix, jam, water, oil and eggs in mixer bowl. Beat at medium speed for 4 minutes, scraping bowl occasionally. Fold in mixture of raisins, black walnuts and flour. Spoon into 3 greased and floured 9-inch cake pans. Bake at 350 degrees for 30 minutes or until layers test done. Cool in pans for 5 minutes. Remove to wire rack to cool completely. Spread your favorite caramel frosting between layers and over top and side of cake. Soak raisins in apple juice or bourbon for added flavor; drain before adding to batter.

Approx Per Serving: Cal 480; Prot 7 g; Carbo 80 g; T Fat 16 g; 30% Calories from Fat; Chol 71 mg; Fiber 2 g; Sod 452 mg

Lynne Bowling, My New Kentucky Home HFH, Bardstown, KY

Lazy Man's Cake

Yield: 8 servings

1½ cups flour
1 cup sugar
3 tablespoons baking cocoa
1 teaspoon baking soda
1 teaspoon baking powder
1 teaspoon salt
5 tablespoons vegetable oil
1 teaspoon vanilla extract
1 teaspoon vinegar
1 cup water
½ cup confectioners' sugar

Combine flour, sugar, baking cocoa, baking soda, baking powder and salt in bowl; mix well. Spread in ungreased 8- or 9-inch cake pan. Make 3 wells in dry ingredients. Pour oil, vanilla and vinegar in separate wells. Pour water over top; mix well. Bake at 350 degrees for 35 to 40 minutes or until cake tests done. Let stand until cool. Invert onto cake plate. Sprinkle with confectioners' sugar.

Approx Per Serving: Cal 292; Prot 3 g; Carbo 52 g; T Fat 9 g; 27% Calories from Fat; Chol 0 mg; Fiber 1 g; Sod 411 mg

Lucille Zabawski, Greater Cleveland HFH, Bay Village, OH

Living in the small town of Bardstown, you feel that you know almost everyone. However, as I was working on a recent home for our affiliate, I became acquainted with so many wonderful people from St. John AME Zion church. I think I received much more than I gave.

LYNNE BOWLING
MY NEW KENTUCKY HOME HFH

Newman's Very Own Lemon Blueberry Cake

Yield: 6 servings

This delicious recipe was awarded the Charity Award by The Make a Wish Foundation.

2 cups fresh or frozen
   blueberries
1/2 cup shortening
1/4 cup butter or margarine,
   softened
3/4 cup sugar
2 eggs
1/4 teaspoon lemon extract
2 teaspoons Newman's Own
   Old-Fashioned Roadside
   Virgin Lemonade

2 cups flour
11/4 teaspoons baking powder
1/4 teaspoon salt
1/2 cup milk
1/2 cup warm water
11/2 cups Newman's Own
   Old-Fashioned Roadside
   Virgin Lemonade
11/2 tablespoons butter

Sprinkle blueberries in bottom of greased 9x9-inch cake pan. Beat shortening, 1/4 cup butter and sugar in mixer bowl until light and fluffy. Add eggs 1 at a time, beating well after each addition. Stir in lemon extract and 2 teaspoons lemonade. Add mixture of flour, baking powder and salt alternately with milk, beating well after each addition. Reserve 1/2 cup of the batter. Spoon remaining batter over blueberries. Bake at 350 degrees for 25 to 35 minutes or until cake tests done. Combine reserved batter with mixture of warm water and 11/2 cups lemonade in saucepan; mix well. Cook over medium heat until thickened, stirring constantly. Remove from heat. Stir in 11/2 tablespoons butter until blended. Drizzle each serving with lemonade sauce. Garnish with additional blueberries and mint sprigs. Serve warm or cold.

Photo by Julie A. Lopez

PAUL NEWMAN

Approx Per Serving: Cal 583; Prot 8 g; Carbo 72 g; T Fat 31 g; 47% Calories from Fat; Chol 102 mg; Fiber 2 g; Sod 302 mg

Ann Marshall, Hudson, MA

Habitat for Humanity is building much more than houses. By building hope it is building relationships, strengthening communities and nurturing families.

PAUL NEWMAN
HABITAT SUPPORTER

Lemon Pudding Cake

Yield: 9 servings

Lemon Pudding Cake is a favorite dessert of President and Mrs. Gerald R. Ford and is served at many of their family gatherings in Vail.

1/2 cup plus 1 tablespoon sugar	3 egg yolks, at room
1/4 cup flour	temperature
1/8 teaspoon salt	1 1/2 cups whipping cream, at
3 tablespoons melted butter	room temperature
3 tablespoons plus 2 teaspoons	3 egg whites, at room
grated lemon rind	temperature
6 tablespoons fresh lemon juice	3 tablespoons sugar

Combine 1/2 cup plus 1 tablespoon sugar, flour and salt in mixer bowl; mix well. Stir in butter, lemon rind and lemon juice. Add mixture of egg yolks and cream. Beat at medium-low speed for 15 seconds or until batter is smooth. Beat egg whites at medium-high speed in mixer bowl for 30 seconds or until frothy. Add 3 tablespoons sugar gradually. Beat for 45 seconds or until stiff peaks form. Fold into flour mixture. Spoon into buttered 8x8-inch cake pan. Place in larger baking pan with water to reach halfway up sides of pan. Bake at 350 degrees on middle rack of oven for 30 to 40 minutes or until brown and top springs back when touched. Serve warm or cool.

Approx Per Serving: Cal 277; Prot 3 g; Carbo 22 g; T Fat 20 g; 64% Calories from Fat; Chol 135 mg; Fiber <1 g; Sod 105 mg

Lorraine M. Ornelas
Chef for Former President and Mrs. Gerald R. Ford

Lemony Pudding Cake

Yield: 6 servings

3 tablespoons butter, softened	1/4 teaspoon salt
3/4 cup sugar	3 tablespoons flour
4 egg yolks	1 cup milk
1/3 cup fresh lemon juice	4 egg whites, stiffly beaten
2 teaspoons grated lemon rind	

Cream butter and sugar in mixer bowl until light and fluffy. Beat in egg yolks until blended. Add lemon juice, lemon rind, salt and flour; mix well. Stir in milk. Fold in egg whites. Spoon into nonstick 5x9-inch loaf pan. Place in baking pan filled with 1-inch hot water. Bake at 325 degrees for 40 minutes; increase temperature to 350 degrees. Bake for 10 minutes longer or until brown. Serve warm or chilled. May add 1/3 cup toasted slivered almonds to batter.

Approx Per Serving: Cal 241; Prot 6 g; Carbo 32 g; T Fat 11 g; 39% Calories from Fat; Chol 162 mg; Fiber <1 g; Sod 209 mg

Harriet B. Holtz, Springfield, VT Area HFH, Bellows Falls, VT

Mississippi Mud Cake
Yield: 15 servings

1 cup margarine or butter,
  softened
4 eggs, beaten
1 teaspoon vanilla extract
$^1/_3$ cup baking cocoa
2 cups sugar
1$^1/_4$ cups flour
$^1/_8$ teaspoon salt
1 teaspoon baking powder
1 cup chopped pecans

1 cup flaked coconut
1 (16-ounce) jar marshmallow
  creme
$^1/_2$ cup melted margarine
$^1/_3$ cup baking cocoa
$^1/_3$ cup Milnot
1 teaspoon vanilla extract
1 (1-pound) package
  confectioners' sugar

Cream 1 cup margarine in mixer bowl until light and fluffy. Add eggs and 1 teaspoon vanilla; mix well. Add mixture of $^1/_3$ cup baking cocoa, sugar, flour, salt and baking powder; mix well. Stir in pecans and coconut. Spoon into greased and floured 9x13-inch cake pan. Bake at 350 degrees for 30 to 35 minutes; center will fall when removed from oven. Spread warm cake with marshmallow creme. Let stand until cool. Beat $^1/_2$ cup melted margarine, $^1/_3$ cup baking cocoa, Milnot, 1 teaspoon vanilla and confectioners' sugar in mixer bowl until of spreading consistency, scraping bowl occasionally. Spread over prepared layers.

Approx Per Serving: Cal 630; Prot 5 g; Carbo 96 g; T Fat 28 g; 38% Calories from Fat; Chol 57 mg; Fiber 3 g; Sod 301 mg

Judy Ann Edwards-Burrus, Callaway County HFH, Fulton, MO

Only-Four-Steps Cake
Yield: 20 servings

1 cup butter, softened
2 cups sugar
4 eggs
3 cups cake flour
$^1/_4$ teaspoon salt

1 cup (or more) milk
1 teaspoon vanilla extract
1 teaspoon (rounded) baking
  powder

Cream butter and sugar in mixer bowl until light and fluffy. Add eggs 1 at a time, beating well after each addition. Beat in sifted mixture of flour and salt. Add milk and vanilla, beating until smooth. Stir in baking powder. Spoon into 2 nonstick 9-inch cake pans and 8 paper-lined muffin cups immediately. Bake at 350 degrees for 25 minutes or until layers and cupcakes test done. Let stand until cool. Spread with your favorite frosting.

Approx Per Serving: Cal 240; Prot 3 g; Carbo 30 g; T Fat 13 g; 47% Calories from Fat; Chol 69 mg; Fiber <1 g; Sod 209 mg

Carolyn Davis, Rabun County HFH, Clayton, GA

Orange Slice Cake

Yield: 16 servings

1 (16-ounce) package orange
   slice candy, finely chopped
2 cups finely chopped pecans
1/2 cup flour
1 cup margarine, softened
2 cups sugar
4 eggs
1/2 cup buttermilk

3 cups flour
1 teaspoon baking soda
1 (8-ounce) package pitted
   dates, finely chopped
1 (3-ounce) can flaked coconut
1/2 cup confectioners' sugar
2 tablespoons (or more) milk

Toss candy and chopped pecans with 1/2 cup flour in bowl. Cream margarine and sugar in mixer bowl until light and fluffy, scraping bowl occasionally. Add eggs 1 at a time, beating well after each addition. Beat in buttermilk until blended. Add sifted mixture of 3 cups flour and baking soda; mix well. Fold in candy mixture, dates and coconut. Spoon into nonstick bundt pan. Bake at 350 degrees for 1 1/2 hours or until cake tests done. Invert onto wire rack. Drizzle with mixture of confectioners' sugar and milk.

Approx Per Serving: Cal 599; Prot 6 g; Carbo 90 g; T Fat 25 g; 37% Calories from Fat; Chol 54 mg; Fiber 4 g; Sod 233 mg

Nola Bernstein, Henderson HFH, Henderson, KY

Mandarin Orange Cake

Yield: 8 servings

1 cup sugar
1 cup flour
1 teaspoon baking soda
1/4 teaspoon salt
1 egg

1 (11-ounce) can mandarin
   oranges
1/2 cup packed brown sugar
1/2 cup flaked coconut
1/2 cup chopped pecans

Sift sugar, flour, baking soda and salt into bowl; mix well. Add egg; mix well. Stir in undrained mandarin oranges. Spoon into ungreased 9-inch cake pan. Sprinkle with brown sugar, coconut and pecans. Bake at 350 degrees for 35 minutes.

Approx Per Serving: Cal 291; Prot 3 g; Carbo 55 g; T Fat 7 g; 22% Calories from Fat; Chol 27 mg; Fiber 2 g; Sod 185 mg

Kathleen Smith, HFH of Miami County OH, Piqua, OH

Plum Cake

Yield: 21 servings

2 cups sugar
2 cups flour
1 teaspoon baking soda
1 teaspoon baking powder
1 teaspoon salt
1 teaspoon cinnamon
1 teaspoon ground cloves

1 cup vegetable oil
3 eggs
3 (4-ounce) jars baby food
  plums
1 cup confectioners' sugar
2 tablespoons lemon juice

Combine sugar, flour, baking soda, baking powder, salt, cinnamon and cloves in bowl; mix well. Stir in oil, eggs and plums until blended. Spoon into bundt pan sprayed with nonstick cooking spray. Bake at 325 degrees for 55 minutes. Cool in pan on wire rack to 5 minutes. Invert onto serving plate. Drizzle hot cake with mixture of confectioners' sugar and lemon juice. May add 1 cup chopped walnuts.

Approx Per Serving: Cal 254; Prot 2 g; Carbo 37 g; T Fat 11 g; 39% Calories from Fat; Chol 30 mg; Fiber <1 g; Sod 167 mg

Diane W. Kirkpatrick, HFH Louisville, Louisville, KY

Poor Man's Cake

Yield: 15 servings

1 (15-ounce) package raisins
2 cups water
1 cup cold water
1/4 cup shortening
1 tablespoon baking soda
1 1/2 cups sugar

4 cups flour
1/2 teaspoon salt
1/2 teaspoon nutmeg
1 teaspoon cinnamon
1/4 teaspoon ground cloves

Combine raisins and 2 cups water in saucepan. Cook for 15 minutes, stirring occasionally. Remove from heat. Stir in 1 cup cold water. Let stand until lukewarm. Stir in shortening, baking soda and sugar. Add mixture of flour, salt, nutmeg, cinnamon and cloves; mix well. Add to raisin mixture, stirring until combined. Spoon into greased and floured 9x12-inch cake pan. Bake at 350 degrees for 1 hour. May serve with applesauce.

Approx Per Serving: Cal 314; Prot 4 g; Carbo 68 g; T Fat 4 g; 11% Calories from Fat; Chol 0 mg; Fiber 2 g; Sod 240 mg

Shirley A. House, Southern Portage County HFH
Mogadore/Randolph, OH

Poppy Seed Cake

Yield: 16 servings

1/3 cup poppy seeds
1 cup milk
1 teaspoon vanilla extract
3/4 cup butter, softened
1 1/2 cups sugar
2 cups flour
2 teaspoons baking powder
1/2 teaspoon salt
4 egg whites, stiffly beaten
3/4 cup sugar

4 egg yolks
2 1/2 tablespoons cornstarch
1 1/3 cups milk
1/4 teaspoon salt
1/2 cup chopped pecans
1 teaspoon vanilla extract
1/4 cup butter
1/2 cup packed brown sugar
1/4 cup milk
1 to 2 cups confectioners' sugar

Combine poppy seeds, 1 cup milk and 1 teaspoon vanilla in bowl; mix well. Let stand for 30 to 60 minutes. Beat 3/4 cup butter in mixer bowl until creamy. Add 1 1/2 cups sugar gradually, beating until light and fluffy. Add sifted mixture of flour, baking powder and 1/2 teaspoon salt alternately with poppy seed mixture, mixing well after each addition. Fold in egg whites. Spoon into 2 greased and floured 9-inch cake pans. Bake at 350 degrees for 30 minutes. Cool in pans for 5 minutes. Remove to wire rack to cool completely. Combine 3/4 cup sugar, egg yolks, cornstarch, 1 1/3 cups milk and 1/4 teaspoon salt in saucepan; mix well. Cook over medium heat for 5 minutes, whisking constantly. Let stand until cool. Stir in pecans and 1 teaspoon vanilla. Arrange 1 cake layer on cake plate. Spread with pecan mixture. Top with remaining cake layer. Bring 1/4 cup butter, brown sugar and 1/4 cup milk to a rolling boil in saucepan. Boil for 1 minute, stirring frequently. Remove from heat. Beat in confectioners' sugar until of spreading consistency. Spread over top layer of cake.

Approx Per Serving: Cal 461; Prot 5 g; Carbo 65 g; T Fat 21 g; 40% Calories from Fat; Chol 97 mg; Fiber 1 g; Sod 326 mg

Sandy Hughes, Holston HFH, Kingsport, TN

Photo by Tally Lancaster

Pound Cake

Yield: 16 servings

1 cup butter, softened
1/2 cup shortening
3 cups sugar
5 eggs
3 cups flour

1/2 teaspoon baking powder
1 cup milk
1 teaspoon vanilla extract
1 teaspoon lemon extract

Cream butter and shortening in mixer bowl. Add sugar, beating constantly until light and fluffy. Add eggs 1 at a time, beating well after each addition. Add sifted mixture of flour and baking powder alternately with milk, mixing well after each addition. Stir in flavorings. Spoon into greased and floured 10-inch tube pan. Place in cold oven. Bake at 325 to 350 degrees for 1 1/4 hours or until cake tests done; do not peek. Invert on funnel to cool completely. Loosen cake from side of pan. Invert onto cake plate.

Approx Per Serving: Cal 422; Prot 5 g; Carbo 56 g; T Fat 20 g; 43% Calories from Fat; Chol 99 mg; Fiber 1 g; Sod 156 mg

Leslie Auld, Butler County HFH, Zelienople, PA

Black Walnut Coconut Pound Cake

Yield: 16 servings

2 cups sugar
1 cup vegetable oil
4 eggs, beaten
3 cups flour
1/2 teaspoon baking soda
1/2 teaspoon baking powder
1 cup buttermilk

1 cup chopped black walnuts
1 cup flaked coconut
2 teaspoons coconut extract
1/2 cup water
1 cup sugar
2 tablespoons butter
1 teaspoon coconut extract

Beat 2 cups sugar, oil and eggs in mixer bowl until blended. Add mixture of flour, baking soda and baking powder alternately with buttermilk, mixing well after each addition. Stir in black walnuts, coconut and 2 teaspoons coconut flavoring. Spoon into greased and floured bundt or tube pan. Bake at 325 degrees for 1 hour and 5 minutes or until cake tests done. Bring water, 1 cup sugar and butter to a boil in saucepan, stirring frequently. Boil for 5 minutes, stirring occasionally. Stir in 1 teaspoon coconut flavoring. Pour over hot cake in pan. Let stand for 4 to 8 hours. Heat cake in oven for several minutes to release sides. Loosen cake from side of pan. Invert onto cake plate.

Approx Per Serving: Cal 461; Prot 6 g; Carbo 60 g; T Fat 23 g; 44% Calories from Fat; Chol 57 mg; Fiber 2 g; Sod 85 mg

Pat Brown, HFH East Regional Office, McGaheysville, VA

Butter Pound Cake

Yield: 16 servings

2 cups butter, softened
1 (1-pound) package
   confectioners' sugar
3 cups flour

6 eggs
1 teaspoon baking powder
1 teaspoon vanilla extract

Cream butter and confectioners' sugar in mixer bowl until light and fluffy. Add 2 cups of the flour and 4 of the eggs; mix well. Add the remaining flour and eggs, beating until smooth. Add baking powder; mix well. Stir in vanilla. Spoon into greased and floured tube pan. Bake at 350 degrees for 1 hour or until cake tests done.

Approx Per Serving: Cal 427; Prot 5 g; Carbo 46 g; T Fat 25 g; 52% Calories from Fat; Chol 142 mg; Fiber 1 g; Sod 279 mg

Pinkie Daniel, HFH of Anderson County, Oak Ridge, TN

Buttermilk Pound Cakes

Yield: 16 servings

1 cup butter, softened
2³/₄ cups sugar
4 egg yolks
3 cups sifted flour

¹/₄ teaspoon baking soda
1 cup buttermilk
2 tablespoons vanilla extract
4 egg whites, stiffly beaten

Beat butter and sugar in mixer bowl until light and fluffy. Add egg yolks; mix well. Add sifted mixture of flour and baking soda alternately with buttermilk, mixing well after each addition. Add vanilla; mix well. Fold in egg whites. Spoon into 2 greased and floured loaf pans. Bake at 350 degrees for 1 hour or until cakes pull from sides of pans. Cool in pans.

Approx Per Serving: Cal 344; Prot 4 g; Carbo 52 g; T Fat 13 g; 34% Calories from Fat; Chol 85 mg; Fiber 1 g; Sod 162 mg

Emily Diamond, HFH St. Tammany West, Covington, LA

Chocolate Pound Cake

Yield: 16 servings

3 cups sifted flour
¹/₂ cup baking cocoa
¹/₂ teaspoon baking powder
¹/₂ teaspoon salt
1 cup butter, softened

¹/₂ cup shortening
3 cups sugar
5 eggs
1 cup milk
2 teaspoons vanilla extract

Combine flour, baking cocoa, baking powder and salt in bowl; mix well. Cream butter, shortening and sugar in mixer bowl until light and fluffy. Add eggs and milk alternately with flour mixture, mixing well after each addition. Stir in vanilla. Spoon into nonstick tube or bundt pan. Bake at 325 degrees for 1 hour and 25 minutes.

Approx Per Serving: Cal 421; Prot 5 g; Carbo 56 g; T Fat 21 g; 43% Calories from Fat; Chol 99 mg; Fiber 1 g; Sod 223 mg

Betty Hill, HFH of Calhoun County, Anniston, AL

I'll always remember the people of the Habitat organization and their willingness to help others to live in a better environment.

PINKIE DANIEL
HFH OF ANDERSON COUNTY

Caramel Nut Pound Cake

Yield: 18 servings

1 cup butter, softened
1/2 cup shortening
**1 (1-pound) package light
  brown sugar**
1 cup sugar
5 eggs
3 cups sifted flour
1/2 teaspoon salt
1/2 teaspoon baking powder

1 cup milk
1 tablespoon vanilla extract
1 cup finely chopped pecans
1/2 cup butter or margarine
1 cup packed light brown sugar
1/4 cup milk
**1 3/4 to 2 cups confectioners'
  sugar**

Beat 1 cup butter, shortening and 1 pound brown sugar in mixer bowl until creamy. Add sugar gradually, beating until light and fluffy. Add eggs 1 at a time, beating well after each addition. Add sifted mixture of flour, salt and baking powder alternately with 1 cup milk, beginning and ending with flour mixture. Stir in vanilla and pecans. Spoon into greased and floured 10-inch tube pan. Bake at 325 degrees for 1 1/2 hours or until cake tests done. Cool in pan for 15 minutes. Invert onto cake plate. Heat 1/2 cup butter in saucepan until melted. Stir in 1 cup brown sugar. Boil over low heat for 2 minutes, stirring constantly. Add 1/4 cup milk; mix well. Bring to a boil, stirring constantly. Remove from heat. Let stand until cool. Add confectioners' sugar gradually, beating until of spreading consistency. Spread over top and side of cake.

Approx Per Serving: Cal 561; Prot 5 g; Carbo 76 g; T Fat 28 g; 44% Calories from Fat; Chol 103 mg; Fiber 1 g; Sod 265 mg

Cherry W. Clements, Atlanta HFH, Atlanta, GA

Easy Pound Cake

Yield: 16 servings

2 cups butter, softened
3 cups sugar
8 eggs

4 cups flour
3/4 cup milk
1 tablespoon bourbon

Cream butter in mixer bowl for 10 minutes, scraping bowl occasionally. Add sugar. Beat for 5 minutes, scraping bowl occasionally. Add eggs 1 at a time, beating well after each addition. Add flour 1 cup at a time alternately with milk, beginning and ending with flour; mix well after each addition. Stir in bourbon. Spoon into greased 10-inch tube pan. Bake at 325 degrees for 1 3/4 hours. Cool in pan for 20 minutes. Invert onto a cake plate.

Approx Per Serving: Cal 509; Prot 7 g; Carbo 62 g; T Fat 26 g; 46% Calories from Fat; Chol 170 mg; Fiber 1 g; Sod 273 mg

Rita T. Foust, HFH of Castle Country, Price, UT

Sour Cream Pound Cake

Yield: 16 servings

2³/₄ cups sugar
1 cup margarine, softened
5 eggs
3 cups sifted flour
¹/₂ teaspoon salt

¹/₄ teaspoon baking soda
1 cup sour cream
¹/₂ teaspoon lemon extract
¹/₂ teaspoon orange extract
¹/₂ teaspoon vanilla extract

Cream sugar and margarine in mixer bowl until light and fluffy, scraping bowl occasionally. Add eggs 1 a time, beating well after each addition. Add sifted mixture of flour, salt and baking soda alternately with sour cream, mixing well after each addition. Stir in flavorings. Spoon into greased and floured 10-inch tube pan. Bake at 350 degrees for 1¹/₂ hours or until cake tests done. Cool in pan for 15 minutes. Invert onto cake plate. Frost with your favorite icing or sprinkle with confectioners' sugar as desired.

Approx Per Serving: Cal 368; Prot 5 g; Carbo 52 g; T Fat 16 g; 39% Calories from Fat; Chol 73 mg; Fiber 1 g; Sod 242 mg

Lucia A. Bryson, Greenwood Area HFH, Greenwood, SC

Company Sour Cream Pound Cake

Yield: 16 servings

This cake is enjoyed by all who attend our "Habi-Chats", informal community meetings at local churches.

1 cup butter, softened
3 cups sugar
6 eggs, at room temperature
3 cups flour
¹/₄ teaspoon salt

¹/₄ teaspoon baking soda
1 cup sour cream
¹/₂ teaspoon almond extract
¹/₂ teaspoon lemon extract
2 teaspoons vanilla extract

Beat butter in mixer bowl until creamy. Add sugar gradually. Beat at medium speed until light and fluffy, scraping bowl occasionally. Add eggs 1 at a time, beating well after each addition. Add mixture of flour, salt and baking soda alternately with sour cream, beginning and ending with flour mixture; mix just until blended. Stir in flavorings. Spoon into greased and floured 10-inch tube pan. Bake at 325 degrees for 55 to 60 minutes or until cake tests done. Cool in pan for 10 to 15 minutes. Invert onto wire rack to cool completely. May substitute cake flour sifted 3 times for all-purpose flour.

Approx Per Serving: Cal 393; Prot 5 g; Carbo 56 g; T Fat 17 g; 38% Calories from Fat; Chol 117 mg; Fiber 1 g; Sod 195 mg

Helena Patton, HFH of Nacogdoches, Nacogdoches, TX

My trip to India in 1988 with a Global Village work camp is my favorite memory. Being close to people's lives as we were was a great contrast to being tourists and looking at things and people. Habitat gives you the opportunity to share in others' lives.

EMILY DIAMOND
HFH ST. TAMMANY WEST

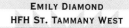

Lemony Sour Cream Pound Cake

Yield: 16 servings

6 egg yolks
3 cups sugar
1 cup butter, softened
3 cups flour
1/4 teaspoon baking soda
1/4 teaspoon baking powder

1/4 teaspoon salt
1 cup sour cream
2 tablespoons lemon juice
Grated lemon rind to taste
6 egg whites, stiffly beaten

Beat egg yolks, sugar and butter in mixer bowl until light and fluffy. Add sifted mixture of flour, baking soda, baking powder and salt alternately with sour cream, mixing well after each addition. Beat in lemon juice and lemon rind. Fold in egg whites. Spoon into greased and floured 10-inch tube pan. Bake at 300 degrees for 1 1/2 to 1 3/4 hours or until cake tests done. Cool in pan for 20 minutes. Invert onto cake plate to cool completely.

Approx Per Serving: Cal 392; Prot 5 g; Carbo 56 g; T Fat 17 g; 38% Calories from Fat; Chol 117 mg; Fiber 1 g; Sod 200 mg

Pam LeFils, Southwest Volusia HFH, Osteen, FL

Prune Cake

Yield: 16 servings

1 cup vegetable oil
2 cups sugar
3 eggs
2 cups flour
1 teaspoon baking soda
1 teaspoon salt
1 teaspoon cinnamon
1 teaspoon ground cloves
1 teaspoon nutmeg

1 teaspoon allspice
1 cup buttermilk
1 cup chopped prunes
1 teaspoon vanilla extract
1 cup sugar
1/2 cup buttermilk
1 tablespoon dark corn syrup
1/2 teaspoon baking soda
6 tablespoons butter

Combine oil, 2 cups sugar, eggs, flour, 1 teaspoon baking soda, salt, cinnamon, cloves, nutmeg, allspice, buttermilk, prunes and vanilla in order listed in bowl; mix well. Spoon into greased 10x15-inch cake pan. Bake at 325 degrees for 40 to 45 minutes or until cake tests done. Pierce cake with fork. Bring 1 cup sugar, buttermilk, corn syrup, 1/2 teaspoon baking soda and butter to a boil in saucepan, stirring frequently. Pour over warm cake.

Approx Per Serving: Cal 435; Prot 4 g; Carbo 64 g; T Fat 19 g; 39% Calories from Fat; Chol 52 mg; Fiber 2 g; Sod 294 mg

Melissa Wise, Dallas HFH, Dallas, TX

Raisin Loaf Cake

Yield: 8 servings

1 cup raisins
1 cup water
1/3 cup shortening
1 cup sugar
1 1/2 cups flour

1/2 teaspoon cinnamon
1/2 teaspoon ground cloves
1/2 teaspoon baking soda
1/2 teaspoon baking powder

Combine raisins and water in saucepan. Cook for 10 minutes. Drain, reserving raisins and liquid. Combine reserved liquid with enough water to measure 1 cup. Cream shortening and sugar in mixer bowl until light and fluffy. Add flour; mix well. Add cinnamon, cloves, baking soda and baking powder; mix well. Stir in raisins and liquid. Spoon into greased and floured 5x9-inch loaf pan. Bake at 350 degrees for 40 to 45 minutes or until loaf tests done.

Approx Per Serving: Cal 320; Prot 3 g; Carbo 59 g; T Fat 9 g; 24% Calories from Fat; Chol 0 mg; Fiber 2 g; Sod 75 mg

Gail Means, Greater Cleveland HFH, Richmond Heights, OH

Rompin' Rutabaga Cake

Yield: 15 servings

1/2 cup margarine, softened
1 1/2 cups packed brown sugar
3 eggs
2 cups flour
1 teaspoon baking powder
1 teaspoon baking soda

1 teaspoon salt
1 teaspoon cinnamon
1 1/2 cups mashed cooked
   rutabagas
3/4 cup raisins
1 teaspoon maple extract

Cream margarine and brown sugar in mixer bowl until light and fluffy. Add eggs 1 at a time, beating well after each addition. Stir in sifted mixture of flour, baking powder, baking soda, salt and cinnamon gradually. Add rutabagas, raisins and maple flavoring; mix well. Spoon into greased 9x13-inch cake pan. Bake at 325 degrees for 35 minutes or until cake tests done. Cool in pan on wire rack. Sprinkle with confectioners' sugar or serve with low-fat yogurt or whipped topping.

Approx Per Serving: Cal 233; Prot 4 g; Carbo 39 g; T Fat 7 g; 28% Calories from Fat; Chol 42 mg; Fiber 1 g; Sod 316 mg

Suzanne Runyan Moore, HFH of Grayson County, Sherman, TX

I took my friend, Linda, to hear Millard Fuller speak at the Cleveland HFH meeting. Impressed that anyone could work for Habitat (even, as Millard said, as a "bad example"), Linda immediately volunteered. Upon meeting Millard, she told him of her enthusiasm but confessed to little construction ability. "I guess I'd be our designated bad example," Linda said. Millard promptly dubbed her the D.B.E.—a title she still wears proudly.

**GAIL MEANS
GREATER CLEVELAND HFH**

Scripture Cake

Yield: 16 servings

3¹/₂ cups sifted flour
  (1 Kings 4:22)
1 tablespoon baking powder
  (Revelation 5:9)
¹/₄ teaspoon salt (Leviticus 2:13)
1¹/₂ teaspoons cinnamon
¹/₂ teaspoon nutmeg
¹/₂ teaspoon ground cloves
1 teaspoon allspice
  (1 Kings 10:2)
1 (8-ounce) package dates,
  chopped (Deuteronomy 34:3)

2 cups raisins (1 Samuel 30:12)
1 cup chopped walnuts
  (Song of Solomon 6:11)
6 eggs (Luke 11:12)
2 tablespoons honey
  (Exodus 16:31)
1 cup butter, softened
  (Judges 5:25)
2 cups packed brown sugar
  (Jeremiah 6:20)
1 cup milk (Judges 5:25)

Sift dry ingredients together. Combine dates, raisins and walnuts in bowl; mix well. Add ¹/₄ cup of the flour mixture to the date mixture, tossing to coat. Beat eggs, honey, butter and brown sugar in mixer bowl for 3 minutes or until light and fluffy. Add remaining flour mixture alternately with milk, beating well after each addition. Stir in date mixture. Spoon into greased and floured 10-inch tube pan. Bake at 325 degrees for 1¹/₂ hours or until top springs back when lightly touched. Cool in pan on wire rack for 20 minutes. Loosen cake from side of pan with sharp knife. Invert onto wire rack.

Approx Per Serving: Cal 474; Prot 8 g; Carbo 73 g; T Fat 19 g; 35% Calories from Fat; Chol 113 mg; Fiber 3 g; Sod 256 mg

Mrs. Willie Jo LaGroone, Greenwood Area HFH, Hodges, SC

Snackin' Cake

Yield: 15 servings

1¹/₂ cups hot water
1 cup rolled oats
1 cup packed brown sugar
1 cup sugar
1 cup vegetable oil
2 eggs
1¹/₂ cups flour
1 teaspoon baking soda

1 teaspoon cinnamon
¹/₂ teaspoon salt
6 tablespoons margarine
³/₄ cup packed brown sugar
1 tablespoon milk
1 (3-ounce) can flaked coconut
1 cup chopped pecans

Pour hot water over oats in bowl. Let stand until cool. Cream 1 cup brown sugar, sugar and oil in mixer bowl until light and fluffy. Beat in eggs until blended. Add flour, baking soda, cinnamon and salt; mix well. Stir in oat mixture. Spoon into nonstick 9x13-inch cake pan. Bake at 350 degrees for 35 minutes or until cake tests done. Bring margarine, ³/₄ cup brown sugar and milk to a boil in saucepan, stirring frequently. Stir in coconut and pecans. Pour over cake. Broil for 3 to 4 minutes or until brown.

Approx Per Serving: Cal 372; Prot 2 g; Carbo 43 g; T Fat 22 g; 52% Calories from Fat; Chol 28 mg; Fiber 1 g; Sod 198 mg

Karyl Rister, Abilene HFH, Abilene, TX

Texas Sheet Cake

Yield: 24 servings

2 cups flour
2 cups sugar
$^1/_2$ cup margarine
$^1/_2$ cup shortening
1 cup dark baking cocoa
1 cup strong brewed coffee
$^1/_2$ cup buttermilk
1 teaspoon vanilla extract

2 eggs, lightly beaten
1 teaspoon baking soda
$^1/_2$ cup margarine
3 tablespoons baking cocoa
$^1/_4$ cup milk
$3^1/_2$ cups confectioners' sugar
1 teaspoon vanilla extract

Combine flour and sugar in bowl; mix well. Bring $^1/_2$ cup margarine, shortening, 1 cup baking cocoa and coffee to a boil in saucepan, stirring occasionally. Pour over flour mixture; mix well. Stir in buttermilk, 1 teaspoon vanilla, eggs and baking soda until blended. Spoon into greased sheet cake pan. Bake at 400 degrees for 20 minutes or until cake tests done. Bring $^1/_2$ cup margarine, 3 tablespoons baking cocoa and milk to a boil in saucepan, stirring frequently. Combine with confectioners' sugar in bowl, stirring until mixture is of pouring consistency. Stir in 1 teaspoon vanilla. Pour over hot cake.

Approx Per Serving: Cal 296; Prot 3 g; Carbo 45 g; T Fat 13 g; 38% Calories from Fat; Chol 18 mg; Fiber 2 g; Sod 137 mg

Kimberly B. Bayless, HFH of Ashtabula County, Ashtabula, OH

Tomato Soup Cake

Yield: 8 servings

1 cup sugar
2 teaspoons butter, softened
1 egg
1 teaspoon cinnamon
1 teaspoon nutmeg
1 (10-ounce) can tomato soup
1 teaspoon baking soda
$1^3/_4$ cups sifted flour

$^1/_2$ teaspoon baking powder
$^1/_4$ to $^1/_2$ cup raisins
$^1/_4$ to $^1/_2$ cup chopped pecans
1 cup (or more) confectioners'
   sugar
1 tablespoon butter, softened
1 tablespoon (or more) hot
   water

Beat sugar, 2 teaspoons butter, egg, cinnamon and nutmeg in mixer bowl until blended. Stir in mixture of tomato soup and baking soda. Add mixture of flour and baking powder; mix well. Stir in raisins and pecans. Spoon into nonstick loaf pan. Bake at 350 degrees for 1 hour. Remove to wire rack to cool. Beat confectioners' sugar, 1 tablespoon butter and hot water in mixer bowl until of spreading consistency. Spread over cake.

Approx Per Serving: Cal 382; Prot 5 g; Carbo 73 g; T Fat 9 g; 20% Calories from Fat; Chol 33 mg; Fiber 2 g; Sod 404 mg

Barbara C. Gustafson, Wythe County HFH, Wytheville, VA

Turtle Cake

Yield: 15 servings

1/2 cup baking cocoa	1 1/2 teaspoons vanilla extract
1 cup boiling water	2 eggs
1/2 cup butter, softened	1 (14-ounce) can sweetened
1 1/4 cups sugar	condensed milk
1/2 cup sour milk	1 (14-ounce) package caramels
1 1/2 teaspoons baking soda	1 to 2 cups chocolate chips
2 cups flour	1 cup chopped pecans

Dissolve baking cocoa in boiling water in bowl; mix well. Stir in butter and sugar until blended. Add mixture of sour milk and baking soda; mix well. Stir in flour, vanilla and eggs. Spoon 1/2 of the batter into buttered 9x13-inch cake pan. Bake at 350 degrees for 15 minutes. Remove to wire rack to cool. Combine condensed milk and caramels in saucepan. Cook until smooth, stirring constantly. Spread evenly over baked layer. Sprinkle with chocolate chips and pecans. Top with remaining batter. Bake for 15 to 20 minutes longer or until cake tests done. May substitute 1 prepared package German chocolate cake mix for first 9 ingredients. May substitute walnuts for pecans.

Approx Per Serving: Cal 548; Prot 8 g; Carbo 82 g; T Fat 24 g; 38% Calories from Fat; Chol 57 mg; Fiber 4 g; Sod 259 mg

Carolyn Reed, HFH of Evansville Inc., Evansville, IN

Swedish Walnut Cake

Yield: 15 servings

2 eggs	1/4 cup butter or margarine,
2 cups sugar	softened
2 cups flour	1 teaspoon vanilla extract
2 teaspoons baking soda	6 ounces cream cheese,
1 teaspoon vanilla extract	softened
1 (20-ounce) can juice-pack	2 cups (about) confectioners'
crushed pineapple	sugar
1/2 cup chopped black walnuts	1/2 cup chopped black walnuts

Beat eggs and sugar in bowl until smooth. Add flour, baking soda, 1 teaspoon vanilla and undrained pineapple; mix well. Stir in 1/2 cup walnuts. Spoon into ungreased 9x13-inch cake pan. Bake at 350 degrees for 40 to 45 minutes or until cake tests done. Beat butter, 1 teaspoon vanilla and cream cheese in mixer bowl until light and fluffy. Add confectioners' sugar, beating until of spreading consistency. Spread over baked layer; sprinkle with 1/2 cup walnuts. May substitute whipped topping for cream cheese frosting.

Approx Per Serving: Cal 377; Prot 5 g; Carbo 63 g; T Fat 13 g; 30% Calories from Fat; Chol 49 mg; Fiber 1 g; Sod 185 mg

Neva Hagemeier, Knox County HFH, Freelandville, IN

Zucchini Chocolate Cake   *Yield: 15 servings*

2 cups flour	2 cups sugar
1 teaspoon baking powder	$1/2$ cup vegetable oil
1 teaspoon baking soda	2 cups shredded unpeeled
1 teaspoon cinnamon	zucchini
$1/2$ teaspoon salt	$3/4$ cup buttermilk
$1/2$ teaspoon nutmeg	1 cup chopped pecans
$1/4$ cup baking cocoa	$1/2$ cup flaked coconut
3 eggs	1 teaspoon vanilla extract

Combine flour, baking powder, baking soda, cinnamon, salt, nutmeg and baking cocoa in bowl; mix well. Beat eggs in mixer bowl until lemon colored. Add sugar gradually, beating until blended. Add oil; mix well. Add flour mixture alternately with zucchini and buttermilk, mixing well after each addition. Fold in pecans, coconut and vanilla. Spoon into greased 9x13-inch cake pan. Bake at 350 degrees for 45 to 50 minutes or until cake tests done. May freeze for future use.

Approx Per Serving: Cal 321; Prot 5 g; Carbo 44 g; T Fat 15 g; 41% Calories from Fat; Chol 43 mg; Fiber 2 g; Sod 176 mg

Jean Tallman, South Puget Sound HFH, Olympia, WA

Black Bottom Cupcakes   *Yield: 18 servings*

8 ounces cream cheese,	$1/4$ cup baking cocoa
softened	1 teaspoon baking soda
1 egg	$1/2$ teaspoon salt
$1/3$ cup sugar	1 teaspoon vanilla extract
$1/8$ teaspoon salt	1 cup water
1 cup chocolate chips	$1/3$ cup vegetable oil
$1^1/2$ cups flour	1 tablespoon vinegar
1 cup sugar	

Beat cream cheese, egg, $1/3$ cup sugar and $1/8$ teaspoon salt in mixer bowl until smooth. Stir in chocolate chips. Beat flour, 1 cup sugar, baking cocoa, baking soda, $1/2$ teaspoon salt, vanilla, water, oil and vinegar in mixer bowl until blended. Fill muffin cups $1/2$ full. Spoon 1 tablespoon of the cream cheese mixture into the center of each prepared muffin cup. Bake at 375 degrees for 10 to 15 minutes or until cupcakes test done.

Approx Per Serving: Cal 227; Prot 3 g; Carbo 30 g; T Fat 12 g; 45% Calories from Fat; Chol 26 mg; Fiber 1 g; Sod 162 mg

Martha J. Camp, Norristown HFH, North Wales, PA

Command those who are rich in this present world not to be arrogant nor to put their hope in wealth, which is so uncertain, but to put their hope in God, who richly provides us with everything for our enjoyment . . . In this way they will lay up treasures to themselves as a firm foundation for the coming age, so that they may lay hold of the life that is truly life.

1 TIMOTHY 6: 17–19

Castle Cakes with Cream Sauce

Yield: 12 servings

This recipe is like Habitat houses—simple, decent sweetness.

1 cup flour	1 teaspoon vanilla extract
2 teaspoons baking powder	2 tablespoons butter or
1/2 cup sugar	margarine
1/8 teaspoon salt	2 tablespoons flour
3 tablespoons butter or	Dash of salt
margarine, softened	3 tablespoons sugar
1 egg, lightly beaten	2 cups milk
2 tablespoons milk	1 teaspoon vanilla extract

Sift 1 cup flour, baking powder, 1/2 cup sugar and 1/8 teaspoon salt into bowl; mix well. Cut in 3 tablespoons butter until crumbly. Stir in mixture of egg, milk and 1 teaspoon vanilla. Spoon into muffin cups sprayed with nonstick cooking spray. Bake at 375 degrees for 15 minutes or until brown and cracked on top. Heat 2 tablespoons butter in saucepan until melted. Stir in 2 tablespoons flour. Cook over low heat until thickened, stirring constantly. Add dash of salt and 3 tablespoons sugar; mix well. Stir in milk gradually. Cook until thickened, stirring constantly. Stir in 1 teaspoon vanilla. Serve warm over Castle Cakes. May prepare cupcakes and sauce in advance and reheat just before serving.

Approx Per Serving: Cal 163; Prot 3 g; Carbo 23 g; T Fat 7 g; 37% Calories from Fat; Chol 37 mg; Fiber <1 g; Sod 153 mg

Amy Bullard, South Atlantic Regional Center HFH, Greenville, SC

Chocolate Coffee Cupcakes

Yield: 30 servings

2 cups sugar	1/2 cup cold brewed coffee
1/2 cup margarine, softened	2 cups flour
2 eggs, at room temperature	1 teaspoon baking soda
1/4 teaspoon salt	1 cup warm water
1/2 cup baking cocoa	1 tablespoon vanilla extract

Cream sugar and margarine in mixer bowl until light and fluffy. Add eggs, salt and baking cocoa; mix well. Add coffee, mixture of flour and baking soda and warm water alternately, mixing well after each addition. Stir in vanilla. Spoon into muffin cups. Bake at 350 degrees for 40 to 50 minutes or until cupcakes test done.

Approx Per Serving: Cal 119; Prot 2 g; Carbo 21 g; T Fat 4 g; 27% Calories from Fat; Chol 14 mg; Fiber 1 g; Sod 86 mg

Gwen Gipple, HFHI, Washington, IA

Truly Different Cupcakes

Yield: 24 servings

4 (1-ounce) squares semisweet
  chocolate
1 cup butter or margarine
¼ teaspoon butter flavoring
1½ cups chopped pecans

1¾ cups sugar
4 eggs
1 teaspoon vanilla extract
1 cup flour

Combine chocolate and butter in saucepan. Cook over low heat until smooth, stirring frequently. Add butter flavoring and chopped pecans, stirring until pecans are coated. Combine sugar, eggs, vanilla and flour in bowl, stirring just until blended; do not beat. Stir in chocolate mixture just until mixed. Spoon into paper-lined muffin cups. Bake at 325 degrees for 25 minutes.

Approx Per Serving: Cal 228; Prot 2 g; Carbo 23 g; T Fat 15 g; 57% Calories from Fat; Chol 56 mg; Fiber 1 g; Sod 90 mg

Jill H. Raukko, Foothills HFH, Loomis, CA

Ersatz Whipped Cream Frosting

Yield: 15 servings

1 cup milk
5 tablespoons flour
1 cup butter or margarine,
  softened

1 tablespoon shortening
1 cup sugar
1 tablespoon vanilla extract

Combine milk and flour in saucepan; mix well. Cook over low heat until thickened, stirring constantly. Let stand until cool. Cream butter, shortening and sugar in mixer bowl until light and fluffy. Add flour mixture gradually, beating well after each addition. Stir in vanilla. Spread over sides and top of 9x13-inch cake. May add food coloring or baking cocoa to frosting. Store frosted cake in refrigerator. Store remaining frosting in refrigerator or freeze for future use.

Approx Per Serving: Cal 190; Prot 1 g; Carbo 16 g; T Fat 14 g; 64% Calories from Fat; Chol 35 mg; Fiber <1 g; Sod 133 mg

Meryl Perlstrom, Lake County IL HFH, Lake Villa, IL

"Tally: Habitat 27, Andrew 0," was the banner headline on a story in the Miami Herald in August 1992 when Hurricane Andrew devastated thousands of homes in south Florida but all 27 Habitat houses in the storm's path emerged standing and virtually unscathed.

Death by Chocolate

Yield: 15 servings

Start with a good cake mix. Prepare the cake using package directions, but with as many of these ideas as you wish.

Add ¹/₂ teaspoon vanilla extract (regardless of the cake flavor), as vanilla is a flavor enhancer.

Add one 4-ounce package instant pudding mix of a flavor compatible with the cake and substitute milk for the water. The baking time will need to be extended about 20 percent.

Enhance the base flavor with ¹/₂ to 1 teaspoon butter extract.

Consider using butter instead of the vegetable oil.

Vary the cake firmness by varying the size of the eggs used. Use extra-large eggs, except when substituting margarine for the oil; then use medium eggs. Make the cake in layers so you can surprise the eater with one of the lovely premixed frostings or make your own frosting.

Consider using a fruit preserve between the layers.

Consider adding candies such as chocolate chips, white chocolate chips, "M & M's" Chocolate Candies, etc., to the mix. These may cause your wooden pick to come out moist, so try more than one spot when testing for doneness. Do not overbake.

Consider adding firm or moistened dried fruit to the cake or using chunky fruit purée such as applesauce (milk powder instead of milk) or shredded carrot, using larger and additional eggs. The texture will be that of a spice cake, or if you have a large amount of moisture in the fruit, the texture will be like that of a coffee cake.

Frost the cake with a commercial frosting, ice cream topping with added confectioners' sugar or a fruit preserve. Consider decorating the cake with attractive, colorful candies or canned fruit.

If you use a bundt cake pan, you can hide a flavor surprise in the hole by covering it with frosting, or leave it open for a colorful flavor treat such as the frostings or fruit.

When you do all these things—use a double chocolate/pudding-recipe cake mix, non-sweetened non-store-brand instant pudding, vanilla, chocolate bits, butter, medium eggs, modified cook time, frosting between layers, a different chocolate or raspberry preserve in the hole you cut to simulate a bundt appearance, a different chocolate flavor for the external frosting, and patterns of chocolate candies around the outside—you have what my family calls "Death by Chocolate."

If you are surprised by the outcome, do not worry because your family will ask you to make more "Disasters." But work with the approaches before you make a cake for company.

Nutritional information for this recipe is not available.

John Blaisdell, Greater Columbus HFH, Columbus, OH

Photograph at right by HFHI

PIES, COBBLERS, & PUDDINGS

"Build houses and dwell in them;

plant gardens and eat their fruit."

-Jeremiah 29:5

Flaky Golden Angel Pie

Yield: 6 servings

3 egg whites
1/8 teaspoon cream of tartar
1/2 cup sugar
1 teaspoon vanilla extract
1/2 cup flaked coconut
3/4 cup sugar
1/4 teaspoon salt
1/3 cup flour
1 cup flaked coconut
3 egg yolks, lightly beaten

2 cups milk
1 teaspoon vanilla extract
1 tablespoon cornstarch
2 tablespoons cold water
1/2 cup boiling water
3 egg whites
6 tablespoons sugar
1/2 teaspoon salt
1 teaspoon vanilla extract

Beat 3 egg whites in mixer bowl until frothy. Add cream of tartar; mix well. Add 1/2 cup sugar gradually, beating constantly until smooth and glossy. Fold in 1 teaspoon vanilla and 1/2 cup coconut. Pat 1/4 inch thick over side and bottom of buttered 9-inch pie plate. Bake at 275 degrees for 1 hour. Let stand until cool. Combine 3/4 cup sugar, 1/4 teaspoon salt, flour and 1 cup coconut in saucepan; mix well. Stir in egg yolks, milk and 1 teaspoon vanilla. Cook until thickened, stirring constantly. Spoon into pie shell. Dissolve cornstarch in cold water in saucepan; mix well. Stir in boiling water. Cook until thickened, stirring constantly. Beat 3 egg whites in mixer bowl until soft peaks form. Add 6 tablespoons sugar, 1/2 teaspoon salt and vanilla gradually, beating constantly until stiff peaks form. Add cornstarch mixture; beat until blended. Spread over pie, sealing to edge. Bake at 350 degrees for 20 minutes.

Approx Per Serving: Cal 421; Prot 9 g; Carbo 73 g; T Fat 11 g; 24% Calories from Fat; Chol 117 mg; Fiber 2 g; Sod 369 mg

Sandra L. Struve-Seberger, Black Hills Area HFH, Rapid City, SD

Homemade Apple Pie

Yield: 6 servings

2 cups flour
1 teaspoon salt
2/3 cup plus 2 tablespoons
    shortening
1/4 cup ice water

8 medium cooking apples,
    peeled, sliced into wedges
3/4 cup sugar
Cinnamon to taste
1 tablespoon sugar

Combine flour and salt in bowl; mix well. Cut in shortening until crumbly. Add ice water 1 tablespoon at a time, mixing with fork until mixture forms a ball. Divide into 2 portions. Roll each portion into a 12-inch circle on lightly floured waxed paper. Fit half the pastry into pie plate. Spoon mixture of apples, 3/4 cup sugar and cinnamon into pastry-lined pie plate. Top with remaining pastry, sealing edge and cutting vents. Sprinkle with 1 tablespoon sugar. Bake at 425 degrees for 40 to 45 minutes or until brown.

Approx Per Serving: Cal 593; Prot 5 g; Carbo 84 g; T Fat 28 g; 42% Calories from Fat; Chol 0 mg; Fiber 4 g; Sod 356 mg

Robin F. Monaghan

Apple Crumb Pie

Yield: 8 servings

**5 to 7 tart apples, peeled, cut
  into eighths**
1 unbaked (9-inch) pie shell
¹/₂ cup sugar

³/₄ teaspoon cinnamon
¹/₃ cup sugar
³/₄ cup flour
6 tablespoons butter

Arrange apples in pie shell. Sprinkle with mixture of ¹/₂ cup sugar and cinnamon. Combine ¹/₃ cup sugar and flour in bowl; mix well. Cut in butter until crumbly. Sprinkle over prepared layers. Bake at 400 degrees for 35 to 40 minutes or until brown and bubbly. Let stand until cool. Garnish with whipped cream and a sprinkling of additional cinnamon and sugar mixture. Cover edge of pie shell with foil if excess browning occurs during baking. May substitute 2 drained 20-ounce cans sliced apples for fresh apples.

Approx Per Serving: Cal 382; Prot 3 g; Carbo 57 g; T Fat 17 g; 39% Calories from Fat; Chol 23 mg; Fiber 3 g; Sod 210 mg

Mamie Cravens, Macon Area HFH, Macon, GA
Mary K. Ruegg, Northern Straits HFH, St. Ignace, MI

No-Crust Apple Pie

Yield: 4 servings

5 apples, peeled, thinly sliced
1 teaspoon cinnamon
1 teaspoon nutmeg
**4 slices white bread, cut
  into quarters**
1 cup sugar

1 egg, beaten
¹/₂ cup melted margarine

Arrange apples in buttered 8x8-inch baking dish. Sprinkle with mixture of cinnamon and nutmeg. Top with bread. Combine sugar, egg and margarine in bowl; mix well. Pour over prepared layers. Bake at 350 degrees for 45 to 50 minutes or until brown.

Approx Per Serving: Cal 584; Prot 5 g; Carbo 88 g; T Fat 26 g; 38% Calories from Fat; Chol 54 mg; Fiber 4 g; Sod 427 mg

Robert Dessell,
Pensacola HFH, Pensacola, FL

Photo by Susie Estill

On my first visit to Americus, Georgia and Habitat's international headquarters, I viewed the thirty homes that were blitz built the summer of 1994, before the floods. I could not believe how close the floods came to wiping out all of those homes! God had better plans for those homes I think.

MAMIE CRAVENS
MACON AREA HFH

Sugar-Free Apple Pie

Yield: 8 servings

1 (20-ounce) can unsweetened
  sliced apples
1 recipe (2-crust) pie pastry
$1/2$ cup aspertame
2 tablespoons cornstarch

$3/4$ teaspoon cinnamon
$3/4$ teaspoon nutmeg
1 tablespoon butter or
  margarine

Drain apples, reserving juice. Combine reserved juice with enough water to measure $1/4$ cup. Spread apples in pastry-lined 8-inch pie plate; pour juice over apples. Sprinkle with mixture of aspertame, cornstarch, cinnamon and nutmeg; dot with butter. Top with remaining pastry; seal edge and cut vents. Bake at 425 degrees for 30 to 35 minutes or until brown.

Approx Per Serving: Cal 284; Prot 3 g; Carbo 34 g; T Fat 16 g; 49% Calories from Fat; Chol 4 mg; Fiber 2 g; Sod 234 mg

Jean A. Bell, Warren County HFH, Front Royal, VA

Blackberry Pie

Yield: 6 servings

3 cups whole wheat flour
$1 1/2$ cups oat bran flour
$1/2$ teaspoon salt
1 cup canola or safflower oil
13 tablespoons cold water

5 tablespoons oat or wheat flour
4 cups (heaping) blackberries
$1/2$ to 1 cup honey
1 tablespoon butter or
  margarine

Sift whole wheat flour, $1 1/2$ cups oat bran flour and salt into bowl; mix well. Stir in mixture of canola oil and cold water until mixture forms a ball. Divide into 2 portions. Roll each portion between sheets of waxed paper to fit 9-inch pie plate. Arrange $1/2$ of the pastry in greased pie plate; trim edges, allowing some overlap. Sprinkle 5 tablespoons oat flour over blackberries in bowl. Pour honey over mixture; mix well. Spoon into pastry-lined pie plate; dot with butter. Top with remaining pastry; trim edges, allowing generous overlap. Fold top pastry edge under edge of bottom pastry; flute edges and cut vents. Bake at 400 degrees for 40 to 50 minutes or until brown. Let cool before serving. May substitute whole wheat flour for oat bran flour.

Approx Per Serving: Cal 841; Prot 14 g; Carbo 122 g; T Fat 42 g; 41% Calories from Fat; Chol 5 mg; Fiber 17 g; Sod 224 mg

Reverend Jon Stasney, Midland HFH, Midland, TX

Blueberry 'n Cheese Pie

Yield: 8 servings

1/4 cup finely chopped pecans
1 unbaked (9-inch) pie shell
8 ounces cream cheese,
    softened
2 cups confectioners' sugar

l envelope whipped topping mix
1/2 cup low-fat milk
1/2 teaspoon vanilla extract
1 (21-ounce) can blueberry pie
    filling

Press pecans into side and bottom of pie shell. Bake at 400 degrees for 15 minutes or until light brown. Let stand until cool. Beat cream cheese and confectioners' sugar in mixer bowl until light and fluffy. Spread over bottom of pie shell. Prepare whipped topping according to package directions, using 1/2 cup low-fat milk and 1/2 teaspoon vanilla and beating until stiff peaks form. Spread over cream cheese mixture. Chill. Top each slice with a spoonful of pie filling.

Approx Per Serving: Cal 474; Prot 5 g; Carbo 65 g; T Fat 23 g; 43% Calories from Fat; Chol 33 mg; Fiber 2 g; Sod 238 mg

Marjorie Griffin, Rabun County HFH, Rabun Gap, GA

Caramel Pies

Yield: 12 servings

1 cup chopped pecans
1 (7-ounce) can flaked coconut
2 tablespoons melted margarine
1 (14-ounce) can sweetened
    condensed milk
8 ounces cream cheese,
    softened

16 ounces whipped topping
1 (20-ounce) jar caramel ice
    cream topping
2 unbaked (10-inch) deep-dish
    pie shells

Combine pecans, coconut and margarine in bowl; mix well. Spread on baking sheet. Toast in moderate oven until light brown, stirring occasionally. Beat condensed milk and cream cheese in mixer bowl until smooth. Fold in whipped topping. Layer cream cheese mixture, ice cream topping and pecan and coconut mixture 1/2 at a time in each pie shell. Chill until serving time.

Approx Per Serving: Cal 749; Prot 9 g; Carbo 83 g; T Fat 45 g; 53% Calories from Fat; Chol 32 mg; Fiber 4 g; Sod 520 mg

Lynda Goble, Loudon County HFH Inc., Loudon, TN

My favorite memory is of seeing and hearing eighty (plus)-year-old Louis Littlejohn end last year's "Raise the Roof Rally" by singing "His Eye is on the Sparrow." There were few dry eyes and everyone left humming or singing that song.

**REVEREND JON STASNEY
MIDLAND HFH**

Cherry Surprise

Yield: 8 servings

1 cup flour
1/4 cup packed brown sugar
1/2 cup margarine, softened
1/2 cup chopped pecans
1 envelope whipped topping mix

3 ounces cream cheese, softened
1/2 cup confectioners' sugar
1 (21-ounce) can cherry pie filling

Combine flour, brown sugar, margarine and pecans in bowl; mix well. Spread on baking sheet. Bake at 350 degrees for 15 minutes or until brown. Let stand until cool. Crumble into 9-inch pie plate. Prepare whipped topping in mixer bowl using package directions. Add cream cheese and confectioners' sugar, beating until smooth. Spoon into prepared pie plate. Spread with cherry pie filling. Chill until set. Chill overnight to enhance flavor.

Approx Per Serving: Cal 422; Prot 4 g; Carbo 51 g; T Fat 23 g; 49% Calories from Fat; Chol 14 mg; Fiber 1 g; Sod 220 mg

Debra Valentine, HFH of Cabarrus County, Concord, NC

Best-in-Town Cherry Pie

Yield: 6 servings

2 (21-ounce) cans cherry pie filling
1 recipe (2-crust) pie pastry

1 egg white, lightly beaten
1/2 cup sugar

Spoon pie filling into pastry-lined pie plate. Top with remaining pastry; seal edge and cut large "C" in top of pastry. Brush with egg white; sprinkle with sugar. Bake at 350 degrees for 25 to 30 minutes or until burned. Throw away pie. Drive to Schulers' Bakery and buy "The Best Cherry Pie in Town."

Nutritional information for this recipe is not available.

Tim Melfi, Clark County Community HFH, Springfield, OH

Chess Pie

Yield: 6 servings

1 1/3 cups sugar
1/2 cup margarine
1 cup raisins
1/2 cup chopped pecans

1 teaspoon vanilla extract
3 egg yolks, beaten
3 egg whites, stiffly beaten
1 unbaked (9-inch) pie shell

Beat sugar and margarine in mixer bowl until light and fluffy. Stir in raisins, pecans and vanilla. Add egg yolks; mix well. Fold in egg whites. Spoon into pie shell. Bake at 350 degrees until center is set.

Approx Per Serving: Cal 653; Prot 7 g; Carbo 82 g; T Fat 35 g; 47% Calories from Fat; Chol 106 mg; Fiber 3 g; Sod 376 mg

Lennie Elliott, Butler County HFH, El Dorado, KS

Chocolate Pie

Yield: 6 servings

³/₄ cup sugar
3 egg whites
1 teaspoon vinegar
1 teaspoon vanilla extract
8 (1-ounce) squares semisweet
   chocolate

3 egg yolks, beaten
¹/₂ cup sugar
1 teaspoon water
1 cup whipping cream, whipped

Add ³/₄ cup sugar gradually to egg whites in mixer bowl, beating constantly until stiff peaks form. Add vinegar and vanilla; mix well. Spread evenly over side and bottom of buttered pie plate. Bake at 275 degrees for 1 hour. Let stand until cool. Melt chocolate in double boiler over hot water, stirring until smooth. Combine egg yolks and ¹/₂ cup sugar in bowl; mix well. Stir in water. Add to chocolate, stirring until blended. Let stand until cool. Fold in whipped cream. Spoon into meringue pie shell. Chill for 6 hours.

Approx Per Serving: Cal 517; Prot 6 g; Carbo 67 g; T Fat 29 g; 47% Calories from Fat; Chol 160 mg; Fiber 2 g; Sod 51 mg

Margie Mahoney, HFH of Oshkosh Inc., Oshkosh, WI

Any-Occasion Chocolate Pie

Yield: 6 servings

2 (1-ounce) squares
   unsweetened chocolate
2¹/₂ cups milk
1 cup sugar
6 tablespoons flour
¹/₂ teaspoon salt
2 egg yolks, lightly beaten

2 tablespoons butter
1 teaspoon vanilla extract
1 (9-inch) graham cracker pie
   shell
¹/₂ cup whipping cream,
   whipped
1 or 2 drops of food coloring

Heat chocolate and milk in double boiler over hot water until smooth, stirring frequently. Beat with rotary beater until blended. Stir in mixture of sugar, flour and salt gradually. Cook until thickened, stirring constantly. Cook for 10 minutes longer, stirring occasionally. Stir a small amount of hot mixture into egg yolks; stir egg yolks into hot mixture. Cook for 5 minutes, stirring occasionally. Stir in butter and vanilla. Cool for 5 minutes, stirring 1 or 2 times. Spoon into pie shell. Chill until set. Tint whipped cream with food coloring. Spread over pie in desired shape. Garnish with chopped nuts and chocolate chips.

Approx Per Serving: Cal 658; Prot 9 g; Carbo 83 g; T Fat 35 g; 46% Calories from Fat; Chol 122 mg; Fiber 3 g; Sod 587 mg

Tamara Palys, Pinellas HFH, St. Petersburg, FL

There is no way I could have ever bought with money any of the things I have learned or felt by working on this house.

NANCY BOYD
HFH VOLUNTEER, BEND, OR

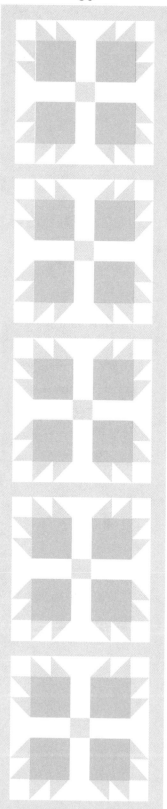

Chocolate Banana Pecan Pie

Yield: 6 servings

3 eggs, beaten
1 cup packed light brown sugar
$1/2$ cup light corn syrup
2 tablespoons flour
$1/4$ cup melted butter

1 banana, chopped
$1/2$ cup chocolate chips
1 cup chopped pecans
1 (10-inch) deep-dish graham
   cracker pie shell

Combine eggs, brown sugar, corn syrup, flour and butter in bowl; mix well. Stir in banana, chocolate chips and pecans. Spoon into pie shell. Bake at 350 degrees for 1 hour.

Approx Per Serving: Cal 702; Prot 7 g; Carbo 93 g; T Fat 37 g; 45% Calories from Fat; Chol 127 mg; Fiber 4 g; Sod 364 mg

Linda Cawley, HFH of Cabarrus County, Concord, NC

French Silk Chocolate Pie

Yield: 8 servings

$1/2$ cup melted margarine
1 cup flour
$1/2$ cup chopped walnuts
1 cup margarine, softened
$1 1/2$ cups sugar

2 teaspoons vanilla extract
3 (1-ounce) squares
   unsweetened chocolate,
   melted
4 eggs

Combine $1/2$ cup margarine, flour and walnuts in bowl; mix well. Pat over side and bottom of 9-inch pie plate. Bake at 325 degrees for 15 minutes. Let stand until cool. Cream 1 cup margarine and sugar in mixer bowl until light and fluffy. Add vanilla and chocolate; mix well. Add eggs 1 at a time, beating for 5 minutes after each addition. Spoon into pie shell. Chill until serving time.

Approx Per Serving: Cal 649; Prot 7 g; Carbo 54 g; T Fat 47 g; 63% Calories from Fat; Chol 106 mg; Fiber 2 g; Sod 436 mg

Mary Howe, Ashtabula County HFH, Jefferson, OH

Chocolate Chip Pie

Yield: 6 servings

1/2 cup melted butter or
   margarine, cooled
1 cup sugar
2 eggs
1/2 cup flour

1 tablespoon vanilla extract
1 cup semisweet chocolate chips
3/4 cup chopped pecans
1 unbaked (9-inch) pie shell

Combine margarine and sugar in bowl; mix well. Add eggs, stirring until blended. Stir in flour and vanilla. Add chocolate chips and pecans; mix well. Spoon into pie shell. Bake at 350 degrees for 45 minutes or until golden brown. Serve warm with ice cream.

Approx Per Serving: Cal 727; Prot 8 g; Carbo 77 g; T Fat 46 g; 55% Calories from Fat; Chol 112 mg; Fiber 4 g; Sod 344 mg

Diane Cooke, West Plains Area HFH, West Plains, MO

Easy-as-Pie

Yield: 8 servings

1/4 cup butter or margarine,
   softened
1 1/2 cups sugar
3 tablespoons baking cocoa

2 eggs
1 (5-ounce) can evaporated milk
1 teaspoon vanilla extract
1 unbaked (9-inch) pie shell

Cream butter in mixer bowl. Add sugar, beating until light and fluffy. Beat in baking cocoa until blended. Add eggs 1 at a time, beating well after each addition. Add evaporated milk and vanilla; mix well. Spoon into pie shell. Bake at 325 degrees for 50 minutes. Let stand until cool. Add 1 tablespoon lemon juice and omit baking cocoa and vanilla for Lemon Chess Pie. Substitute 1 cup grated or shredded coconut for baking cocoa and vanilla for Coconut Chess Pie.

Approx Per Serving: Cal 362; Prot 5 g; Carbo 51 g; T Fat 16 g; 40% Calories from Fat; Chol 74 mg; Fiber 1 g; Sod 216 mg

Tom and Pat Row, HFH of Anderson County TN, Oak Ridge, TN

Last summer I coordinated lunches for the Saturday Habitat work crews. Our seven-year-old daughter gave a tour of the unfinished Habitat house to neighborhood residents while the Habitat family smiled and followed along. Our daughter had watched the house come up from the ground and was proud to show people around.

DIANE COOKE
WEST PLAINS AREA HFH

Japanese Fruit Pie

Yield: 6 servings

1/2 cup margarine, softened
2 cups sugar
3 eggs
1/2 cup chopped pecans
1/2 cup drained crushed
  pineapple
1/2 cup flaked coconut
1 teaspoon vanilla extract
1 teaspoon cider vinegar
1/4 teaspoon salt
1 unbaked (9-inch) pie shell

Beat margarine, sugar and eggs in mixer bowl until smooth. Stir in pecans, pineapple and coconut. Add vanilla, vinegar and salt; mix well. Spoon into pie shell. Bake at 325 degrees for 45 minutes.

Approx Per Serving: Cal 695; Prot 6 g; Carbo 88 g; T Fat 37 g; 47% Calories from Fat; Chol 106 mg; Fiber 2 g; Sod 464 mg

Stella Pieper, Knox County HFH, Edwardsport, IN

Mocha Fudge Pie

Yield: 8 servings

1/3 cup hot water
2 teaspoons instant coffee
  granules
1/2 (20-ounce) package light
  fudge brownie mix
1 teaspoon vanilla extract
2 egg whites
3/4 cup 1% milk
2 tablespoons Kahlúa
1 teaspoon instant coffee
  granules
1 teaspoon vanilla extract
1 (4-ounce) package chocolate
  instant pudding mix
3 cups light whipped topping,
  thawed
1 tablespoon Kahlúa
1 teaspoon instant coffee
  granules

Combine hot water and 2 teaspoons coffee granules in bowl, stirring until dissolved. Stir in brownie mix, 1 teaspoon vanilla and egg whites until blended. Spoon into 9-inch pie plate coated with nonstick cooking spray. Bake at 325 degrees for 22 minutes. Let stand until cool. Combine milk, 2 tablespoons Kahlúa, 1 teaspoon coffee granules, 1 teaspoon vanilla and pudding mix in mixer bowl. Beat at medium speed for 1 minute. Fold in 1 1/2 cups of the whipped topping. Spoon into prepared pie plate. Combine 1 tablespoon Kahlúa and 1 teaspoon coffee granules in bowl; mix well. Fold in remaining whipped topping. Spread evenly over top, sealing to edge. Garnish with chocolate curls. Serve immediately or store, loosely covered, in refrigerator. Prepare nonalcoholic version by substituting 2 tablespoons 1% milk for the Kahlúa in pudding mixture and omitting Kahlúa in topping and dissolving coffee granules in 1 tablespoon hot water.

Approx Per Serving: Cal 284; Prot 3 g; Carbo 52 g; T Fat 6 g; 20% Calories from Fat; Chol 1 mg; Fiber <1 g; Sod 350 mg

Debbie Prynoski, Burlington County NJ HFH, Bordentown, NJ

Bob Hope's Favorite Lemon Pie

Yield: 6 servings

1 cup plus 2 tablespoons sugar
3 tablespoons cornstarch
1 cup boiling water
1/4 cup lemon juice
2 tablespoons butter
4 egg yolks, lightly beaten

Grated rind of 1 lemon
1/8 teaspoon salt
1 baked (9-inch) pie shell
3 egg whites
2 tablespoons sugar

Combine 1 cup plus 2 tablespoons sugar and cornstarch in saucepan; mix well. Add boiling water gradually, stirring until blended. Add lemon juice, butter, egg yolks, lemon rind and salt; mix well. Cook for 2 to 3 minutes or until of the desired consistency. Spoon into pie shell. Beat egg whites in mixer bowl until soft peaks form. Add 2 tablespoons sugar, beating constantly until stiff peaks form. Spread over pie, sealing to edge. Bake at 250 to 300 degrees for 15 minutes or until light brown.

Photo by Carolyn DeMeriott

JIMMY CARTER AND BOB HOPE

Approx Per Serving:
Cal 419; Prot 6 g; Carbo 61 g;
T Fat 18 g; 37% Calories from Fat;
Chol 152 mg; Fiber 1 g; Sod 279 mg

Bob Hope, Actor and Comedian, Palm Springs, CA

Lemon Sponge Pie

Yield: 6 servings

3 tablespoons flour
1 cup sugar
1/4 cup melted butter
3 egg yolks, lightly beaten
Grated rind and juice of 1 lemon

1 1/2 cups milk, heated
3 egg whites
1/8 teaspoon salt
1 unbaked (9-inch) pie shell

Combine flour, sugar and butter in bowl; mix well. Stir in egg yolks, lemon rind and lemon juice. Add milk; mix well. Beat egg whites and salt in mixer bowl until stiff peaks form. Fold into lemon mixture. Spoon into pie shell. Bake at 400 degrees for 10 minutes. Reduce oven temperature to 325 degrees. Bake for 45 minutes longer.

Approx Per Serving: Cal 447; Prot 8 g; Carbo 54 g; T Fat 23 g;
45% Calories from Fat; Chol 135 mg; Fiber 1 g; Sod 347 mg

Peg Mullaney, Black Hills Area HFH, Rapid City, SD

Lime Pie
Yield: 6 servings

1 (14-ounce) can sweetened
　condensed milk
1/2 cup lime juice

2 eggs, beaten
1 (9-inch) graham cracker pie
　shell

Combine condensed milk and lime juice in bowl; mix well. Stir in eggs. Pour into pie shell. Bake at 350 degrees for 10 to 15 minutes or until set. May add grated lime or lemon rind to taste. May substitute lemon juice or Key lime juice for lime juice.

Approx Per Serving: Cal 510; Prot 10 g; Carbo 73 g; T Fat 21 g; 36% Calories from Fat; Chol 93 mg; Fiber 2 g; Sod 414 mg

Joyce Frohn, University of Wisconsin Oshkosh HFH, Oshkosh, WI

Northern Key Lime Pie
Yield: 10 servings

16 graham crackers, crushed
1/4 cup butter, softened
1/4 cup sugar
1 (3-ounce) package lime gelatin
3/4 cup boiling water

1/2 cup sugar
Juice of 2 lemons
1 can Milnot, chilled, whipped
1 to 2 cups whipping cream,
　whipped

Combine graham crackers, butter and sugar in bowl; mix well. Pat into 10-inch pie plate or 9x13-inch baking dish. Bake in moderate oven for 8 minutes. Dissolve gelatin in boiling water in bowl; mix well. Stir in sugar and lemon juice. Chill until partially set. Fold in Milnot. Spoon into prepared pie plate. Chill until set. Spread evenly with whipped cream. Garnish with tinted sugar or chocolate curls. May substitute evaporated milk for Milnot.

Approx Per Serving: Cal 356; Prot 3 g; Carbo 34 g; T Fat 24 g; 59% Calories from Fat; Chol 78 mg; Fiber <1 g; Sod 165 mg

Iola K. Brown, Greater Keokuk Area HFH, Keokuk, IA

Oatmeal Pie
Yield: 6 servings

3 eggs, beaten
3/4 cup light pancake syrup
3/4 cup rolled oats
1/4 cup margarine
3/4 cup packed brown sugar

1 teaspoon vanilla extract
1/2 cup grated coconut
1/4 cup chopped pecans
1 unbaked (9-inch) pie shell

Combine eggs, syrup, oats, margarine, brown sugar, vanilla, coconut and pecans in bowl; mix well. Spoon into pie shell. Bake at 350 degrees for 40 minutes. Let stand until cool. Serve with whipped topping or frozen yogurt. May substitute egg substitute for whole eggs.

Approx Per Serving: Cal 509; Prot 7 g; Carbo 63 g; T Fat 27 g; 46% Calories from Fat; Chol 106 mg; Fiber 3 g; Sod 373 mg

Bonnie Orton, HFHI, Area #5, Chicago, IL

Peach Cream Pie

Yield: 6 servings

³/₄ cup sugar
¹/₄ cup flour
¹/₄ teaspoon salt
¹/₄ teaspoon nutmeg

4 cups sliced peaches
1 unbaked (9-inch) pie shell
³/₄ cup half-and-half

Combine sugar, flour, salt and nutmeg in bowl; mix well. Add peaches, tossing to coat. Spoon into pie shell. Pour half-and-half over peach mixture. Bake at 400 degrees for 45 minutes. Serve warm with ice cream or whipped cream.

Approx Per Serving: Cal 362; Prot 4 g; Carbo 57 g; T Fat 14 g; 34% Calories from Fat; Chol 11 mg; Fiber 2 g; Sod 264 mg

Robbie Barnes, Oconee County HFH, Salem, SC

Peach Custard Pie

Yield: 6 servings

3 fresh peaches, peeled, sliced
1 unbaked (9-inch) pie shell
4 eggs, lightly beaten
¹/₂ cup sugar

¹/₄ teaspoon salt
¹/₂ teaspoon vanilla extract
2¹/₂ cups milk, scalded

Arrange peaches in pie shell. Combine eggs, sugar, salt and vanilla in bowl, stirring until blended. Stir in milk gradually. Pour over peaches. Bake at 350 degrees for 35 to 45 minutes or until set. Let stand until cool. Chill until serving time. May substitute one 16-ounce can drained peaches for fresh peaches. May sprinkle pie with 1 teaspoon nutmeg before baking.

Approx Per Serving: Cal 353; Prot 10 g; Carbo 41 g; T Fat 17 g; 43% Calories from Fat; Chol 155 mg; Fiber 1 g; Sod 343 mg

Susan M. Parsel-Armagost, Blue Spruce HFH, Evergreen, CO

Peanut Butter Pie

Yield: 6 servings

¹/₂ cup peanut butter
³/₄ cup confectioners' sugar
1 baked (9-inch) pie shell

1 (6-ounce) package vanilla or chocolate instant pudding mix, prepared, chilled
8 ounces whipped topping

Combine peanut butter and confectioners' sugar in bowl, stirring until crumbly. Sprinkle ²/₃ cup of the crumb mixture into pie shell. Spoon pudding over crumb mixture; top with whipped topping. Sprinkle with remaining crumb mixture. Chill until serving time.

Approx Per Serving: Cal 624; Prot 12 g; Carbo 70 g; T Fat 35 g; 49% Calories from Fat; Chol 16 mg; Fiber 2 g; Sod 680 mg

Karen Kruzel, Maumee Valley HFH, Toledo, OH

My favorite times as a Habitat volunteer are when I am sharing the loving feelings of thanks with our new homeowners.

**SUSAN M. PARSEL-ARMAGOST
BLUE SPRUCE HFH**

Raisin Cream Pie

Yield: 6 servings

2 cups raisins
1 cup water
1/2 cup cream
1/2 cup milk
1 cup packed brown sugar
3 1/2 tablespoons flour
1/2 teaspoon cinnamon

3 egg yolks, beaten
1 baked (9-inch) pie shell
3 egg whites
1/2 teaspoon vanilla extract
1/4 teaspoon cream of tartar
6 tablespoons sugar

Combine raisins and water in saucepan. Cook until soft. Stir in cream and milk. Add mixture of brown sugar, flour and cinnamon; mix well. Stir in egg yolks. Cook until thickened, stirring constantly. Pour into pie shell. Beat egg whites with vanilla and cream of tartar in mixer bowl until soft peaks form. Add sugar gradually, beating constantly until stiff peaks form. Spread over raisin mixture, sealing to edge. Bake at 350 degrees for 12 to 15 minutes or until brown.

Approx Per Serving: Cal 621; Prot 8 g; Carbo 105 g; T Fat 21 g; 30% Calories from Fat; Chol 136 mg; Fiber 4 g; Sod 230 mg

Eleanor C. Pease, Jasper County HFH, Colfax, IA

Sour Cream Raisin Pie

Yield: 6 servings

1 unbaked (9-inch) pie shell
1 1/3 cups raisins
1 cup water
3/4 cup sugar
3 egg yolks, beaten
1/8 teaspoon salt
1/4 cup sugar
1 tablespoon (heaping) cornstarch

1 1/2 cups sour cream
1/2 teaspoon cinnamon
1/4 teaspoon ground cloves
1 tablespoon vanilla extract
3 egg whites
1/4 teaspoon salt
1/4 teaspoon cream of tartar
6 tablespoons sugar

Bake pie shell at 450 degrees for 10 minutes. Combine raisins, water and 3/4 cup sugar in saucepan. Bring to a boil. Boil, covered, over medium heat until raisins plump. Stir in mixture of egg yolks, 1/8 teaspoon salt, 1/4 cup sugar, cornstarch, sour cream, cinnamon and cloves. Cook until thickened, stirring constantly. Stir in vanilla. Spoon into pie shell. Beat egg whites, 1/4 teaspoon salt and cream of tartar in mixer bowl until soft peaks form. Add 6 tablespoons sugar 1 tablespoon at a time, beating constantly until stiff peaks form. Spread over pie, sealing to edge. Bake at 350 degrees for 12 to 15 minutes or until brown.

Approx Per Serving: Cal 619; Prot 8 g; Carbo 94 g; T Fat 25 g; 36% Calories from Fat; Chol 132 mg; Fiber 2 g; Sod 362 mg

Gary Rowland, Butler County HFH, Andover, KS

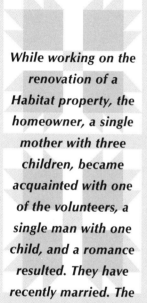

While working on the renovation of a Habitat property, the homeowner, a single mother with three children, became acquainted with one of the volunteers, a single man with one child, and a romance resulted. They have recently married. The community has been blessed by this family.

ELEANOR C. PEASE
JASPER COUNTY HFH

Raspberry Pie

Yield: 6 servings

1 teaspoon salt
2 cups flour
²/₃ cup shortening
¹/₄ cup ice water
1 tablespoon vinegar
4 cups raspberries

1 cup sugar
3¹/₂ tablespoons instant tapioca
¹/₂ teaspoon ground orange rind
2 tablespoons lemon juice
¹/₄ cup cold water

Combine salt and flour in bowl; mix well. Cut in shortening until crumbly. Add ¹/₄ cup ice water and vinegar, mixing with fork until mixture forms a ball. Divide dough into 2 portions. Let stand while preparing filling. Combine raspberries, sugar, tapioca, orange rind, lemon juice and ¹/₄ cup cold water in bowl; mix well. Roll each dough portion into a 12-inch circle on lightly floured surface. Fit 1 pastry circle into 9-inch pie plate. Spoon raspberry mixture into pie shell. Top with remaining pastry, sealing edge and cutting vents. Bake at 400 degrees for 45 to 60 minutes.

Approx Per Serving: Cal 543; Prot 5 g; Carbo 80 g; T Fat 24 g; 39% Calories from Fat; Chol 0 mg; Fiber 5 g; Sod 357 mg

Fred Giese, Green County HFH, Monroe, WI

Raspberry Cream Pie

Yield: 6 servings

1 cup sugar
2 tablespoons (heaping) flour
1 cup whipping cream

2 cups raspberries
1 unbaked (9-inch) pie shell

Combine sugar and flour in bowl; mix well. Add whipping cream; mix well. Fold in raspberries. Spoon into pie shell. Bake at 450 degrees for 10 to 15 minutes; reduce oven temperature to 350 degrees. Bake for 35 to 50 minutes longer or until set.

Approx Per Serving: Cal 454; Prot 3 g; Carbo 55 g; T Fat 25 g; 49% Calories from Fat; Chol 54 mg; Fiber 3 g; Sod 178 mg

Janet Viau, Bay de Noc HFH, Brampton, MI

All of the smiles, love, and bonding that occurs through the fellowship of working on Habitat projects, as well as working behind the scenes with our affiliate board and committee members, makes it all worthwhile.

GARY ROWLAND
BUTLER COUNTY HFH

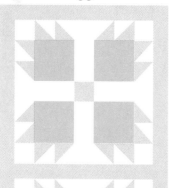

Strawberry Pie

Yield: 6 servings

3 tablespoons strawberry gelatin
3 tablespoons cornstarch
1 cup sugar
2 cups water

1 teaspoon red food coloring
2 cups strawberries
1 baked (10-inch) pie shell

Combine gelatin, cornstarch and sugar in 2-quart saucepan; mix well. Stir in water and food coloring. Cook over medium heat until thickened and clear, stirring constantly. Cool to lukewarm. Fold in strawberries. Spoon into pie shell. Chill for 30 minutes or until set. Serve with whipped topping. Store in refrigerator.

Approx Per Serving: Cal 348; Prot 3 g; Carbo 59 g; T Fat 12 g; 30% Calories from Fat; Chol 0 mg; Fiber 2 g; Sod 191 mg

Ella L. Smith, Appalachia HFH, Elgin, TN

Mom's Sugar Pies

Yield: 12 servings

3 cups packed light brown sugar
3 tablespoons flour
3 eggs, lightly beaten
1/2 cup melted butter

1 cup milk
1/2 teaspoon lemon extract
2 unbaked (9-inch) pie shells

Combine brown sugar, flour and eggs in bowl; mix well. Stir in butter, milk and lemon extract. Pour into pie shells. Bake at 350 degrees for 1 hour or until set.

Approx Per Serving: Cal 434; Prot 4 g; Carbo 61 g; T Fat 20 g; 41% Calories from Fat; Chol 77 mg; Fiber 1 g; Sod 284 mg

Barbara L. Saunders, Lynchburg HFH, Lynchburg, VA

Toll House Pie

Yield: 6 servings

2 eggs
1/2 cup flour
1/2 cup sugar
1/2 cup packed brown sugar

1 cup melted butter, cooled
1 cup chocolate chips
1 cup chopped pecans
1 unbaked (9-inch) pie shell

Beat eggs in mixer bowl until foamy. Add flour, sugar and brown sugar, beating until blended. Stir in butter. Add chocolate chips and pecans; mix well. Spoon into pie shell. Bake at 325 degrees for 1 hour. May substitute walnuts for pecans.

Approx Per Serving: Cal 881; Prot 8 g; Carbo 75 g; T Fat 65 g; 64% Calories from Fat; Chol 154 mg; Fiber 4 g; Sod 506 mg

Kelle Shultz, Knoxville HFH, Knoxville, TN

Pie Pastry

Yields: 12 servings

2 cups flour
1 teaspoon salt

²/₃ cup vegetable oil
3 tablespoons cold water

Combine flour, salt and oil in bowl, stirring with fork until blended. Sprinkle cold water over flour mixture, mixing with fork until mixture forms a ball. Divide into 2 portions. Roll each portion between sheets of plastic wrap to fit 8-inch pie plate. Fit into pie plates; prick with fork. Bake at 450 degrees for 10 minutes or until light brown. Reduce oven temperature to 425 degrees for 2-crust pie.

Approx Per Serving: Cal 183; Prot 2 g; Carbo 16 g; T Fat 12 g; 61% Calories from Fat; Chol 0 mg; Fiber 1 g; Sod 178 mg

Irene Hartley, HFH of Miami County, Piqua, OH

Easy Pastry

Yield: 6 servings

1¹/₂ cups flour
1¹/₂ teaspoons sugar
³/₄ teaspoon salt

¹/₂ cup salad oil
2 tablespoons milk

Combine flour, sugar and salt in bowl, stirring with fork until mixed. Add mixture of oil and milk, stirring with fork until moistened. Pat over side and bottom of 9-inch pie plate; flute edge. Prick with fork at 1-inch intervals. Bake at 425 degrees for 10 to 15 minutes or until light brown.

Approx Per Serving: Cal 281; Prot 3 g; Carbo 25 g; T Fat 19 g; 60% Calories from Fat; Chol 1 mg; Fiber 1 g; Sod 270 mg

Patricia Koch, Marion County HFH, Marion, SC

Photo by HFHI

Hal Ketchum's Maple-Glazed Apple Tart

Yield: 10 servings

1 teaspoon dry yeast
1 tablespoon maple syrup
1/2 cup (105- to 115-degree) water
1 1/2 cups bread flour
1 teaspoon salt

1 tablespoon walnut or vegetable oil
1 pound Granny Smith apples, peeled, thinly sliced
1/4 cup chopped walnuts
1/2 cup maple syrup

Combine yeast, 1 tablespoon maple syrup and warm water in bowl; mix well. Let stand for 10 minutes. Combine flour and salt in food processor container. Add yeast mixture and 2 1/2 teaspoons of the walnut oil gradually, processing constantly until mixture forms a ball. Knead gently on lightly floured surface 4 times. Place in bowl coated with nonstick cooking spray, turning to coat surface. Let rise, covered, in warm place for 45 minutes or until doubled in bulk. Punch dough down. Roll into 12-inch circle on lightly floured surface. Place on baking sheet sprayed with nonstick cooking spray. Brush dough with remaining walnut oil. Let rise for 30 minutes or until puffy. Arrange apple slices in overlapping circular pattern over dough. Bake at 425 degrees for 10 minutes. Sprinkle with walnuts. Bake for 10 minutes longer. Heat 1/2 cup maple syrup in saucepan over medium-high heat to 230 degrees on candy thermometer, spun-thread stage. Cool for 1 minute. Drizzle over warm tart. Serve immediately.

Approx Per Serving: Cal 173; Prot 3 g; Carbo 34 g; T Fat 4 g; 18% Calories from Fat; Chol 0 mg; Fiber 2 g; Sod 216 mg

Hal Ketchum, Nashville, TN

Butter Tarts

Yield: 12 servings

1 egg, beaten
1 cup packed brown sugar
1 cup raisins

1 teaspoon vanilla extract
4 teaspoons butter or margarine
12 unbaked tart shells

Combine egg, brown sugar, raisins, vanilla and butter in bowl; mix well. Spoon into tart shells. Bake at 375 degrees for 15 minutes or until light brown. May double or triple recipe.

Approx Per Serving: Cal 512; Prot 6 g; Carbo 58 g; T Fat 29 g; 50% Calories from Fat; Chol 21 mg; Fiber 2 g; Sod 206 mg

Gayle Evans, Alpena Area HFH Inc., Alpena, MI

Apple Dumplings

Yield: 8 servings

2 cups flour
2 teaspoons baking powder
3/4 teaspoon salt
5 tablespoons shortening, beaten
3/4 cup milk
6 apples, finely chopped

1/2 cup sugar
Cinnamon to taste
3/4 cup water
1 cup sugar
1/4 teaspoon salt
1/4 teaspoon cinnamon
1 teaspoon butter

Combine flour, baking powder and 3/4 teaspoon salt in bowl; mix well. Add shortening; mix well. Stir in milk until soft dough forms. Roll into 1/2-inch thick rectangle on lightly floured surface. Spread with apples; sprinkle with 1/2 cup sugar and cinnamon to taste. Roll as for jelly roll; cut into 11/2- to 2-inch slices. Arrange cut side up in greased 8x8-inch baking pan. Bring water, 1 cup sugar, 1/4 teaspoon salt, 1/4 teaspoon cinnamon and butter to a boil in saucepan, stirring occasionally. Pour over dumplings. Bake at 375 degrees for 45 minutes or until golden brown. Serve with milk or ice cream.

Approx Per Serving: Cal 404; Prot 4 g; Carbo 77 g; T Fat 10 g; 22% Calories from Fat; Chol 4 mg; Fiber 3 g; Sod 366 mg

Bonnie Hoover, Northwest IN HFH, New Buffalo, MI

Old-Fashioned Apple Dumplings

Yield: 4 servings

1 cup packed brown sugar
1 cup hot water
2 teaspoons butter
1 recipe (1-crust) pie pastry mix

1 to 2 teaspoons baking powder
4 tart apples, peeled, cut into quarters
4 teaspoons sugar

Combine brown sugar, hot water and butter in saucepan. Cook until of syrupy consistency, stirring frequently. Pour into 8- or 9-inch baking pan. Prepare pie pastry, adding baking powder to recipe. Divide pastry into 4 portions. Roll each portion into circle large enough to enclose 1 apple. Stand 4 apple quarters up in shape of apple on each pastry circle; spoon 1 teaspoon sugar into center of each apple. Fold dough over to enclose apples; moisten edges to seal. Arrange dumplings in prepared baking pan, spooning some of the syrup over the top. Bake at 450 degrees for 10 minutes; reduce oven temperature to 350 degrees. Bake for 20 to 25 minutes or until apples are tender and dumplings are brown.

Approx Per Serving: Cal 516; Prot 3 g; Carbo 89 g; T Fat 18 g; 30% Calories from Fat; Chol 5 mg; Fiber 3 g; Sod 446 mg

Mary A. DeArmond, Joplin Area HFH, Joplin, MO

My favorite memory is of a partner family's change from despair to hope when selected to be a Habitat family. The recipient had just gone on disability due to a progressive illness and could not see how he was going to provide for his young family. When told of his selection, his response "Praise The Lord" was with special meaning.

**BONNIE HOOVER
NORTHWEST INDIANA HFH**

Baked Apple Rolls
Yield: 10 servings

4 cups flour
4 teaspoons baking powder
2 teaspoons salt
$1/4$ cup vegetable oil
$1^1/_2$ cups milk
4 to 6 Rome, Granny Smith or
  Yellow Delicious apples,
  sliced

$1/2$ cup sugar
$1/2$ to 1 teaspoon cinnamon
$1^1/_2$ cups sugar
3 tablespoons cornstarch
1 cup corn syrup
3 cups water
$1/4$ cup butter
Nutmeg to taste

Combine flour, baking powder and salt in bowl; mix well. Add oil and milk, stirring until blended. Roll into $1/4$- to $3/8$-inch thick rectangle on lightly floured surface. Spread with apples; sprinkle with $1/2$ cup sugar and cinnamon. Roll as for jelly roll; cut into $1^1/_2$-inch slices. Arrange in 9x13-inch baking pan. Combine $1^1/_2$ cups sugar and cornstarch in saucepan; mix well. Stir in corn syrup, water, butter and nutmeg. Cook for 5 minutes, stirring frequently. Pour over rolls. Bake at 350 degrees for 30 to 40 minutes or until apples are tender. Serve warm with ice cream.

Approx Per Serving: Cal 595; Prot 7 g; Carbo 119 g; T Fat 12 g; 18% Calories from Fat; Chol 17 mg; Fiber 3 g; Sod 664 mg

Shirley Patterson, HFH of East King County, Canation, WA

Apple Crisp
Yield: 12 servings

$1/4$ cup packed brown sugar
3 tablespoons flour
$1^1/_2$ teaspoons cinnamon
4 cups sliced peeled apples
1 egg, beaten
1 cup flour

1 cup sugar
1 teaspoon baking powder
$1/4$ teaspoon salt
$1/2$ cup melted butter or
  margarine

Combine brown sugar, flour and cinnamon in bowl; mix well. Add apples; mix well. Spoon into buttered 9x13-inch baking dish. Combine egg, flour, sugar, baking powder and salt in bowl, stirring with fork until crumbly. Sprinkle over apples; drizzle with butter. Bake at 375 degrees for 45 minutes or until brown and bubbly.

Approx Per Serving: Cal 219; Prot 2 g; Carbo 35 g; T Fat 8 g; 33% Calories from Fat; Chol 38 mg; Fiber 1 g; Sod 157 mg

Elaine McCune, HFH of Butler County, Saxonburg, PA

Easy Apple Crisp

Yield: 8 servings

6 large apples, peeled, sliced
1¹/₂ cups sugar
Cinnamon to taste
³/₄ cup flour
¹/₂ cup butter, softened

Arrange apples in ungreased 8x8-inch baking pan. Sprinkle with ¹/₂ cup of the sugar and cinnamon. Combine the remaining sugar and flour in bowl; mix well. Cut in butter until crumbly. Sprinkle over apples; pat down. Sprinkle with cinnamon. Bake at 375 degrees for 30 minutes or until brown and bubbly.

Approx Per Serving: Cal 329; Prot 2 g; Carbo 70 g; T Fat 6 g; 17% Calories from Fat; Chol 16 mg; Fiber 3 g; Sod 59 mg

Cedi Cover, Dixon HFH, Dixon, IL

Divine Apple Crisp

Yield: 12 servings

6 to 8 apples, peeled, sliced
¹/₄ to ¹/₂ cup sugar
¹/₂ to 1 teaspoon cinnamon
³/₄ cup packed brown sugar
¹/₂ cup flour
1 cup rolled oats
¹/₂ cup melted butter or margarine

Toss apples with mixture of sugar and cinnamon in bowl. Arrange in 9x12-inch baking dish. Combine brown sugar, flour, oats and butter in bowl, stirring until crumbly. Spread over apples. Bake at 350 degrees for 45 to 50 minutes or until brown and bubbly.

Approx Per Serving: Cal 236; Prot 2 g; Carbo 40 g; T Fat 8 g; 31% Calories from Fat; Chol 21 mg; Fiber 2 g; Sod 83 mg

Lucy Darr, Clark County Community HFH, Springfield, OH

Apple and Pear Cheese Crisp

Yield: 8 servings

3 cups sliced peeled apples
3 cups sliced peeled pears
1 teaspoon cinnamon
1 tablespoon lemon juice
¹/₂ cup corn syrup
¹/₂ cup sugar
²/₃ cup sifted flour
¹/₄ teaspoon salt
¹/₃ cup butter or margarine, softened
1 cup shredded sharp Cheddar cheese

Arrange apples and pears in greased baking dish; sprinkle with cinnamon. Drizzle with lemon juice and corn syrup. Mix sugar, flour and salt in bowl. Cut in butter until crumbly. Add cheese; mix gently. Sprinkle over prepared layers. Bake at 350 degrees for 1 hour or until apples are tender. Serve warm. May use apples or pears excusively.

Approx Per Serving: Cal 326; Prot 5 g; Carbo 51 g; T Fat 13 g; 34% Calories from Fat; Chol 36 mg; Fiber 3 g; Sod 257 mg

Kimberley P. Fogle, Warren County HFH, Front Royal, VA

One of our founding members died shortly after we dedicated our first Habitat home. Since that time, we have planted a tree in his remembrance in the front yard of that home. It never ceases to remind us of Howard's dedication to serving mankind.

CEDI COVER
DIXON HFH

Easy Apple Macaroon
Yield: 6 servings

3 medium apples, cut into
   quarters
3/4 cup sugar
1 teaspoon cinnamon

1/2 cup flour
1/2 teaspoon salt
1/2 teaspoon baking powder
2 eggs

Arrange apples in buttered 9-inch pie plate. Sprinkle with 1/4 cup of the sugar and cinnamon. Combine remaining sugar, flour, salt and baking powder in bowl; mix well. Beat in eggs until blended. Spread over apples. Bake at 350 degrees for 30 minutes.

Approx Per Serving: Cal 196; Prot 3 g; Carbo 43 g; T Fat 2 g; 9% Calories from Fat; Chol 71 mg; Fiber 2 g; Sod 226 mg

Phyllis A. Parks, Cumberland Valley HFH, Carlisle, PA

Blueberry Buckle
Yield: 6 servings

This makes an impressive and delicious breakfast dessert. Serve with fresh fruit, bacon and an egg casserole.

1/2 cup sugar
1/4 cup melted margarine
1 egg, beaten
1 cup flour
1 1/2 teaspoons baking powder
1/4 teaspoon salt

1/3 cup milk
1 cup blueberries
1/2 cup melted margarine
1/2 cup sugar
1/3 cup flour
1/2 teaspoon cinnamon

Cream 1/2 cup sugar and 1/4 cup margarine in mixer bowl. Add egg, 1 cup flour, baking powder, salt and milk, beating until smooth. Spread in 8x8-inch greased baking pan. Sprinkle with blueberries. Top with mixture of 1/2 cup margarine, 1/2 cup sugar, 1/3 cup flour and cinnamon. Bake at 350 degrees for 45 minutes.

Approx Per Serving: Cal 470; Prot 5 g; Carbo 59 g; T Fat 25 g; 46% Calories from Fat; Chol 37 mg; Fiber 1 g; Sod 458 mg

Kay Hewitt Holmes, Arkansas Valley HFH, Ft. Smith, AR

Blueberry Cobbler

Yield: 8 servings

3 cups fresh blueberries
1/4 teaspoon almond extract
1 cup sifted flour
1 cup sugar

1/2 teaspoon salt
1 egg, beaten
6 tablespoons melted margarine

Spread blueberries in 6x10-inch baking dish sprayed with nonstick cooking spray. Drizzle with almond flavoring. Sift flour, sugar and salt into bowl; mix well. Add egg, stirring until crumbly. Sprinkle over blueberries; drizzle with margarine. Bake at 375 degrees for 40 minutes. Serve with ice cream or whipped cream.

Approx Per Serving: Cal 265; Prot 3 g; Carbo 44 g; T Fat 10 g; 32% Calories from Fat; Chol 27 mg; Fiber 2 g; Sod 245 mg

Ann R. Hartman, Calcasieu Area HFH, Lake Charles, LA

Blueberry Kuchen

Yield: 8 servings

1 cup flour
2 tablespoons sugar
1/4 teaspoon salt
1/2 cup butter, softened
1 tablespoon white vinegar

2 tablespoons flour
1 cup sugar
1/4 teaspoon cinnamon
3 cups blueberries
Confectioners' sugar to taste

Combine 1 cup flour, 2 tablespoons sugar and salt in bowl; mix well. Cut in butter with pastry blender until crumbly. Stir in vinegar. Press over bottom and 1 inch up side of 9-inch springform pan. Combine 2 tablespoons flour, 1 cup sugar and cinnamon in bowl. Fold in 2 cups of the blueberries. Spoon into prepared pan. Bake at 400 degrees for 1 hour. Sprinkle with remaining blueberries. Let stand until cool. Remove ring. Sprinkle with confectioners' sugar. May serve with whipped cream or ice cream.

Approx Per Serving: Cal 305; Prot 2 g; Carbo 49 g; T Fat 12 g; 34% Calories from Fat; Chol 31 mg; Fiber 2 g; Sod 188 mg

Sandra Oudheusden, Westchester County HFH, Valhalla, NY

The idea behind Habitat is not to provide charity for the poor, but to help provide the capital and experience needed to effect long-term change in the community. When the community of need has ownership of and partnership in a project, it supports the project and provides the positive input and work necessary for long-term success.

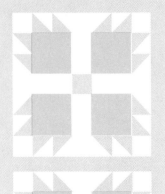

Cherry Cobbler

Yield: 10 servings

1/2 cup shortening	1/2 teaspoon salt
1 cup sugar	2 cups cherries
1 cup milk	1 cup sugar
11/2 cups flour	11/2 cups boiling water
2 teaspoons baking powder	2 tablespoons butter

Cream shortening and 1 cup sugar in mixer bowl until light and fluffy. Add milk; mix well. Beat in flour, baking powder and salt until smooth. Spread in 9x13-inch baking dish. Top with cherries; sprinkle with 1 cup sugar. Pour boiling water over prepared layers; dot with butter. Bake at 350 degrees for 45 minutes.

Approx Per Serving: Cal 371; Prot 3 g; Carbo 60 g; T Fat 14 g; 33% Calories from Fat; Chol 10 mg; Fiber 1 g; Sod 208 mg

Deb Hillman, Southwest Iowa HFH, Shenandoah, IA

Cherry Delight

Yield: 10 servings

1/2 cup margarine	3/4 cup milk
1 cup sugar	1 (16-ounce) can pitted red
1 cup flour	cherries
2 teaspoons baking powder	1/2 cup sugar

Heat margarine in 9x13-inch baking pan until melted, swirling pan to cover. Combine 1 cup sugar, flour, baking powder and milk in bowl; mix well. Spread in prepared pan; do not stir. Pour undrained cherries over top; do not stir. Sprinkle with 1/2 cup sugar; do not stir. Bake at 325 degrees for 1 hour.

Approx Per Serving: Cal 293; Prot 2 g; Carbo 50 g; T Fat 10 g; 30% Calories from Fat; Chol 2 mg; Fiber 1 g; Sod 184 mg

Susan Latham, HFH of Henderson, Henderson, KY

Peach Cobbler

Yield: 6 servings

2 tablespoons margarine	1¹/₂ cups sugar
6 tablespoons shortening	3 tablespoons flour
1¹/₂ cups flour	Nutmeg to taste
3 tablespoons water	Cinnamon to taste
4 cups sliced peeled peaches	6 tablespoons margarine

Cut 2 tablespoons margarine and shortening into 1¹/₂ cups flour in bowl until crumbly. Add water, stirring until mixture forms a ball. Divide pastry into 2 portions. Roll 1 portion into 8-inch square on lightly floured surface. Place on baking sheet. Bake at 400 degrees for 15 to 20 minutes or until light brown. Arrange ¹/₂ of the peaches in 8x8-inch baking dish. Combine sugar and 3 tablespoons flour in bowl; mix well. Sprinkle peaches with ¹/₂ of the flour mixture. Sprinkle lightly with nutmeg and cinnamon; dot with 3 tablespoons of the margarine. Top with baked pastry. Layer remaining peaches, remaining flour mixture, nutmeg, cinnamon and remaining margarine in prepared baking dish. Roll remaining pastry portion into 8-inch square on lightly floured surface. Place on prepared layers, sealing to edges of pan. Cut four 1-inch slits in pastry. Bake at 400 degrees for 20 to 25 minutes or until light brown.

Approx Per Serving: Cal 619; Prot 5 g; Carbo 89 g; T Fat 29 g; 41% Calories from Fat; Chol 0 mg; Fiber 3 g; Sod 180 mg

Sandy Swinney, HFH of Ouochita Inc., Monroe, LA

Apple Pudding

Yield: 4 servings

1 egg	1 teaspoon vanilla extract
³/₄ cup sugar	¹/₂ cup chopped walnuts
¹/₃ cup flour	1¹/₂ cups chopped apples
2 teaspoons baking powder	

Beat egg and sugar in mixer bowl until light and fluffy. Fold in sifted mixture of flour and baking powder. Fold in vanilla, walnuts and apples. Spoon into buttered 8x10-inch baking pan. Bake at 300 degrees for 15 minutes. Increase oven temperature to 375 degrees. Bake for 15 minutes longer. Serve warm plain or with whipped cream.

Approx Per Serving: Cal 328; Prot 5 g; Carbo 56 g; T Fat 11 g; 29% Calories from Fat; Chol 53 mg; Fiber 2 g; Sod 182 mg

Martha S. Corbett, HFH of the Lehigh Valley, Emmaus, PA

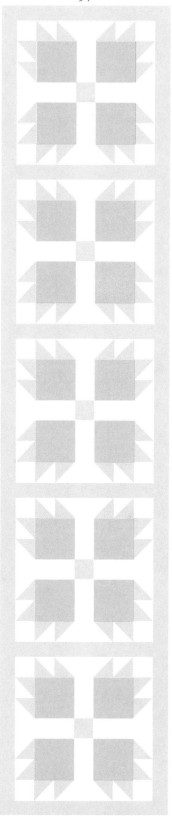

Baked Apple Pudding   *Yield: 8 servings*

1/3 cup margarine, softened	1/4 teaspoon salt
1 cup sugar	1/4 teaspoon nutmeg
1 egg	1/4 teaspoon cinnamon
1 1/2 teaspoons vanilla extract	2 cups grated unpeeled apples
1 cup flour	1/2 cup coarsely chopped
1 teaspoon baking soda	walnuts

Combine margarine, sugar, egg and vanilla in mixer bowl, beating until smooth. Add mixture of flour, baking soda, salt, nutmeg and cinnamon; mix well. Stir in apples and walnuts. Spoon into ungreased 8x8-inch baking pan. Bake at 350 degrees for 35 minutes or until wooden pick inserted in center comes out clean. Serve warm with whipped cream or ice cream.

Approx Per Serving: Cal 311; Prot 4 g; Carbo 47 g; T Fat 13 g; 37% Calories from Fat; Chol 27 mg; Fiber 2 g; Sod 268 mg

Dolores M. Bahr, HFH of Oshkosh Inc., Oshkosh, WI

Do-Ahead Apricot Dessert   *Yield: 8 servings*

1 cup baking mix	1 1/4 cups confectioners' sugar
1 tablespoon sugar	1/2 cup butter, softened
2 tablespoons butter	3 ounces cream cheese,
1 cup dried apricots	softened
2 cups water	1 cup whipping cream, whipped
1/2 cup sugar	

Combine baking mix and 1 tablespoon sugar in bowl; mix well. Cut in 2 tablespoons butter until crumbly. Press into 9x9-inch baking pan. Bake at 375 degrees for 10 minutes or until light brown. Let stand until cool. Bring apricots and water to a boil in saucepan; reduce heat. Simmer for 20 minutes or until water is absorbed and apricots are tender, stirring occasionally. Remove from heat. Beat in 1/2 cup sugar until mixture is of uniform consistency. Let stand until cool. Combine confectioners' sugar, 1/2 cup butter and cream cheese in mixer bowl. Beat at medium speed until smooth, scraping bowl frequently. Spread evenly over baked layer; top with apricot mixture. Spread with whipped cream. Chill, covered, for 8 hours.

Approx Per Serving: Cal 494; Prot 3 g; Carbo 53 g; T Fat 31 g; 56% Calories from Fat; Chol 91 mg; Fiber 1 g; Sod 372 mg

Terrie Kragenbrink, HFH of Oshkosh Inc., Oshkosh, WI

Banana Pudding

Yield: 8 servings

3/4 cup sugar
1/4 cup flour
1/2 teaspoon salt
3 egg yolks, beaten
2 cups milk

1 teaspoon vanilla extract
1 (16-ounce) package vanilla
  wafers
3 bananas, sliced
Cinnamon and sugar to taste

Combine 3/4 cup sugar, flour and salt in saucepan; mix well. Stir in egg yolks and milk. Cook until thickened, stirring constantly. Stir in vanilla. Layer vanilla wafers, bananas, custard mixture, cinnamon and sugar to taste alternately in dish until all ingredients are use. Garnish with whipped cream. Chill for several hours before serving.

Approx Per Serving: Cal 435; Prot 7 g; Carbo 76 g; T Fat 13 g; 26% Calories from Fat; Chol 121 mg; Fiber 1 g; Sod 344 mg

Shirley Skirvin, Pueblo HFH, Pueblo, CO

Creamy Banana Pudding

Yield: 10 servings

3 bananas, sliced
1/4 cup lemon juice concentrate
1 (14-ounce) can sweetened
  condensed milk
1 1/2 cups cold water

1 (4-ounce) package vanilla
  instant pudding mix
16 ounces whipped topping
36 vanilla wafers

Dip bananas in lemon juice concentrate. Combine condensed milk and cold water in mixer bowl; mix well. Add pudding mix. Beat until blended. Chill for 5 minutes. Fold in whipped topping. Spread 1 cup of the pudding mixture in 2 1/2-quart glass serving bowl. Layer vanilla wafers, bananas and remaining pudding mixture 1/3 at a time in prepared bowl, ending with pudding. Chill, covered, until serving time. Store in refrigerator.

Approx Per Serving: Cal 404; Prot 5 g; Carbo 60 g; T Fat 17 g; 38% Calories from Fat; Chol 22 mg; Fiber 1 g; Sod 250 mg

Margaret Ann Piner, Carteret County HFH, Morehead City, NC

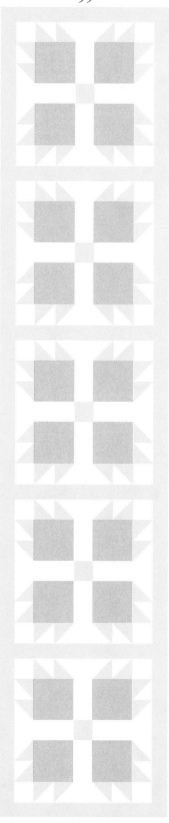

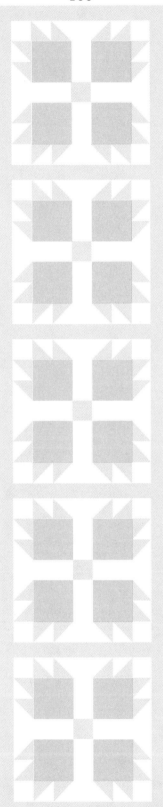

Bread Pudding with Rum Sauce

Yield: 10 servings

4 cups milk
2 cups sugar
4 eggs, beaten
1 tablespoon vanilla extract
1 to 1¹/2 cups chopped peeled
   apples
1 cup raisins

1 (16-ounce) loaf dry French
   bread, torn into bite-size
   pieces
2 eggs
¹/4 cup rum
1 cup confectioners' sugar
1 cup whipping cream, whipped

Beat milk, sugar and 4 eggs in mixer bowl until blended. Stir in vanilla, apples and raisins. Pour over bread in bowl; mix well. Let stand until bread absorbs milk, stirring occasionally. Spoon into greased 9x9-inch baking pan. May chill at this point and bake just before serving. Bake at 350 degrees for 30 to 40 minutes or until pudding tests done. Beat 2 eggs in saucepan. Add rum and confectioners' sugar; mix well. Cook over low heat until of the desired consistency. Remove from heat. Fold in whipped cream. Serve warm bread pudding with rum sauce or vanilla ice cream. May substitute rum extract for rum.

Approx Per Serving: Cal 590; Prot 12 g; Carbo 97 g; T Fat 17 g; 25% Calories from Fat; Chol 173 mg; Fiber 3 g; Sod 373 mg

Larry Arney, HFH Atlanta, Atlanta, GA

Chocolate Walnut Bread Pudding

Yield: 8 servings

1 cup semisweet chocolate chips
3 cups milk
¹/2 teaspoon salt
3 eggs, lightly beaten
³/4 cup sugar
1 teaspoon vanilla extract

³/4 teaspoon cinnamon
8 slices dry bread, crusts
   trimmed, cut into ¹/2-inch
   cubes
¹/2 cup walnut pieces

Combine chocolate chips and 1 cup of the milk in double boiler. Cook over hot water, stirring until smooth. Stir in remaining milk. Remove from heat. Combine salt, eggs, sugar, vanilla and cinnamon in bowl; mix well. Stir in chocolate mixture. Pour chocolate mixture over bread cubes in 1¹/2-quart baking dish; mix gently to saturate bread cubes. Sprinkle with walnuts. Place in larger pan filled with warm water. Bake at 350 degrees for 1 to 1¹/4 hours or until knife inserted in center comes out clean. Let stand until cool. Serve with whipped cream or ice cream.

Approx Per Serving: Cal 359; Prot 9 g; Carbo 48 g; T Fat 17 g; 40% Calories from Fat; Chol 92 mg; Fiber 2 g; Sod 306 mg

Louise Twaddle, Androscoggin County HFH, Auburn, ME

Great-Grandmother's Bread Pudding

Yield: 6 servings

4 slices bread	2 eggs, beaten
3 tablespoons butter	2 cups milk
5 cups water	1/2 cup sugar
1 cup packed brown sugar	1/8 teaspoon salt
1/4 cup raisins	1 teaspoon vanilla extract

Spread bread with 2 tablespoons of the butter; cut into cubes. Pour water in bottom pan of double boiler. Coat side and bottom of top pan of double boiler with remaining butter. Place top pan over bottom pan. Add brown sugar and raisins to buttered pan; do not mix. Add bread cubes; do not mix. Pour mixture of eggs, milk, sugar, salt and vanilla over top; do not stir. Steam, covered, over medium heat for 1 hour.

Approx Per Serving: Cal 375; Prot 7 g; Carbo 65 g; T Fat 11 g; 25% Calories from Fat; Chol 98 mg; Fiber 1 g; Sod 272 mg

Deborah Schulte, Southeast New Hampshire HFH, New Castle, NH

Cherry Pudding

Yield: 6 servings

1 cup sugar	3/4 cup milk
2 tablespoons margarine, softened	2 to 3 cups fresh tart pitted cherries
1 cup flour	1/2 cup water
1/8 teaspoon salt	1/4 cup sugar
1 teaspoon baking powder	

Cream 1 cup sugar and margarine in mixer bowl until light and fluffy. Add mixture of flour, salt and baking powder alternately with milk, mixing well after each addition. Spoon into greased 8x8-inch baking pan. Bring cherries and water to a boil in saucepan. Stir in sugar. Pour over prepared layer. Bake at 350 degrees for 30 minutes or until top springs back when touched. Serve with milk or ice cream. May substitute one 16-ounce can cherries for fresh cherries and 1/2 cup cherry juice for water.

Approx Per Serving: Cal 343; Prot 4 g; Carbo 71 g; T Fat 6 g; 15% Calories from Fat; Chol 4 mg; Fiber 1 g; Sod 160 mg

Betty Clark, Greater Cleveland HFH, Cleveland Heights, OH

Habitat is the spiritual center of my life. I can't listen to a sermon, prayer, or scripture reading without thinking of Habitat. I feel God's presence at every project.

TOM SCHMIDT
HFH VOLUNTEER

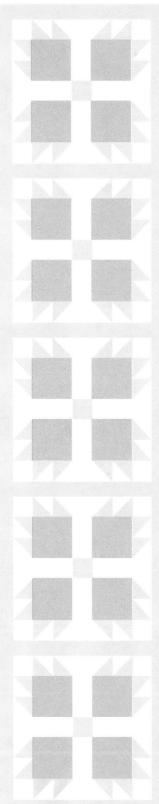

Chocolate Dessert

Yield: 12 servings

¹/2 cup margarine, softened
1 cup flour
¹/2 cup chopped walnuts
8 ounces cream cheese, softened
8 to 16 ounces whipped topping
1 cup confectioners' sugar

1 (4-ounce) package vanilla instant pudding mix
1 (4-ounce) package chocolate instant pudding mix
2¹/2 cups milk
1 (2-ounce) chocolate candy bar, shaved

Cut margarine into flour in bowl until crumbly. Stir in walnuts. Pat into 8x12-inch baking pan. Bake at 350 degrees for 20 minutes. Let stand until cool. Beat cream cheese, 1 cup of the whipped topping and confectioners' sugar in mixer bowl until smooth. Spread over baked layer. Combine pudding mixes and milk in bowl, stirring until blended. Pour over cream cheese layer. Top with remaining whipped topping. Sprinkle with shaved chocolate. Chill for 3 hours or until set.

Approx Per Serving: Cal 478; Prot 6 g; Carbo 48 g; T Fat 30 g; 56% Calories from Fat; Chol 29 mg; Fiber 1 g; Sod 421 mg

Lee Anne Caswell, HFH of Ottawa County, Port Clinton, OH
Mary Jane Fields, Knox County HFH, Wheatland, IN
Bonnie Wallace, Macon County HFH, Otto, NC

Chocolate Fudge Upside-Down Dessert

Yield: 6 servings

³/4 cup sugar
1 tablespoon butter, softened
¹/2 cup milk
1 cup flour
¹/4 teaspoon salt
1 teaspoon baking powder

1¹/2 tablespoons baking cocoa
¹/2 cup chopped walnuts
¹/2 cup sugar
¹/2 cup packed brown sugar
¹/4 cup baking cocoa
1¹/4 cups boiling water

Cream ³/4 cup sugar and butter in mixer bowl until light and fluffy. Stir in milk. Add sifted mixture of flour, salt, baking powder and 1¹/2 tablespoons baking cocoa; mix well. Spread in buttered 9x9-inch baking pan. Sprinkle with walnuts. Sprinkle with mixture of ¹/2 cup sugar, brown sugar and ¹/4 cup baking cocoa. Pour boiling water over top; do not stir. Bake at 350 degrees for 45 minutes. Let stand until cool. Serve upside down with whipped topping.

Approx Per Serving: Cal 400; Prot 5 g; Carbo 78 g; T Fat 10 g; 21% Calories from Fat; Chol 8 mg; Fiber 3 g; Sod 182 mg

Hedy Sands, HFH of Knox County, Galesburg, IL

Hot Fudge Pudding Cake   *Yield: 8 servings*

1 cup flour
2 teaspoons baking powder
1/4 teaspoon salt
2 tablespoons baking cocoa
3/4 cup sugar
1/2 cup milk
2 tablespoons salad oil

1 teaspoon vanilla extract
1 cup chopped pecans
1 cup packed brown sugar
1/4 cup baking cocoa
13/4 cups hot water
1 quart vanilla ice cream
8 maraschino cherries

Combine flour, baking powder, salt, 2 tablespoons baking cocoa and sugar in bowl; mix well. Stir in milk, oil and vanilla until blended. Add pecans; mix well. Spoon into ungreased 10x10-inch baking pan. Sprinkle with mixture of brown sugar and 1/4 cup baking cocoa. Pour hot water over top; do not stir. Bake at 350 degrees for 40 minutes. Let stand for 15 minutes. Serve hot over ice cream; top with maraschino cherries or other favorite topping.

Approx Per Serving: Cal 503; Prot 6 g; Carbo 76 g; T Fat 22 g; 38% Calories from Fat; Chol 31 mg; Fiber 3 g; Sod 219 mg

Teresa R. Street, Carteret County HFH, Morehead City, NC

Drumstick Dessert   *Yield: 10 servings*

2 cups crushed vanilla wafers
3/4 cup crushed Spanish peanuts
1/2 cup melted margarine
1 cup confectioners' sugar
1/3 cup peanut butter
8 ounces cream cheese,
  softened

16 ounces whipped topping
2 (4-ounce) packages chocolate
  instant pudding mix
3 cups milk
1/2 cup crushed Spanish peanuts
1 (2-ounce) chocolate candy
  bar, shredded

Combine vanilla wafers, 3/4 cup peanuts and margarine in bowl; mix well. Pat over bottom of 9x13-inch baking pan. Bake at 350 degrees for 10 minutes. Let stand until cool. Beat confectioners' sugar, peanut butter and cream cheese in mixer bowl until smooth. Fold in 1/2 of the whipped topping. Spread over baked layer. Combine pudding mix and milk in bowl, stirring until blended. Pour over cream cheese layer. Spread with remaining whipped topping. Sprinkle with 1/2 cup peanuts and shredded candy bar. Chill until serving time.

Approx Per Serving: Cal 709; Prot 13 g; Carbo 65 g; T Fat 47 g; 58% Calories from Fat; Chol 47 mg; Fiber 2 g; Sod 605 mg

Amy Sticha, HFH of Oshkosh Inc., Oshkosh, WI

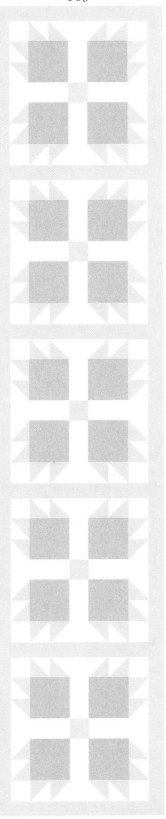

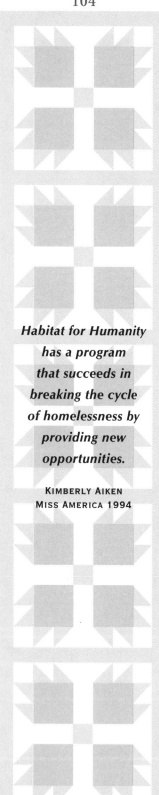

Ozark Pudding
Yield: 6 servings

³/₄ cup sugar
³/₄ cup flour
¹/₂ teaspoon salt
1¹/₄ teaspoons baking powder

1 egg, beaten
1 cup chopped peeled apple
1 cup pecan pieces
1 teaspoon vanilla extract

Combine sugar, flour, salt and baking powder in bowl; mix well. Stir in egg. Add apple, pecans and vanilla; mix well. Spoon into greased 8x8-inch baking dish. Bake at 350 degrees for 30 to 35 minutes or until brown and bubbly. Serve plain or with vanilla ice cream.

Approx Per Serving: Cal 312; Prot 4 g; Carbo 44 g; T Fat 15 g; 40% Calories from Fat; Chol 35 mg; Fiber 2 g; Sod 257 mg

Rozelle E. Dinwiddie, Augusta/CSRA HFH, Augusta, GA

Amazing Peach Pudding
Yield: 6 servings

3 cups sliced peeled fresh
  peaches
³/₄ cup sugar
¹/₂ teaspoon salt
1 cup flour
1 teaspoon baking powder

¹/₄ cup butter, softened
¹/₂ cup milk
1 cup sugar
1 tablespoon flour
¹/₂ teaspoon cinnamon
1 cup boiling water

Arrange peaches in 8x8-inch baking dish. Combine ³/₄ cup sugar, salt, 1 cup flour and baking powder in mixer bowl; mix well. Add butter and milk, beating until smooth. Spread evenly over peaches. Sift mixture of 1 cup sugar, 1 tablespoon flour and cinnamon over prepared layers. Pour boiling water over top; do not stir. Bake at 325 degrees for 1 hour. Serve warm with cream or ice cream. May substitute cherries or apples for peaches if desired.

Approx Per Serving: Cal 424; Prot 4 g; Carbo 86 g; T Fat 9 g; 18% Calories from Fat; Chol 24 mg; Fiber 2 g; Sod 322 mg

Sylvia D. Stock, Sweet Home HFH, Sweet Home, OR

Surprise Pudding
Yield: 4 servings

¹/₄ cup chocolate chips
¹/₂ cup miniature marshmallows

1 (4-serving) package tapioca
  pudding mix

Mix chocolate chips and marshmallows in 1-quart serving dish. Prepare tapioca using package directions. Pour hot pudding over marshmallow mixture. Let stand until cool.

Approx Per Serving: Cal 230; Prot 5 g; Carbo 39 g; T Fat 7 g; 27% Calories from Fat; Chol 17 mg; Fiber 1 g; Sod 175 mg

Vicky Pinto, Holston HFH, Kingsport, TN

Photograph at right by Julie A. Lopez

CHEESECAKES & TORTES

"There is nothing better for a man than
that he should eat and drink, and that his
soul should enjoy good in his labor. This
also, I saw, was from the hand of God."

-Ecclesiastes 2:24

Amaretto Almond Cheesecake

Yield: 8 servings

16 ounces cream cheese
1/2 cup sugar
1/2 teaspoon vanilla extract
2 eggs
2 tablespoons amaretto
1 (9-inch) graham cracker pie shell

1 cup whipping cream
4 to 5 tablespoons confectioners' sugar
1 tablespoon amaretto
12 almond slivers

Beat softened cream cheese, sugar and vanilla in mixer bowl until light and fluffy. Add eggs, beating until blended. Beat in 2 tablespoons amaretto. Spoon into pie shell. Bake at 350 degrees for 40 minutes or until center is almost set. Let cool. Chill for 3 hours. Cut into 8 slices, leaving cheesecake intact. Beat whipping cream in mixer bowl until soft peaks form. Add confectioners' sugar and 1 tablespoon amaretto; mix well. Pipe 1 swirl onto each slice; place 1 almond sliver on each swirl. Swirl remaining whipped cream onto center of cheesecake; top with remaining almond slivers. Drizzle with additional amaretto.

Approx Per Serving: Cal 607; Prot 8 g; Carbo 49 g; T Fat 42 g; 62% Calories from Fat; Chol 156 mg; Fiber 1 g; Sod 427 mg

Mischelle Paton, Springfield, VT Area HFH, Springfield, VT

Chocolate Amaretto Cheesecake

Yield: 16 servings

15 (2 1/2x5-inch) graham crackers, crushed
2 tablespoons sugar
1 (1-ounce) square unsweetened chocolate, melted
5 tablespoons melted butter
3 1/2 ounces marzipan, chopped

1/3 cup amaretto
24 ounces cream cheese, softened
1/2 cup sugar
6 (1-ounce) squares semisweet chocolate, melted
4 eggs
1/2 cup whipping cream

Combine graham cracker crumbs and 2 tablespoons sugar in bowl; mix well. Stir in unsweetened chocolate and butter. Press into 10-inch springform pan. Process marzipan and amaretto in food processor until blended. Beat cream cheese in mixer bowl until smooth. Add 1/2 cup sugar, marzipan mixture and semisweet chocolate, beating well after each addition. Add eggs 1 at a time, beating just until blended after each addition. Add whipping cream. Beat just until smooth. Spoon into prepared pan. Bake at 350 degrees for 50 minutes. Chill for 5 hours.

Approx Per Serving: Cal 359; Prot 6 g; Carbo 24 g; T Fat 27 g; 66% Calories from Fat; Chol 120 mg; Fiber 1 g; Sod 222 mg
Nutritional information does not include marzipan.

Linda Thomas, Bay Area HFH/Houston, Houston, TX

Becoming a part of Habitat has been a goal of mine for over ten years. As a mother of six, I had to wait. I have now been involved for seven months and love it. As a Christian, I find it falls into my lifestyle.

MISCHELLE PATON
SPRINGFIELD, VT AREA HFH

Company Cheesecake

Yield: 12 servings

1³/4 cups cinnamon crisp
    graham cracker crumbs
1/4 cup finely chopped walnuts
2 tablespoons sugar
1/3 cup butter, softened
3 eggs, beaten
16 ounces cream cheese,
    softened

1 cup sugar
1/4 teaspoon salt
2 teaspoons vanilla extract
1/2 teaspoon almond extract
3 cups sour cream

Combine graham cracker crumbs, walnuts, 2 tablespoons sugar and butter in bowl; mix well. Press over bottom and side of 9-inch spring-form pan. Combine eggs, cream cheese, 1 cup sugar, salt and flavorings in mixer bowl, beating until blended. Add sour cream; mix well. Spoon into prepared pan. Bake at 375 degrees for 35 minutes or just until light brown and top cracks. Turn off oven. Let stand in oven with door slightly ajar until cool.

Approx Per Serving: Cal 478; Prot 8 g; Carbo 38 g; T Fat 34 g; 63% Calories from Fat; Chol 134 mg; Fiber 1 g; Sod 372 mg

Janet Cornell, Westchester NY HFH, Valhalla, NY

Easy Cheesecake

Yield: 9 servings

1 cup confectioners' sugar
8 ounces cream cheese,
    softened
8 ounces whipped topping

1 (9-inch) graham cracker pie
    shell
1 (21-ounce) can cherry pie
    filling

Beat confectioners' sugar and cream cheese in mixer bowl until blended. Fold in whipped topping. Spoon into pie shell. Top with pie filling. Chill for 2 hours or longer.

Approx Per Serving: Cal 477; Prot 4 g; Carbo 62 g; T Fat 25 g; 46% Calories from Fat; Chol 28 mg; Fiber 1 g; Sod 321 mg

Mary E. Kinney, Winter Park/Maitland HFH, Altamonte Springs, FL

My affiliate has built eight houses on the same street. I enjoy seeing the children from the families, both those living in the completed homes as well as those whose homes aren't built yet, playing basketball on the driveways while the older children and adults construct the next HFH home.

LINDA THOMAS
BAY AREA HFH/HOUSTON

Jessica's Cheesecake
Yield: 8 servings

1 1/2 cups graham cracker crumbs
2 tablespoons sugar
1/4 cup melted butter or margarine
11 ounces cream cheese, softened

2 eggs, beaten
1/2 cup sugar
1 1/2 teaspoons vanilla extract
2 cups sour cream
1/4 cup sugar
1 to 2 teaspoons almond essence

Combine graham cracker crumbs, 2 tablespoons sugar and butter in bowl; mix well. Pat over bottom and side of 9-inch pie plate. Bake at 350 degrees for 5 minutes. Let stand until cool. Beat cream cheese in mixer bowl until smooth. Add 1/2 of the eggs, beating until blended. Add remaining egg; mix well. Add 1/2 cup sugar and vanilla gradually, beating until smooth. Spoon over baked layer. Bake for 20 minutes. Spread with mixture of sour cream, 1/4 cup sugar and almond essence. Turn off oven. Let stand in oven with door closed for 4 minutes. Remove from oven. Let stand until cool. Chill until serving time.

Approx Per Serving: Cal 508; Prot 8 g; Carbo 43 g; T Fat 35 g; 61% Calories from Fat; Chol 137 mg; Fiber 1 g; Sod 356 mg

Angela Lansbury, Corymore Productions, Universal City, CA

Lemon Cheesecake
Yield: 15 servings

1 (3-ounce) package lemon gelatin
1 cup boiling water
22 graham crackers, crushed
1/2 cup margarine, softened

8 ounces cream cheese, softened
1 cup sugar
1 teaspoon vanilla extract
1 (12-ounce) can Milnot

Dissolve gelatin in boiling water; mix well. Let stand until room temperature. Combine graham cracker crumbs and margarine in bowl; mix well. Press 1/2 of the crumb mixture into 9x13-inch baking pan. Bake at 250 degrees until brown. Beat cream cheese and sugar in mixer bowl until light and fluffy. Add vanilla; mix well. Beat Milnot in mixer bowl until stiff peaks form. Add gelatin and cream cheese mixture. Beat for 1 minute. Spoon over prepared layer; sprinkle with remaining crumb mixture. Chill for several hours or until set.

Approx Per Serving: Cal 239; Prot 3 g; Carbo 28 g; T Fat 13 g; 49% Calories from Fat; Chol 17 mg; Fiber <1 g; Sod 207 mg

Dorothy Imle, Knox County HFH, Vincennes, IN

No-Bake Lemon Cheesecake

Yield: 12 servings

1 (14-ounce) can evaporated milk
1 (6-ounce) package lemon gelatin
2 cups boiling water
1½ cups cold water
2 cups graham cracker crumbs
½ cup melted margarine
2 tablespoons sugar
8 ounces cream cheese, softened
1 cup sugar
2 teaspoons vanilla extract

Chill evaporated milk in freezer for 2 hours or until partially frozen. Dissolve gelatin in boiling water in bowl; mix well. Stir in cold water. Chill until partially set. Combine graham cracker crumbs, margarine and 2 tablespoons sugar in bowl; mix well. Reserve ¼ cup of the crumb mixture. Press remaining crumb mixture over bottom of 9x13-inch dish. Beat evaporated milk in mixer bowl until stiff peaks form. Beat cream cheese, 1 cup sugar and vanilla in mixer bowl until light and fluffy. Beat in gelatin mixture until blended. Fold in evaporated milk. Spread in prepared dish; sprinkle with reserved crumb mixture. Chill for 2 hours or longer.

Approx Per Serving: Cal 390; Prot 6 g; Carbo 51 g; T Fat 19 g; 42% Calories from Fat; Chol 31 mg; Fiber 1 g; Sod 337 mg

Becky Brown, Norristown HFH, Norristown, PA

Mini Cheesecakes

Yield: 12 servings

12 vanilla wafers
16 ounces cream cheese, softened
½ cup sugar
1 teaspoon vanilla extract
2 eggs

Line muffin cups with foil liners. Place 1 vanilla wafer in each muffin cup. Combine cream cheese, sugar and vanilla in mixer bowl. Beat at medium speed until light and fluffy, scraping bowl occasionally. Add eggs; mix well. Fill muffin cups ¾ full. Bake at 325 degrees for 25 minutes. Cool in pan. Chill until serving time. Top with fruit, preserves, chopped nuts or chocolate.

Approx Per Serving: Cal 194; Prot 4 g; Carbo 12 g; T Fat 15 g; 67% Calories from Fat; Chol 79 mg; Fiber 0 g; Sod 135 mg

April McGinnis, HFHI, Campus Chapters, Americus, GA

Praline Cheesecake

Yield: 12 servings

2 cups graham cracker crumbs
1/2 cup margarine, softened
35 ounces cream cheese, softened
2 cups packed brown sugar

1/2 teaspoon vanilla extract
4 eggs
2 cups sour cream
1 cup chopped walnuts

Combine graham cracker crumbs and margarine in bowl; mix well. Press over bottom and side of springform pan. Beat cream cheese and brown sugar in mixer bowl until light and fluffy. Add vanilla, eggs and sour cream, beating until blended. Stir in walnuts. Spoon into prepared pan. Bake at 400 degrees for 10 minutes. Reduce oven temperature to 300 degrees. Bake for 40 minutes longer. Turn off oven. Let stand in oven with door closed for 30 minutes. Chill for 2 hours or longer.

Approx Per Serving: Cal 726; Prot 12 g; Carbo 51 g; T Fat 54 g; 66% Calories from Fat; Chol 179 mg; Fiber 1 g; Sod 508 mg

Anna Lynn Floyd, Williamsburg HFH, Kingstree, SC

Easy Praline Cheesecake

Yield: 12 servings

2 cups graham cracker crumbs
1/2 cup melted butter
3 tablespoons dark brown sugar
1/2 cup ground walnuts
1/2 teaspoon cinnamon
3 cups sour cream

16 ounces cream cheese, softened
1 1/2 cups sugar
3 eggs
2 teaspoons vanilla extract

Combine graham cracker crumbs, butter, brown sugar, walnuts and cinnamon in bowl; mix well. Reserve 1 tablespoon of the crumb mixture. Press remaining crumb mixture over bottom of 9-inch springform pan. Chill for 15 minutes. Beat sour cream, cream cheese, sugar, eggs and vanilla in mixer bowl until blended. Spread over chilled layer. Place on center rack of oven. Bake at 325 degrees for 1 hour or until set. Sprinkle reserved crumb mixture over top of cheesecake. Let stand until cool. Chill until serving time.

Approx Per Serving: Cal 552; Prot 9 g; Carbo 47 g; T Fat 38 g; 61% Calories from Fat; Chol 141 mg; Fiber 1 g; Sod 358 mg

Julie McHugh, Morris HFH, Madison, NJ

Lee's Praline Cheesecake

Yield: 10 servings

1¼ cups graham cracker crumbs
¼ cup sugar
¼ cup butter, softened
24 ounces cream cheese, softened
2 tablespoons flour

1¼ cups packed dark brown sugar
1½ teaspoons vanilla extract
3 eggs
¾ cup finely chopped pecans
¼ cup maple syrup

Combine graham cracker crumbs, sugar and butter in bowl; mix well. Press into 8x11-inch baking pan. Bake at 375 degrees for 8 to 10 minutes or until brown. Let stand until cool. Beat cream cheese, flour, brown sugar, vanilla and eggs in mixer bowl until blended. Fold in pecans. Spoon over baked layer. Bake at 350 degrees for 50 to 55 minutes or until cheesecake tests done. Let stand until cool. Chill until serving time. Brush with maple syrup and garnish with pecan halves just before serving.

Approx Per Serving: Cal 555; Prot 9 g; Carbo 49 g; T Fat 37 g; 59% Calories from Fat; Chol 151 mg; Fiber 1 g; Sod 367 mg

Judi Feniger, Greater Cleveland HFH, Chagrin Falls, OH

Secret Cheesecake

Yield: 12 servings

10 graham crackers, crushed
¼ cup sugar
½ cup melted butter
24 ounces cream cheese, softened
1 cup sugar

5 eggs
1½ tablespoons vanilla extract
2 cups sour cream
¼ cup sugar
1½ tablespoons vanilla extract

Combine graham cracker crumbs, ¼ cup sugar and butter in bowl; mix well. Press into 9x13-inch baking pan. Beat cream cheese, 1 cup sugar, eggs and 1½ tablespoons vanilla in mixer bowl until smooth. Spread over prepared layer. Bake at 325 degrees for 30 to 40 minutes or until cheesecake tests done. Spread with mixture of sour cream, ¼ cup sugar and 1½ tablespoons vanilla. Bake at 425 degrees for 5 minutes. Chill for 8 to 10 hours.

Approx Per Serving: Cal 511; Prot 9 g; Carbo 34 g; T Fat 38 g; 67% Calories from Fat; Chol 188 mg; Fiber <1 g; Sod 327 mg

Evelyn Marrison, HFH of Ashtabula County, Jefferson, OH

Chocolate Eclair Torte
Yield: 12 servings

1 cup water
1/2 cup butter
1 cup flour
4 eggs
2 (4-ounce) packages vanilla instant pudding mix
2 1/2 cups milk
1 teaspoon vanilla extract

8 ounces whipped topping
2 (1-ounce) squares semisweet chocolate
2 tablespoons butter
2 tablespoons milk
1 teaspoon vanilla extract
1 cup confectioners' sugar

Bring water and 1/2 cup butter to a rolling boil in saucepan. Stir in flour all at once. Cook over low heat until mixture forms a ball, stirring constantly. Remove from heat. Add eggs 1 at a time, beating well with mixer after each addition. Drop by spoonfuls in circular shape on lightly greased round baking pan. Bake at 400 degrees for 45 to 50 minutes. Let stand until cool. Split horizontally into halves. Combine pudding mix, 2 1/2 cups milk and 1 teaspoon vanilla in bowl; mix well. Fold in whipped topping. Spread over cut side of bottom half. Top with remaining half. Melt chocolate and 2 tablespoons butter in double boiler over hot water, stirring until smooth. Remove from heat. Stir in 2 tablespoons milk and 1 teaspoon vanilla. Add confectioners' sugar, stirring until of glaze consistency. Drizzle over torte. Chill until serving time.

Approx Per Serving: Cal 364; Prot 6 g; Carbo 42 g; T Fat 21 g; 50% Calories from Fat; Chol 104 mg; Fiber 1 g; Sod 388 mg

Judy Martiny, Macon County HFH, Andersonville, GA

Graham Cracker Torte
Yield: 12 servings

2 cups graham cracker crumbs
1 tablespoon (heaping) flour
2 teaspoons baking powder
1 cup sugar
1/2 cup butter, softened
3 egg yolks

1 cup milk
3 egg whites
1 cup chopped Georgia pecans
1/2 cup butter, softened
1 teaspoon vanilla extract
2 tablespoons Kahlúa

Combine graham cracker crumbs, flour and baking powder in bowl; mix well. Cream sugar and 1/2 cup butter in mixer bowl until light and fluffy. Add egg yolks, beating until creamy. Add milk alternately with graham cracker crumb mixture, beating well after each addition. Beat egg whites in mixer bowl until soft peaks form. Fold egg whites and pecans into graham cracker mixture. Spoon into 2 greased and floured 9-inch round baking pans. Bake at 350 degrees for 25 minutes. Beat 1/2 cup butter, vanilla and Kahlúa in mixer bowl until of spreading consistency. May add cream if needed for desired consistency. Spread between layers and over top and side of torte.

Approx Per Serving: Cal 394; Prot 5 g; Carbo 37 g; T Fat 26 g; 58% Calories from Fat; Chol 97 mg; Fiber 1 g; Sod 358 mg

U.S. Senator Bob Graham, Washington, DC

Pavlova

Yield: 12 servings

Millard and I have enjoyed eating Pavlova when visiting Habitat affiliates in Australia and New Zealand. There, they take as much pride in their Pavlova as we in America do in our Apple Pie. This famous dessert was named for the Russian ballerina, Anna Pavlova.

Baked Meringue Shell
1¹/₂ cups whipping cream
3 tablespoons sugar
¹/₂ teaspoon vanilla extract
2 cups strawberry halves

1 (8-ounce) can pineapple
**   tidbits, drained**
1 star fruit, sliced
1 kiwifruit, cut into halves
**   lengthwise, sliced**

Arrange Baked Meringue Shell on serving plate. Beat whipping cream in mixer bowl until soft peaks form. Add sugar and vanilla; mix well. Spread shell with whipped cream. Decorate with strawberries, pineapple, star fruit and kiwifruit. Serve immediately.

Approx Per Serving: Cal 227; Prot 2 g; Carbo 31 g; T Fat 11 g; 43% Calories from Fat; Chol 41 mg; Fiber 2 g; Sod 31 mg

Linda Fuller, Co-Founder HFHI, Americus, GA

Baked Meringue Shell

Yield: 12 servings

4 egg whites
1 cup sugar
¹/₄ cup cornstarch

1¹/₂ teaspoons white vinegar
¹/₂ teaspoon vanilla extract

Grease baking sheet; line with waxed paper and grease waxed paper. Draw 8-inch circle on waxed paper using skewer or wooden pick. Beat egg whites in mixer bowl until soft peaks form. Add sugar gradually, beating constantly until stiff peaks form. Beat in cornstarch, vinegar and vanilla until blended. Spread meringue with rubber spatula over circle on prepared baking sheet, building up sides to form 2-inch rim. Bake at 225 degrees for 2 hours or until surface is dry but not brown. Turn off oven. Let stand in oven with door slightly ajar until cool. May store baked meringue, loosely covered, at room temperature for up to 3 days.

Approx Per Serving: Cal 81; Prot 1 g; Carbo 19 g; T Fat <1 g; <1% Calories from Fat; Chol 0 mg; Fiber <1 g; Sod 19 mg

Linda Fuller, Co-Founder HFHI, Americus, GA

In 1980, Allan Brown went with a group of skilled craftsmen to Americus, Georgia. He wanted to personally meet the people who not only donated their talents and skills to build Habitat homes, but who also paid their own expenses. He helped a woman with no construction skills feel useful by teaching her how to help. Fifteen years later he continues to teach me, Mrs. Allan Brown, so I can serve as Executive Director of Muncie Indiana HFH. He is a Habitat hero!

Sharon Brown
Greater Muncie Indiana HFH

Schaum Tortes
Yield: 8 servings

6 egg whites, at room
  temperature
2 cups sugar
2 tablespoons vinegar

1/2 teaspoon vanilla extract
2 cups raspberries
2 cups whipped cream

Beat egg whites in mixer bowl until soft peaks form. Add sugar gradually, beating constantly until stiff peaks form. Beat in vinegar and vanilla until blended. Spoon into 8 mounds on nonstick baking sheet. Bake at 300 degrees for 30 minutes. Reduce oven temperature to 200 degrees. Bake for 20 minutes longer. (Bottoms will form a 1/2-inch thick sticky pastry and tops will separate.) Remove tops. Fill with raspberries and whipped cream; replace tops. May also fill with ice cream and fruit and top with whipped cream. May substitute strawberries for raspberries.

Approx Per Serving: Cal 324; Prot 4 g; Carbo 55 g; T Fat 11 g; 30% Calories from Fat; Chol 41 mg; Fiber 1 g; Sod 53 mg

Sharon Brown, Greater Muncie Indiana HFH, Farmland, IN

Company Schaum Torte
Yield: 6 servings

3 egg whites
3/4 teaspoon cider vinegar

1/2 teaspoon vanilla
3/4 cup sugar

Combine egg whites and vinegar in mixer bowl. Beat until stiff peaks form. Add vanilla and sugar gradually, beating well after each addition. Spoon into 9-or 10-inch buttered round baking dish. Bake at 300 degrees for 1 1/4 hours. Top with ice cream and fresh or frozen raspberries, strawberries or peaches. May double recipe.

Approx Per Serving: Cal 105; Prot 2 g; Carbo 25 g; T Fat 0 g; 0% Calories from Fat; Chol 0 mg; Fiber 0 g; Sod 28 mg

Ann E. Denton, Thermal Belt HFH, Columbus, NC

Photo by Dennis E. Meola

Photograph at right by HFHI

ICE CREAM, FROZEN DESSERTS, & MOUSSES

"The fruit of the righteous is a tree of
life, and he who wins souls is wise."

-Proverbs 11:30

Alberta referred to our work camp group as her "Indiana Angels" because of the reputation our all-men work camp had made the year before. This was in 1985. The name has stuck and our work camp is still called the "Indiana Angels." We will miss Alberta's bright smile and friendly welcome when we come to Americus again.

WANDA MARMADUKE
KNOX COUNTY HFH

ALBERTA MOORE, DEARLY
LOVED RECEPTIONIST AT
HABITAT INTERNATIONAL
FOR MORE THAN TEN YEARS,
LOST HER BATTLE WITH
CANCER IN THE MONTH OF
DECEMBER 1994.

Banana Split Ice Cream
Yield: 15 servings

1 (14-ounce) can sweetened
  condensed milk
1 (12-ounce) can evaporated
  milk
1 to 1¹/₂ cups sugar
2 eggs, beaten
2 teaspoons vanilla extract
1 (4-ounce) jar maraschino
  cherries, drained

3 or 4 ripe bananas, mashed
¹/₂ cup pecan pieces, toasted
1 (8-ounce) can crushed
  pineapple
1 cup flaked coconut, lightly
  toasted
2 quarts (or more) milk

Combine condensed milk, evaporated milk, sugar, eggs, vanilla, maraschino cherries, bananas, pecans, undrained pineapple and coconut in bowl; mix well. Pour into ice cream freezer container. Add milk to fill line. Freeze using manufacturer's directions.

Approx Per Serving: Cal 380; Prot 10 g; Carbo 58 g; T Fat 14 g; 31% Calories from Fat; Chol 62 mg; Fiber 2 g; Sod 131 mg

Janice Jolley, HFH of Cabarrus County, Concord, NC

Old-Fashioned Homemade Ice Cream
Yield: 24 servings

2 tablespoons cornstarch
2 quarts milk
6 egg yolks, beaten
3¹/₂ cups sugar

1 quart half-and-half
6 egg whites, stiffly beaten
2 tablespoons vanilla extract
1 cup whipping cream

Combine cornstarch with ¹/₄ cup of the milk in 3-quart saucepan; mix well. Stir in egg yolks, sugar, half-and-half and enough of the remaining milk to fill saucepan. Cook over medium heat for 20 minutes, stirring frequently. Let stand until cool. Strain into bowl. Fold in egg whites. Stir in vanilla and whipping cream. Pour into freezer container. Pour in remaining milk to fill line. Freeze using manufacturer's directions.

Approx Per Serving: Cal 274; Prot 6 g; Carbo 36 g; T Fat 12 g; 40% Calories from Fat; Chol 93 mg; Fiber <1 g; Sod 76 mg

Wanda Marmaduke, Knox County HFH, Oaktown, IN

Buster Bar Dessert

Yield: 15 servings

1 (16-ounce) package chocolate
    sandwich cookies, crushed
1/2 cup melted margarine
2 quarts vanilla ice cream,
    softened
1 1/2 cups salted Spanish peanuts

2 cups confectioners' sugar
1 1/2 cups evaporated milk
2/3 cup chocolate chips
1/2 cup butter or margarine
1 teaspoon vanilla extract

Combine cookie crumbs and 1/2 cup margarine in bowl; mix well. Press into 9x13-inch dish. Spread with ice cream; sprinkle with peanuts. Freeze until firm. Bring confectioners' sugar, evaporated milk, chocolate chips and 1/2 cup butter to a boil in saucepan. Boil for 8 minutes, stirring constantly. Remove from heat. Stir in vanilla. Let stand until cool. Drizzle over frozen layers. Freeze until serving time.

Approx Per Serving: Cal 609; Prot 10 g; Carbo 64 g; T Fat 38 g; 53% Calories from Fat; Chol 55 mg; Fiber 3 g; Sod 463 mg

Bonnie J. Howard, Loudon County HFH Inc., Loudon, TN
Karen Reese, Grand Island Area HFH, Grand Island, NE

Coffee Ice Cream Dessert

Yield: 15 servings

2 cups vanilla wafer crumbs
1 cup butter, softened
3 cups confectioners' sugar
3 (1-ounce) squares
    unsweetened chocolate,
    melted

1 teaspoon vanilla extract
3 egg whites, stiffly beaten
1 cup chopped pecans
2 quarts coffee ice cream,
    softened
1/2 cup vanilla wafer crumbs

Spread 2 cups vanilla wafer crumbs in bottom of 9x13-inch dish. Beat butter, confectioners' sugar, chocolate and vanilla in mixer bowl until smooth. Fold in egg whites and pecans. Spread over prepared layer. Freeze for 1 hour or until firm. Spread with ice cream; sprinkle with 1/2 cup vanilla wafer crumbs. Freeze for 2 to 10 hours or until firm.

Approx Per Serving: Cal 494; Prot 5 g; Carbo 54 g; T Fat 31 g; 54% Calories from Fat; Chol 73 mg; Fiber 1 g; Sod 239 mg

Mary Lee Reiff, HFH of Greater Bucks County, Doylestown, PA

Chocolate Mint Cream
Yield: 6 servings

3 tablespoons butter, softened
1¼ cups chocolate wafer
crumbs
2 tablespoons confectioners'
sugar
2 tablespoons half-and-half

1 cup Swedish puffed mints,
finely crushed
1 cup whipping cream, whipped
2 to 4 drops of green food
coloring

Cream butter in mixer bowl. Add some of the chocolate wafer crumbs, confectioners' sugar and half-and half; mix well. Add remaining chocolate wafer crumbs, stirring until crumbly. Spread ½ of the crumb mixture in 8x8-inch dish. Fold whipped cream into mints in bowl. Stir in food coloring. Spread over prepared layer. Top with remaining crumb mixture. Freeze until firm.

Approx Per Serving: Cal 381; Prot 2 g; Carbo 41 g; T Fat 24 g; 55% Calories from Fat; Chol 72 mg; Fiber 0 g; Sod 182 mg

Dot Fredericks, Benton HFH, Corvallis, OR

Crème de Menthe Pie
Yield: 6 servings

1½ cups chocolate sandwich
cookie crumbs
¼ cup melted margarine
¼ cup milk
1 (7-ounce) jar marshmallow
creme
2 or 3 drops of peppermint
extract

2 or 3 drops of green food
coloring
2 cups whipping cream,
whipped
½ cup chocolate sandwich
cookie crumbs

Combine 1½ cups cookie crumbs and margarine in bowl; mix well. Press into 9-inch pie plate. Chill until set. Combine milk and marshmallow creme in bowl; mix well. Stir in peppermint flavoring and food coloring. Fold in whipped cream. Spoon into prepared pie plate; sprinkle with ½ cup cookie crumbs. Freeze until firm.

Approx Per Serving: Cal 643; Prot 4 g; Carbo 58 g; T Fat 46 g; 62% Calories from Fat; Chol 110 mg; Fiber 1 g; Sod 390 mg

Lee Fitzpatrick, HFH of Franklin County, Waynesboro, PA

Daiquiri Delight

Yield: 10 servings

Great luncheon dessert.

2 (3-ounce) packages custard
  mix
2 envelopes daiquiri mix
1 (20-ounce) can crushed
  pineapple

1/4 cup rum
Juice of 1/2 lime
12 ounces whipped topping

Combine custard mix, daiquiri mix, undrained pineapple, rum and lime juice in bowl; mix well. Fold in whipped topping. Spoon into 9x9-inch dish. Freeze until firm. Let stand at room temperature for 10 minutes before serving. Spoon into sherbet glasses or small dessert bowls. May substitute 1 teaspoon rum extract for rum.

Approx Per Serving: Cal 248; Prot 2 g; Carbo 37 g; T Fat 10 g; 34% Calories from Fat; Chol 51 mg; Fiber <1 g; Sod 129 mg

Jim Phillips, HFH of Miami County OH, Troy, OH

Delightful Ice Cream Pie

Yield: 6 servings

1 cup flour
1/4 cup quick-cooking oats
1/4 cup packed brown sugar
1/2 cup butter or margarine
3/4 cup chopped walnuts
5 tablespoons chocolate syrup

1 quart chocolate ice cream,
  softened
1 quart coffee ice cream,
  softened
4 or 5 Heath candy bars,
  crushed

Combine flour, oats and brown sugar in bowl; mix well. Cut in butter until crumbly. Stir in walnuts. Pat into 9x13-inch baking pan. Bake at 400 degrees for 15 minutes; stir. Spread 1/2 of the crumb mixture in 10-inch pie plate; drizzle with chocolate syrup. Layer with chocolate ice cream and coffee ice cream. Sprinkle with remaining crumb mixture; top with crushed candy bars. Freeze until firm. May substitute pecans for walnuts. May use frozen yogurt and fat-free chocolate syrup.

Approx Per Serving: Cal 923; Prot 13 g; Carbo 101 g; T Fat 56 g; 52% Calories from Fat; Chol 130 mg; Fiber 3 g; Sod 388 mg

Dyal Randall, HFH Greater Canton, North Canton, OH

At a Habitat dedication, the new homeowner's two sons were very much in evidence. The younger child, who was two and one-half years old, was asked by someone, "Whose house is this?" His reply was, "My Father's!"

DOROTHY P. McMILLAN
HFH OF SPOKANE

Ice Cream Cake

Yield: 16 servings

1 angel food cake, torn into
   bite-size pieces
4 cups whipping cream,
   whipped
2 quarts vanilla ice cream,
   softened

1 cup chopped walnuts
1 pint lime sherbet, sliced
1 pint orange sherbet, sliced
1 pint raspberry sherbet, sliced

Fold angel food cake into $1/2$ of the whipping cream in bowl until mixed well. Add ice cream; mix well. Stir in walnuts. Layer $1/4$ of the cake mixture, lime sherbet, $1/4$ of the cake mixture, orange sherbet, $1/4$ of the cake mixture, raspberry sherbet and $1/4$ of the cake mixture in tube pan. Freeze, covered, for 8 to 10 hours or until firm. Loosen cake from side of pan with sharp knife. Invert onto serving plate. Spread side and top with remaining whipping cream.

Approx Per Serving: Cal 588; Prot 8 g; Carbo 64 g; T Fat 36 g; 53% Calories from Fat; Chol 114 mg; Fiber 1 g; Sod 407 mg

Dorothy P. McMillan, HFH of Spokane, Spokane, WA

Ice Cream and Chocolate Chip Cookie with Java

Yield: Variable

Begin a search for a grocery store that carries Haagen-Daz Swiss Almond Vanilla Ice Cream. It costs about twice as much as it should so you won't be doing this very often. Once located, bring the ice cream home. Serve generous helpings with the best chocolate chip cookie you can find. Top it off with some really expensive Colombian coffee. If this is too complicated, then after supper pile the whole family into the car and head to the nearest Baskin-Robbins. Once there, instinct will tell you what to do. Afterwards, go home full and thankful for a clean kitchen!

Nutritional information for this recipe is not available.

Buddy Greene, Williamson County HFH, Brentwood, TN

Key Lime Pie

Yield: 8 servings

1¹/₄ cups graham cracker crumbs
3 tablespoons sugar
2 tablespoons grated orange rind
¹/₃ to ¹/₂ cup butter, softened
1 (14-ounce) can sweetened condensed milk

6 egg yolks
¹/₂ cup fresh key lime juice
6 egg whites
¹/₄ cup sugar
1 tablespoon grated orange rind

Combine graham cracker crumbs, 3 tablespoons sugar and 2 table-spoons orange rind in bowl; mix well. Cut in butter until crumbly. Press into 9-inch pie plate sprayed with nonstick cooking spray. Chill until set. Combine condensed milk and egg yolks in bowl; mix well. Stir in lime juice. Spoon into prepared pie shell. Beat egg whites in mixer bowl until soft peaks form. Add ¹/₄ cup sugar gradually, beating constantly until stiff peaks form. Swirl meringue over filling, sealing to edge. Sprinkle with 1 tablespoon orange rind. Bake at 300 degrees for 20 minutes or until light brown. Cool for 30 minutes. Freeze for 8 to 10 hours. Let stand at room temperature for 15 minutes before slicing. Garnish each slice with fresh mint leaves and lime slices.

Approx Per Serving: Cal 446; Prot 10 g; Carbo 55 g; T Fat 22 g; 43% Calories from Fat; Chol 207 mg; Fiber 1 g; Sod 341 mg

Dr. W. Frank Evans, Jr., Sarasota HFH, Sarasota, FL

Lemon Custard

Yield: 12 servings

Enjoy this light dessert after a heavy meal.

³/₄ cup graham cracker crumbs
2 egg yolks
²/₃ cup sugar
¹/₂ teaspoon lemon extract
6 tablespoons lemon juice
¹/₄ teaspoon salt

2 egg whites
²/₃ cup water
1¹/₃ cups instant dry milk powder
¹/₄ cup graham cracker crumbs

Sprinkle ³/₄ cup graham cracker crumbs over bottom of 9x13-inch dish. Combine egg yolks, sugar, lemon extract, lemon juice and salt in mixer bowl, beating until smooth. Beat egg whites, water and milk powder in mixer bowl until soft peaks form. Fold lemon mixture into egg white mixture. Spread over prepared layer. Sprinkle with ¹/₄ cup graham cracker crumbs. Freeze until firm. Cut into squares.

Approx Per Serving: Cal 127; Prot 4 g; Carbo 24 g; T Fat 2 g; 13% Calories from Fat; Chol 37 mg; Fiber <1 g; Sod 157 mg

Peg Clovis, Mon County HFH, Morgantown, WV

Future homeowner Anthony Whitfield and his young son were hammering footings on their future home. All around him could be heard the Habitat symphony of hammers made by the fifty volunteers from his Sarasota First United Methodist Church. Anthony was heard to say, "Son, we're going to have an awful lot to talk to Jesus about tonight!" And that is what Habitat is all about.

**DR. W. FRANK EVANS, JR.
SARASOTA HFH**

Oreo Ice Cream Pies

Yield: 16 servings

1/2 gallon vanilla ice cream, softened
1 (4-ounce) package vanilla instant pudding mix
8 ounces whipped topping, thawed

1/2 (16-ounce) package Oreo cookies, crushed
2 Oreo cookie pie shells

Combine ice cream and pudding mix in bowl; mix well. Fold in whipped topping and cookie crumbs. Spoon into pie shells. Freeze for 2 hours or until firm. Let stand at room temperature for 15 minutes before slicing.

Approx Per Serving: Cal 388; Prot 4 g; Carbo 51 g; T Fat 19 g; 44% Calories from Fat; Chol 29 mg; Fiber <1 g; Sod 331 mg

Yvonne D. Van Duser, Abilene HFH, Abilene, TX

Frozen Peanut Butter Pies

Yield: 12 servings

8 ounces cream cheese, softened
2 cups confectioners' sugar
1 cup smooth or crunchy peanut butter

1 cup milk
16 ounces whipped topping
2 (9-inch) graham cracker pie shells

Beat cream cheese, confectioners' sugar and peanut butter in mixer bowl until blended. Add milk; mix well. Fold in whipped topping. Spoon into pie shells. Freeze for 24 hours or until firm. Let stand at room temperature for several minutes before slicing. May drizzle pies with melted chocolate. May substitute chocolate cookie pie shell for graham cracker pie shell.

Approx Per Serving: Cal 669; Prot 10 g; Carbo 70 g; T Fat 41 g; 54% Calories from Fat; Chol 24 mg; Fiber 3 g; Sod 486 mg

Rita Carbonneau, Jackson County HFH, Marianna, FL
Pat Watson, HFH of Bay County, Panama City, FL

Peanut Butter Yogurt Pie

Yield: 8 servings

1 quart frozen vanilla yogurt, softened
1 cup peanut butter
8 ounces whipped topping
1 (9-inch) chocolate cookie pie shell
1/4 cup chocolate syrup

Mix yogurt and peanut butter in bowl. Fold in whipped topping. Spoon into pie shell. Freeze until firm. Drizzle with chocolate syrup.

Approx Per Serving: Cal 532; Prot 12 g; Carbo 52 g; T Fat 32 g; 53% Calories from Fat; Chol 1 mg; Fiber 2 g; Sod 331 mg

Willie Schick, HFH of Flagstaff, Flagstaff, AZ

Pear Ice Cream Dessert with Raspberry Sauce

Yield: 8 servings

1 (29-ounce) can pear halves in syrup
1/4 cup sugar
1 thin lemon slice
1 quart vanilla ice cream, slightly softened
1 (10-ounce) package frozen raspberries, thawed
1/2 cup seedless red raspberry jam

Drain pears, reserving 1 cup syrup. Bring reserved syrup, sugar and lemon slice to a boil in saucepan. Boil for 10 minutes or until liquid is reduced to 1/2 cup, stirring frequently. Let stand until cool. Discard lemon slice. Reserve 3 pear halves. Process remaining pears in food processor until puréed. Stir in syrup. Pour into 9x9-inch dish. Freeze just until set but not firm. Spoon into bowl. Fold in ice cream. Spoon into 8 cup mold. Freeze, covered, until firm. Process raspberries in blender until puréed. Press through sieve into bowl. Heat raspberry jam in saucepan until melted, stirring frequently. Stir into berries. Let stand until cool. Invert mold onto serving platter. Drizzle with raspberry sauce. Slice reserved pear halves; arrange around outer edge of platter. Garnish with whipped cream and fresh raspberries or strawberries.

Approx Per Serving: Cal 318; Prot 3 g; Carbo 64 g; T Fat 7 g; 20% Calories from Fat; Chol 29 mg; Fiber 4 g; Sod 67 mg

Rebecca Snyder, Androscoggin County HFH, Auburn, ME

Pumpkin Squares

Yield: 24 servings

36 gingersnaps
1 (16-ounce) can pumpkin
1 cup sugar
1 teaspoon salt
1 teaspoon ginger

1/2 teaspoon nutmeg
1 teaspoon cinnamon
1/2 gallon vanilla ice cream,
　softened
1 cup chopped pecans

Crush gingersnaps, reserving 1/3 cup. Press remaining crumbs over bottom of greased 9x13-inch dish. Combine pumpkin, sugar, salt, ginger, nutmeg, cinnamon and ice cream in bowl; mix well. Stir in pecans. Spread over prepared layer; sprinkle with reserved cookie crumbs. Freeze, covered with foil, for 5 hours or longer. Let stand at room temperature for 30 minutes before serving. Cut into squares. Garnish with whipped cream.

Approx Per Serving: Cal 204; Prot 3 g; Carbo 29 g; T Fat 9 g; 40% Calories from Fat; Chol 19 mg; Fiber 1 g; Sod 194 mg

Marilyn Veley, Charlotte County HFH, Port Charlotte, FL

Rainbow Dessert

Yield: 32 servings

8 ounces slivered almonds
1 quart frozen peach yogurt
1 quart frozen vanilla yogurt
1 quart frozen lemon yogurt
1 quart frozen raspberry yogurt

2 quarts vanilla ice cream,
　softened
2 cups whipping cream,
　whipped

Place almonds in shallow baking dish. Toast at 275 degrees for 15 minutes, stirring occasionally. Let stand until cool. Scoop peach, vanilla, lemon and raspberry yogurt into 2 tube pans. Spread with mixture of ice cream and toasted almonds; tap pans to force ice cream to drizzle between scoops of yogurt. Freeze until firm. Place pans on hot towel to loosen 1 hour before serving. Invert onto serving platters. Spread tops and sides with whipped cream. Freeze until serving time. May substitute any flavor ices or ice cream for yogurt. Serve immediately.

Approx Per Serving: Cal 269; Prot 6 g; Carbo 28 g; T Fat 16 g; 51% Calories from Fat; Chol 39 mg; Fiber 1 g; Sod 89 mg

Helen Leigh, Rapid City HFH, Rapid City, SD

Frozen Yummy Dessert

Yield: 15 servings

25 to 30 vanilla wafers
¹/₄ cup butter, softened
2 egg yolks
2 (1-ounce) squares baking chocolate, melted
2 cups confectioners' sugar

2 egg whites, stiffly beaten
1 (12-ounce) can mixed salted nuts
2 quarts vanilla ice cream, softened
¹/₂ cup vanilla wafer crumbs

Line bottom of 9x11-inch dish with vanilla wafers. Beat butter, egg yolks, chocolate and confectioners' sugar in mixer bowl until smooth. Fold in egg whites. Spread over vanilla wafers; sprinkle with nuts. Top with ice cream; sprinkle with vanilla wafer crumbs. Freeze until firm. Let stand at room temperature for 10 to 15 minutes before slicing.

Approx Per Serving: Cal 449; Prot 8 g; Carbo 47 g; T Fat 28 g; 54% Calories from Fat; Chol 74 mg; Fiber 3 g; Sod 278 mg

Donna Beck, Alpena Area HFH, Alpena, MI

Blender Mousse

Yield: 6 servings

2 cups chocolate chips
¹/₂ cup sugar
3 eggs

1 cup milk
3 tablespoons Kahlúa

Combine chocolate chips, sugar and eggs in blender container. Combine milk and Kahlúa in microwave-safe dish. Microwave on High for 1 minute and 20 seconds to 2 minutes or until hot. Pour into blender container. Process until smooth. Spoon into serving bowl or individual dessert bowls. Chill for 2 hours or until set.

Approx Per Serving: Cal 422; Prot 7 g; Carbo 58 g; T Fat 21 g; 41% Calories from Fat; Chol 112 mg; Fiber 4 g; Sod 58 mg

Katy Owens, Cottage Grove Area HFH, Cottage Grove, OR

While working alongside the partnering family, Jean, the wife and mother, looked around at her home in progress and with amazement exclaimed, "My, we are blessed."

CAROL FRANK
MARSHALL COUNTY HFH

Cherries-on-Snow

Yield: 9 servings

1¹/2 cups graham cracker crumbs
1 tablespoon sugar
¹/4 cup melted butter
1 envelope unflavored gelatin
¹/4 cup cold water
¹/4 cup milk
8 ounces cream cheese, softened
¹/2 cup sifted confectioners' sugar
2 teaspoons grated lemon rind
2 envelopes whipped topping mix, prepared
1 (21-ounce) can cherry pie filling

Combine graham cracker crumbs, sugar and butter in bowl; mix well. Press over bottom of 8-inch springform pan. Line side with waxed paper to form collar. Soften gelatin in cold water; mix well. Heat milk in saucepan. Stir in gelatin. Cook until gelatin dissolves, stirring constantly. Beat cream cheese and confectioners' sugar in mixer bowl until smooth. Add gelatin mixture and lemon rind; mix well. Fold in whipped topping. Spoon into prepared pan. Chill until set. Spread pie filling gently over top. Chill until serving time. Flavor enhanced if chilled for 8 to 10 hours.

Approx Per Serving: Cal 397; Prot 6 g; Carbo 48 g; T Fat 21 g; 47% Calories from Fat; Chol 46 mg; Fiber 1 g; Sod 310 mg

Jeri Popke, Waupaca County HFH, New London, WI

Chocolate Truffle Mousse

Yield: 12 servings

16 (1-ounce) squares semisweet chocolate
¹/2 cup light corn syrup
¹/2 cup margarine
¹/2 cup whipping cream
3 egg yolks, beaten
1¹/2 cups whipping cream
¹/4 cup confectioners' sugar
1 teaspoon vanilla extract
1 (10-ounce) package frozen raspberries, thawed
¹/3 cup light corn syrup

Line 5x9-inch loaf pan with plastic wrap. Combine chocolate, ¹/2 cup corn syrup and margarine in saucepan. Cook over medium heat until smooth, stirring constantly. Stir in mixture of ¹/2 cup whipping cream and egg yolks. Cook over medium heat for 3 minutes, stirring constantly. Cool to room temperature. Combine 1¹/2 cups whipping cream, confectioners' sugar and vanilla in mixer bowl. Beat at medium speed until soft peaks form. Fold into chocolate mixture. Spoon into prepared loaf pan. Chill, covered with plastic wrap, for 8 to 10 hours. Purée raspberries in blender or food processor. Press through sieve into bowl. Stir in ¹/3 cup corn syrup. Serve with mousse. May freeze mousse for future use; thaw in refrigerator for 8 hours.

Approx Per Serving: Cal 498; Prot 3 g; Carbo 51 g; T Fat 35 g; 59% Calories from Fat; Chol 107 mg; Fiber 4 g; Sod 138 mg

Joanna Warren, Flagler HFH Inc., Palm Coast, FL

White Chocolate Mousse
Yield: 10 servings

8 ounces white chocolate
3 tablespoons kirsch
3 tablespoons water

3 egg whites, stiffly beaten
8 ounces whipped topping

Combine white chocolate, kirsch and water in double boiler. Cook over hot water just until blended, stirring frequently. Let stand until cool. Fold in egg whites. Fold in whipped topping. Spoon into serving bowl or individual dessert bowls. Chill or freeze for 3 hours or longer. Serve chilled or frozen. Garnish with fresh blueberries, fresh strawberries or fresh raspberries.

Approx Per Serving: Cal 208; Prot 3 g; Carbo 19 g; T Fat 13 g; 54% Calories from Fat; Chol 5 mg; Fiber 0 g; Sod 42 mg

Louise Lawson, Fort Worth Area HFH, Fort Worth, TX

Gone-with-the-Wind
Yield: 8 servings

1 cup graham cracker crumbs
3 tablespoons brown sugar
3 tablespoons melted butter
1 envelope unflavored gelatin
1/2 cup cold water
2 egg yolks, beaten
1 cup sugar

1/2 cup milk
2 egg whites, stiffly beaten
1 cup whipping cream, whipped
1 teaspoon vanilla extract
**1 (20-ounce) can crushed
     pineapple, drained**

Combine graham cracker crumbs, brown sugar and butter in bowl; mix well. Pat 1/2 of the crumb mixture into 9x9-inch dish. Soften gelatin in cold water; mix well. Combine egg yolks, sugar and milk in double boiler. Cook over hot water for 15 minutes, stirring frequently. Add gelatin; mix well. Cook until dissolved, stirring constantly. Chill until thickened, but not set; whip. Fold in egg whites, whipped cream and vanilla. Fold in pineapple. Spread in prepared pan. Top with remaining crumb mixture. Chill for 1 to 2 hours or until set.

Approx Per Serving: Cal 382; Prot 5 g; Carbo 51 g; T Fat 19 g; 43% Calories from Fat; Chol 107 mg; Fiber 1 g; Sod 173 mg

Carol Frank, Marshall County HFH, Lacon, IL

Families apply to local Habitat affiliates. A selection committee chooses families on the basis of housing need, ability to repay the loan, and willingness to participate as a partner in Habitat's ministry. Every project follows a nondiscriminatory policy of family selection. Neither race nor religion are factors in choosing the families that receive Habitat houses.

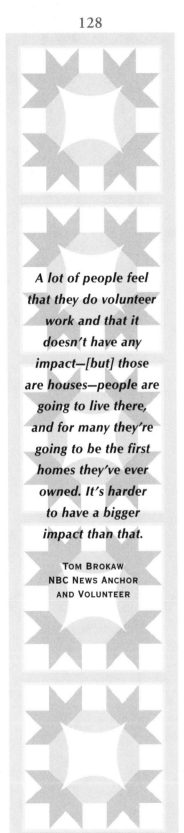

Lemon Mousse

Yield: 6 servings

1 envelope unflavored gelatin
2 tablespoons white grape juice
1/3 cup fresh lemon juice
1 tablespoon grated lemon rind
3 egg yolks
3 tablespoons sugar
3 egg whites

5 tablespoons sugar
1 cup whipping cream, whipped
1 (10-ounce) package frozen
   raspberries, thawed
2 tablespoons sugar
1 tablespoon fresh lemon juice

Sprinkle gelatin over grape juice in bowl. Let stand for 5 minutes or until softened. Stir in 1/3 cup lemon juice and lemon rind. Cook in double boiler over simmering water until gelatin dissolves, stirring constantly. Beat egg yolks and 3 tablespoons sugar in mixer bowl until frothy. Add gelatin mixture gradually, mixing well. Beat egg whites in mixer bowl until frothy. Add 5 tablespoons sugar gradually, beating constantly until soft peaks form. Fold whipped cream into egg yolk mixture. Fold in 1/2 of the meringue. Add mixture to remaining meringue; mix gently. Chill for 2 hours or until set. Drain raspberries, reserving juice. Process raspberries, 2 tablespoons sugar and 1 tablespoon lemon juice in blender until puréed. Press through sieve into bowl. Add just enough reserved raspberry juice to thin slightly. Spoon raspberry sauce onto dessert plate; top with lemon mousse. May freeze mousse for future use.

Approx Per Serving: Cal 315; Prot 5 g; Carbo 37 g; T Fat 17 g; 48% Calories from Fat; Chol 160 mg; Fiber 2 g; Sod 49 mg

Dyal Randall, HFH Greater Canton, North Canton, OH

Raspberry Mousse

Yield: 6 servings

1 cup water
1 (3-ounce) package raspberry
   gelatin
1 (10-ounce) package frozen
   raspberries, partially thawed

3/4 cup whipping cream
1/4 cup whipping cream,
   whipped
1/2 cup slivered almonds

Microwave water in microwave-safe cup just to boiling point. Combine hot water and gelatin in blender. Process on low for 15 seconds. Add undrained raspberries. Process for 5 seconds. Chill for 10 minutes. Add whipping cream. Process for 8 to 10 seconds or until blended. Pour into stemmed dessert glasses. Chill for several hours or until set. Top with whipped cream; sprinkle with almonds.

Approx Per Serving: Cal 305; Prot 5 g; Carbo 29 g; T Fat 21 g; 58% Calories from Fat; Chol 54 mg; Fiber 3 g; Sod 53 mg

Agnes Cartwright, Albany County/Laramie HFH, Laramie, WY

CROWD PLEASERS

"You shall eat in plenty and be satisfied, and
praise the name of the LORD your God,
who has dealt wondrously with you; and my
people shall never be put to shame."

-Joel 2:26

Apple Supreme

Yield: 24 servings

2 (16-ounce) cans juice-pack
  chunk pineapple
2 tablespoons vinegar
2 tablespoons flour
1/2 cup sugar
2 eggs, beaten

16 ounces whipped topping
1 (10-ounce) package miniature
  marshmallows
1 (16-ounce) package Spanish
  peanuts, chopped
12 large apples, chopped

Drain pineapple, reserving juice. Combine reserved pineapple juice, vinegar, flour, sugar and eggs in saucepan; mix well. Cook until thickened, stirring constantly. Let stand for 15 minutes or until cool. Fold in whipped topping. Combine marshmallows, peanuts, apples and pineapple in large serving bowl; mix well. Fold in whipped topping mixture. Chill, covered, until serving time. Stir just before serving. Garnish with additional peanuts.

Approx Per Serving: Cal 317; Prot 6 g; Carbo 44 g; T Fat 15 g; 40% Calories from Fat; Chol 18 mg; Fiber 4 g; Sod 17 mg

Fran Ingram, Dayton Ohio HFH, Beavercreek, OH

Caramel Corn Pops

Yield: 40 servings

1 cup margarine
1 cup packed light brown sugar
1/2 cup light corn syrup

1/2 teaspoon baking soda
1 (8-ounce) package corn pops

Bring margarine, brown sugar and corn syrup to a boil in saucepan; reduce heat. Simmer for 2 minutes, stirring occasionally. Stir in baking soda. Pour over cereal in large baking pan, tossing to coat. Bake at 250 degrees for 40 minutes, stirring every 10 minutes. Turn off oven. Let stand in closed oven for 5 minutes. Spread on waxed paper. Let stand until cool. Break into pieces. Store in airtight container.

Approx Per Serving: Cal 91; Prot <1 g; Carbo 13 g; T Fat 5 g; 44% Calories from Fat; Chol 0 mg; Fiber <1 g; Sod 91 mg

Shirleyann Franks, HFH of Northwest Indiana, Munster, IN

Cherry Fantasy

Yield: 18 servings

6 tablespoons melted margarine
1¹/₂ cups graham cracker crumbs
1 cup (heaping) confectioners' sugar
¹/₄ cup milk
16 ounces cream cheese, softened

1 cup chopped pecans
1 envelope whipped topping mix, prepared
1 (21-ounce) can cherry pie filling
1 teaspoon almond extract

Combine margarine and graham cracker crumbs in bowl; mix well. Pat into bottom of 9x13-inch baking pan. Bake at 350 degrees for 10 minutes. Let stand until cool. Beat confectioners' sugar, milk and cream cheese in mixer bowl until creamy, scraping bowl occasionally. Spread over baked layer; sprinkle with pecans. Spread with whipped topping. Top with mixture of pie filling and almond flavoring. Chill until serving time. May substitute any flavor pie filling for cherry pie filling.

Approx Per Serving: Cal 292; Prot 4 g; Carbo 27 g; T Fat 20 g; 59% Calories from Fat; Chol 29 mg; Fiber 1 g; Sod 204 mg

Kay DeMarea, My New Kentucky Home HFH, Lebanon, KY

Chocolate Applesauce Cake

Yield: 15 servings

¹/₂ cup shortening
1¹/₂ cups sugar
2 tablespoons baking cocoa
¹/₂ teaspoon cinnamon
2 eggs
2 cups flour

1¹/₂ teaspoons baking soda
¹/₂ teaspoon salt
2 cups applesauce
1 cup miniature chocolate chips
¹/₂ cup chopped pecans
2 tablespoons sugar

Beat shortening, 1¹/₂ cups sugar, baking cocoa, cinnamon, eggs, flour, baking soda, salt and applesauce in mixer bowl until blended. Spoon into greased and floured 9x13-inch cake pan. Sprinkle with mixture of chocolate chips, pecans and 2 tablespoons sugar. Bake at 350 degrees for 25 to 30 minutes or until cake tests done.

Approx Per Serving: Cal 354; Prot 4 g; Carbo 53 g; T Fat 15 g; 37% Calories from Fat; Chol 28 mg; Fiber 2 g; Sod 163 mg

Ann B. Meyer, Blount County HFH, Maryville, TN

We were in need of a volunteer to apply vinyl siding to a Habitat house. While having his car serviced, a subcontractor was informed of our need by the owner of the service center. The willing volunteer came to the site and offered his services until he had to report to his job two days later.

KAY DeMAREA
MY NEW KENTUCKY HOME HFH

German Chocolate Caramel Bars

Yield: 36 servings

1/3 cup evaporated milk
1 (14-ounce) package caramels
15 caramels
1 (2-layer) package German
    chocolate cake mix

3/4 cup melted butter
1/3 cup evaporated milk
1 cup semisweet chocolate chips

Combine 1/3 cup evaporated milk and caramels in saucepan. Cook over low heat until smooth, stirring constantly. Combine cake mix, butter and 1/3 cup evaporated milk in bowl; mix well. Spread 1/2 of the cake mixture in greased 9x13-inch baking pan. Bake at 350 degrees for 6 minutes. Sprinkle baked layer with chocolate chips. Pour caramel mixture over chocolate chips; spread evenly. Crumble remaining cake mixture over prepared layers. Bake for 20 minutes. Let stand until cool. Cut into bars.

Approx Per Serving: Cal 177; Prot 2 g; Carbo 26 g; T Fat 8 g; 39% Calories from Fat; Chol 13 mg; Fiber <1 g; Sod 213 mg

Ann Schweers, HFHI, Wisconsin State Coordinator
Cottage Grove, WI

Chocolate Caramel Nut Bars

Yield: 36 servings

1 (14-ounce) package caramels
2/3 cup evaporated milk
1 (2-layer) package
    pudding-recipe German
    chocolate cake mix

1/2 cup melted butter or
    margarine
2 cups semisweet chocolate
    chips
2 cups chopped walnuts

Combine caramels and 1/2 cup of the evaporated milk in saucepan. Cook over medium heat until smooth, stirring constantly. Combine cake mix, butter and remaining evaporated milk in bowl; mix well. Pat half the cake mixture into bottom of greased 9x13-inch baking pan. Bake at 350 degrees for 6 minutes. Sprinkle with chocolate chips and 1/2 of the walnuts; drizzle with caramel mixture. Sprinkle with remaining cake mixture; top with remaining walnuts. Bake for 20 minutes. Chill in refrigerator. Cut into bars.

Approx Per Serving: Cal 219; Prot 3 g; Carbo 28 g; T Fat 12 g; 47% Calories from Fat; Chol 9 mg; Fiber 1 g; Sod 193 mg

Bee Frame, HFHI, Americus, GA, Asheville, NC

Chocolate Nut Brownies
Yield: 36 servings

1 (14-ounce) package caramels
1/2 cup evaporated milk
1 (2-layer) package German
   chocolate cake mix

3/4 cup melted butter
1/3 cup evaporated milk
1 cup chopped pecans
1 cup semisweet chocolate chips

Combine caramels and 1/2 cup evaporated milk in saucepan. Cook over low heat until smooth, stirring constantly. Combine cake mix, butter and 1/3 cup evaporated milk in bowl; mix well. Stir in pecans. Spread 1/2 of the cake mixture in greased 9x13-inch pan. Bake at 350 degrees for 8 minutes. Sprinkle baked layer with chocolate chips. Spread caramel mixture evenly over chocolate chips. Spread remaining cake mixture over top. Bake for 18 to 20 minutes or until edges pull from sides of pan. Let stand until cool. Cut into bars.

Approx Per Serving: Cal 188; Prot 2 g; Carbo 24 g; T Fat 10 g; 46% Calories from Fat; Chol 13 mg; Fiber 1 g; Sod 206 mg

Michelle Tipping, Butler County HFH, Wichita, KS

Chocolate Layer Dessert
Yield: 15 servings

1 cup flour
1/2 cup butter, softened
1/2 cup chopped pecans
12 ounces whipped topping
1 cup confectioners' sugar
8 ounces cream cheese,
   softened

2 (4-ounce) packages chocolate
   instant pudding mix
3 cups milk
1/4 cup chopped pecans, toasted

Combine flour, butter and 1/2 cup pecans; mix well. Press into bottom of 9x13-inch baking pan. Bake at 350 degrees for 20 minutes or until light brown. Let stand until cool. Beat 1 cup of the whipped topping, confectioners' sugar and cream cheese in mixer bowl until smooth. Spread over baked layer. Combine pudding mix and milk in mixer bowl. Beat at low speed for 2 minutes, scraping bowl occasionally. Spread over prepared layers. Top with remaining whipped topping; sprinkle with 1/2 cup toasted pecans. Chill until set.

Approx Per Serving: Cal 364; Prot 5 g; Carbo 37 g; T Fat 23 g; 56% Calories from Fat; Chol 40 mg; Fiber 1 g; Sod 353 mg

Dianne M. Boswell, Pilot Mountain Area HFH, Pilot Mountain, NC
Robert H. Lehman, Flathead Valley Partners HFH, Kalispell, MT
Claudia Methvin, Barbour County HFH, Eufaula, AL

When I went to visit the homeowners of the first Pilot Mountain HFH home, their three little girls came running to the door. They wrapped themselves around my legs and told me they loved their new home. It made all the work involved in building our first Habitat home worthwhile.

DIANNE M. BOSWELL
PILOT MOUNTAIN AREA HFH

Rich Chocolate Chip Cookies

Yield: 36 servings

3/4 cup shortening	13/4 cups flour
11/4 cups packed light brown sugar	1 teaspoon salt
2 tablespoons milk	3/4 teaspoon baking soda
1 teaspoon vanilla extract	1 cup semisweet chocolate chips
1 egg	1 cup chopped pecans

Beat shortening, brown sugar, milk, vanilla and egg in mixer bowl until creamy, scraping bowl occasionally. Add mixture of flour, salt and baking soda; mix well. Stir in chocolate chips and pecans. Drop by rounded tablespoonfuls onto ungreased cookie sheet. Bake at 375 degrees for 8 to 10 minutes for soft cookies or 11 to 13 minutes for crisp cookies. Remove to wire rack to cool.

Approx Per Serving: Cal 131; Prot 1 g; Carbo 14 g; T Fat 8 g; 54% Calories from Fat; Chol 6 mg; Fiber 1 g; Sod 82 mg

Nancy Beach, HFH of Montgomery County IN, Crawfordsville, IN

Chocolate Mint Snaps

Yield: 126 servings

11/4 cups shortening	21/2 tablespoons water
2 cups sugar	2 teaspoons peppermint extract
4 (1-ounce) squares unsweetened chocolate, melted	1 teaspoon vanilla extract
	4 cups flour
	2 teaspoons baking soda
2 eggs	1/2 teaspoon salt
1/3 cup corn syrup	6 tablespoons sugar

Beat shortening in mixer bowl until creamy. Add 2 cups sugar gradually, beating until light and fluffy. Add chocolate, eggs, corn syrup, water and flavorings; mix well. Beat in mixture of flour, baking soda and salt just until blended. Shape into 1-inch balls; roll in 6 tablespoons sugar. Arrange on ungreased cookie sheet. Bake at 350 degrees for 10 minutes. Cool on cookie sheet for 5 minutes. Remove to wire rack to cool completely.

Approx Per Serving: Cal 56; Prot 1 g; Carbo 8 g; T Fat 3 g; 42% Calories from Fat; Chol 3 mg; Fiber <1 g; Sod 24 mg

Marietta Payne, North Webster HFH, Springhill, LA

Chocolate Scotcheroos

Yield: 48 servings

1 cup corn syrup
1 cup sugar
1 cup peanut butter
6 cups crisp rice cereal

2 cups semisweet chocolate
 chips
2 cups butterscotch chips

Combine corn syrup and sugar in saucepan; mix well. Heat just until mixture begins to boil, stirring frequently. Remove from heat. Stir in peanut butter. Add cereal; mix well. Press into buttered 9x13-inch dish. Combine chocolate chips and butterscotch chips in saucepan. Cook over medium heat until smooth, stirring constantly. Spread evenly over prepared layer. Chill for 1 hour or until set. Cut into bars.

Approx Per Serving: Cal 151; Prot 2 g; Carbo 23 g; T Fat 7 g; 38% Calories from Fat; Chol <1 mg; Fiber 1 g; Sod 83 mg

Penni Matthews, Pemi-Valley HFH, Ashland, NH

Chocolate Sheet Cake with Pecan Fudge Frosting

Yield: 24 servings

2 cups sugar
2 cups flour
1/2 cup butter
3 1/2 tablespoons baking cocoa
1 cup water
1/2 cup shortening
1 teaspoon baking soda
1/2 cup buttermilk
2 eggs, lightly beaten

1 teaspoon vanilla extract
1/2 cup butter
6 tablespoons milk
3 1/2 tablespoons baking cocoa
1 (1-pound) package
 confectioners' sugar, sifted
1 teaspoon vanilla extract
1 cup chopped pecans

Combine 2 cups sugar and flour in bowl; mix well. Bring 1/2 cup butter, 3 1/2 tablespoons baking cocoa, water and shortening to a boil in saucepan. Boil for 2 minutes, stirring occasionally. Pour over sugar mixture; mix well. Stir in mixture of baking soda and buttermilk. Beat in eggs and 1 teaspoon vanilla until blended. Spoon into 9x13-inch cake pan. Bake at 300 degrees for 30 minutes or until cake tests done. Bring 1/2 cup butter, milk and 3 1/2 tablespoons baking cocoa to a boil in saucepan, stirring frequently. Boil just until blended, stirring constantly. Remove from heat. Add confectioners' sugar and 1 teaspoon vanilla, beating until of spreading consistency. Stir in chopped pecans. Spread over hot cake.

Approx Per Serving: Cal 329; Prot 3 g; Carbo 46 g; T Fat 16 g; 43% Calories from Fat; Chol 39 mg; Fiber 1 g; Sod 126 mg

Cheryl Dean, Bryan/College Station HFH, College Station, TX

was not available locally. The part was ordered, but was not received until early October after our first frost. Our volunteers installed the part one day before the birth of the baby. I visited the family after the baby came home from the hospital to deliver some gifts from the Habitat volunteers. It was a cold rainy day, but the mother led me to a peacefully sleeping little girl, warm and comfortable with just a light blanket covering her tiny body. I don't have a way with words to describe how I felt, but I knew our Lord Jesus, he who was born in a manger, was pleased His Habitaters had come to Alamo.

NANCY BEACH
HFH OF MONTGOMERY COUNTY IN

Bittersweet Chocolate Torte

Yield: 16 servings

14 ounces bittersweet chocolate, coarsely chopped
1/2 cup butter
1/4 cup milk
5 eggs
1 teaspoon vanilla extract
1/2 cup sugar
1/4 cup flour
1/3 cup seedless red raspberry jam
2 cups fresh red raspberries
1/4 cup confectioners' sugar

Grease bottom of 8- or 9-inch springform pan. Combine chocolate, butter and milk in saucepan. Cook over low heat until smooth, stirring frequently. Cool for 20 minutes. Combine eggs and vanilla in mixer bowl. Beat at low speed until blended. Add sugar and flour. Beat at high speed for 10 minutes, scraping bowl occasionally. Add chocolate mixture; mix well. Spoon into prepared pan. Bake at 325 degrees for 35 minutes or until torte is slightly puffed on outer 1/3 edge. Cool in pan on wire rack for 20 minutes; center will fall 1/4 inch and surface will become crusty. Loosen from edge of pan with sharp knife. Let stand for 2 to 3 hours or until cool. Remove side of pan; wrap torte in foil. Chill for 8 hours to 2 days. Arrange torte on serving plate. Let stand until room temperature. Heat raspberry jam in saucepan until melted. Let stand until cool. Spread evenly on top of torte. Arrange raspberries stem side down in heart design over jam; sift confectioners' sugar over raspberries. Slice using a knife dipped in hot water. May substitute 16 ounces semisweet chocolate chips for bittersweet chocolate.

Approx Per Serving: Cal 257; Prot 4 g; Carbo 28 g; T Fat 17 g; 55% Calories from Fat; Chol 82 mg; Fiber 2 g; Sod 84 mg

Irene W. Sandford, Westchester NY HFH, Armonk, NY

Murder by Chocolate

Yield: 15 servings

1 (2-layer) package chocolate cake mix
1/2 cup Kahlúa
2 (4-ounce) packages chocolate instant pudding mix, prepared
16 ounces whipped topping
6 Skor or Heath candy bars, broken into pieces

Prepare cake mix using package directions. Let stand until cool. Pierce cake with fork. Pour Kahlúa evenly over cake; crumble. Layer cake, pudding, whipped topping and candy 1/2 at a time in large serving bowl. Chill until serving time.

Approx Per Serving: Cal 460; Prot 7 g; Carbo 61 g; T Fat 22 g; 41% Calories from Fat; Chol 48 mg; Fiber 1 g; Sod 581 mg

Sarah Stanley, Lakes Region HFH, West Franklin, NH

Our 1992 work team to Guatemala built a prototype brick stove for Guatemala Habitat homes. These were duplicated and sponsored by various work teams and churches. This idea is being built upon by the World Health Organization.

ROBERT H. LEHMAN
FLATHEAD VALLEY
PARTNERS HFH

Mom's Best Cinnamon Rolls

Yield: 16 servings

2 envelopes dry yeast
2 cups lukewarm milk
2 tablespoons sugar
2 cups flour
1 cup sugar
2 eggs
1/2 cup vegetable oil
1 teaspoon salt
5 cups flour
1 cup margarine, softened

1/2 cup butter, softened
11/2 cups sugar
1/2 cup packed brown sugar
2 tablespoons cinnamon
3 ounces cream cheese, softened
1/3 cup butter, softened
2 cups confectioners' sugar
2 tablespoons milk
1 teaspoon vanilla extract

Dissolve yeast in lukewarm milk. Combine yeast mixture, 2 tablespoons sugar and 2 cups flour in bowl; mix well. Let stand for 30 minutes; stir down. Add 1 cup sugar, eggs, oil and salt; mix well. Add 5 cups flour 1 cup at a time, mixing well after each addition. Knead on lightly floured surface for 5 minutes. Place in greased bowl, turning to coat surface. Let rise until doubled in bulk. Punch dough down. Roll into 1/4- to 1/2-inch thick rectangle on lightly floured surface. Spread with mixture of margarine and 1/2 cup butter; sprinkle with mixture of 11/2 cups sugar and brown sugar. Sprinkle with cinnamon. Roll as for jelly roll to enclose filling; seal edge and ends. Cut into 11/2-inch slices with string or dental floss. Arrange rolls with edges touching in ungreased 9x13-inch baking pan. Let rise, covered, until doubled in bulk. Bake at 400 degrees for 15 minutes or until golden brown. Cool slightly. Beat cream cheese, 1/3 cup butter, confectioners' sugar, milk and vanilla in mixer bowl until of spreading consistency. Spread over warm cinnamon rolls. Serve warm or at room temperature.

Approx Per Serving: Cal 705; Prot 8 g; Carbo 98 g; T Fat 32 g; 40% Calories from Fat; Chol 63 mg; Fiber 2 g; Sod 409 mg

Kathleen N. Bryan, South Puget Sound HFH, Olympia, WA

Photo by HFHI

When my husband, Scott, became unemployed, it sure was nice to have networked while volunteering for the Franklin HFH affiliate. His current employer is also a volunteer.

SARAH STANLEY
LAKES REGION HFH

Nut Rolls

Yield: 192 servings

1 envelope dry yeast
1/2 cup lukewarm water
7 cups flour
2 teaspoons baking powder
1 teaspoon (scant) salt
2 cups shortening
1 teaspoon confectioners' sugar

1 cup evaporated milk
3 eggs
2 pounds pecans, ground
1 1/2 cups confectioners' sugar
1/4 cup lukewarm evaporated milk

Dissolve yeast in lukewarm water; mix well. Sift flour, baking powder and salt into bowl; mix well. Cut in shortening until crumbly. Beat 1 teaspoon confectioners' sugar, 1 cup evaporated milk and eggs in mixer bowl until blended. Stir in yeast mixture. Add to dry ingredients, mixing well. Chill, covered, for 8 to 10 hours. Combine pecans, 1 1/2 cups confectioners' sugar and 1/4 cup evaporated milk in bowl, stirring until of spreading consistency. Separate dough into 3-ounce balls. Roll each ball into thin rounds on lightly floured surface. Spread with pecan mixture. Cut each circle into 8 wedges; roll wedges up from wide end. Arrange on greased baking sheet. Bake at 375 degrees for 12 minutes or until brown. Remove to wire rack to cool.

Approx Per Serving: Cal 74; Prot 1 g; Carbo 5 g; T Fat 6 g; 66% Calories from Fat; Chol 4 mg; Fiber <1 g; Sod 17 mg

Marilyn Chappell, Blount County HFH, Greenback, TN

Coffee Cake

Yield: 16 servings

1 envelope dry yeast
1/2 cup lukewarm water
1/2 cup milk
1/4 cup sugar
1 teaspoon salt
2 tablespoons shortening
2 1/2 cups (or more) flour

1 egg, lightly beaten
1/4 cup melted margarine
1/2 cup sugar
1 teaspoon (or more) cinnamon
2 tablespoons melted margarine
2 tablespoons (or more) sugar

Dissolve yeast in lukewarm water. Scald milk in saucepan. Add 1/4 cup sugar, salt and shortening, stirring until shortening melts. Add flour; mix well. Stir in yeast mixture and egg until blended. Add additional flour if desired for soft dough. Knead dough on lightly floured surface until smooth and elastic. Place in greased bowl, turning to coat surface. Let rise for 1 1/2 hours or until doubled in bulk. Punch dough down. Let rest for 10 minutes. Roll into 10x15-inch rectangle on lightly floured surface; fit into baking pan. Brush with 1/4 cup butter; sprinkle with mixture of 1/2 cup sugar and cinnamon. Let rise for 45 minutes or until doubled in bulk. Bake at 375 degrees for 12 to 14 minutes or until brown. Invert onto serving plate; drizzle with 2 tablespoons butter; sprinkle with 2 tablespoons sugar.

Approx Per Serving: Cal 176; Prot 3 g; Carbo 26 g; T Fat 7 g; 34% Calories from Fat; Chol 14 mg; Fiber 1 g; Sod 192 mg

Clara Short, Southeast New Hampshire HFH, Portsmouth, NH

Philadelphia Danish

Yield: 15 servings

2 (8-count) cans crescent rolls
16 ounces cream cheese,
   softened
1 cup sugar

1 tablespoon vanilla extract
1 egg yolk
1 egg white, lightly beaten

Unroll 1 can of the crescent roll dough. Spread dough in bottom of 9x13-inch baking pan; seal edges and perforations. Beat cream cheese, sugar, vanilla and egg yolk in mixer bowl until smooth. Spread over prepared layer. Unroll remaining can of crescent roll dough. Spread over cream cheese mixture, sealing edges and perforations. Brush with egg white. Bake at 350 degrees for 20 to 30 minutes or until golden brown. May sprinkle baked Danish with confectioners' sugar or top with your favorite fruit topping.

Approx Per Serving: Cal 256; Prot 4 g; Carbo 28 g; T Fat 14 g; 49% Calories from Fat; Chol 50 mg; Fiber 0 g; Sod 360 mg

Steven Crebessa, Meade County HFH, Vine Grove, KY

Cookie Brittle

Yield: 30 servings

1 cup butter, softened
1 1/2 teaspoons vanilla extract
1 teaspoon salt

1 cup sugar
2 cups flour
1 cup chocolate chips

Combine butter, vanilla, salt, sugar and flour in bowl; mix well. Stir in chocolate chips. Pat 1/2 inch thick onto ungreased baking sheet or jelly roll pan; mixture does not have to reach edges of pan. Bake at 375 degrees for 25 minutes. Let stand until cool. Break into pieces.

Approx Per Serving: Cal 137; Prot 1 g; Carbo 17 g; T Fat 8 g; 50% Calories from Fat; Chol 17 mg; Fiber 1 g; Sod 134 mg

Lisa Nielsen, HFHI, Americus, GA

When I'm asked about housing success stories from our inner cities, the first group that comes to mind is Habitat for Humanity.

JACK KEMP
FORMER U.S. SECRETARY
OF HOUSING AND URBAN
DEVELOPMENT

Photo by Julie A. Lopez

JACK KEMP CONGRATULATES ATLANTA HFH HOMEOWNER

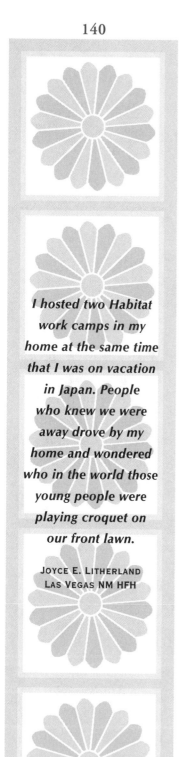

Delight Dessert

Yield: 15 servings

2 cups flour
1 cup melted butter
1 cup chopped pecans
1¼ cups whipping cream
4 ounces cream cheese, softened
½ cup sifted confectioners' sugar

2 (4-ounce) packages vanilla instant pudding mix
2½ cups milk
1 banana, thinly sliced
1 cup whipping cream, whipped
½ cup chopped pecans, toasted
½ cup flaked coconut, toasted

Combine flour, butter and pecans in bowl; mix well. Pat into 9x13-inch baking pan. Bake at 350 degrees for 25 minutes or until light brown. Let stand until cool. Beat whipping cream, cream cheese and confectioners' sugar in mixer bowl until smooth. Spread over baked layer. Chill, covered, in refrigerator. Combine pudding mix and milk in bowl, whisking until thickened. Spread over chilled layer. Chill until set. Arrange banana slices over pudding; spread with mixture of whipped cream and pecans. Sprinkle with coconut. Chill until serving time.

Approx Per Serving: Cal 510; Prot 6 g; Carbo 38 g; T Fat 39 g; 67% Calories from Fat; Chol 96 mg; Fiber 2 g; Sod 399 mg

Genie German, Macon Area HFH, Macon, GA

Layered Fruit Fluff

Yield: 15 servings

4 cups miniature marshmallows
1 cup milk
1¼ cups flour
½ cup packed brown sugar
¼ teaspoon salt

½ cup butter
1 cup whipping cream
½ teaspoon almond extract
1 (21-ounce) can cherry pie filling

Combine marshmallows and milk in double boiler. Cook over hot water until smooth, stirring frequently. Chill until slightly thickened. Combine flour, brown sugar and salt in bowl; mix well. Cut in butter until crumbly. Spread mixture in 8x12-inch baking pan. Bake at 400 degrees for 12 to 14 minutes or until golden brown, stirring occasionally. Let stand until cool. Reserve ½ cup of the crumb mixture; press remainder of crumb mixture over bottom of pan. Beat whipping cream and almond extract in mixer bowl until thickened. Fold in marshmallow mixture. Spread ⅔ of the marshmallow mixture over prepared layer. Spread with pie filling. Top with remaining marshmallow mixture. Sprinkle with reserved crumb mixture. Chill, covered, for 6 to 10 hours.

Approx Per Serving: Cal 266; Prot 2 g; Carbo 36 g; T Fat 13 g; 43% Calories from Fat; Chol 41 mg; Fiber 1 g; Sod 141 mg

Joyce E. Litherland, Las Vegas NM HFH, Las Vegas, NM

Fruit Pizza

Yield: 16 servings

1 (20-ounce) package
   refrigerated sugar cookie
   dough
8 ounces cream cheese
1/3 cup sugar
1/2 teaspoon vanilla extract
1 kiwifruit, sliced

1 (16-ounce) can pineapple
   chunks, drained
1 cup grape halves
1 cup maraschino cherry halves
2 ounces white chocolate,
   melted

Press cookie dough into pizza pan with floured fingers. Bake at 350 degrees until brown. Let stand until cool. Beat cream cheese, sugar and vanilla in mixer bowl until smooth. Spread over baked layer. Arrange kiwifruit, pineapple, grapes and cherries over top; drizzle with white chocolate. Cut into wedges. May substitute your favorite fruits for ones mentioned.

Approx Per Serving: Cal 310; Prot 3 g; Carbo 46 g; T Fat 14 g; 39% Calories from Fat; Chol 27 mg; Fiber 1 g; Sod 196 mg

Tilda Bowling, Appalachia HFH, Sunbright, TN

Company Fruit Pizza

Yield: 16 servings

2 cups baking mix
1/3 cup sugar
1/3 cup margarine
1 egg, beaten
3 ounces light cream cheese,
   softened
1 cup whipping cream
1/3 cup sugar

1/2 teaspoon vanilla extract
1 cup sliced strawberries
1 banana, sliced
1 (16-ounce) can pineapple
   chunks, drained
2 kiwifruit, sliced
1 cup red grape halves

Combine baking mix and 1/3 cup sugar in bowl; mix well. Cut in margarine until crumbly. Stir in egg until blended. Pat into greased and floured 16-inch pizza pan. Bake at 350 degrees for 12 minutes or until light brown. Let stand until cool. Beat cream cheese and whipping cream in mixer bowl until peaks form. Stir in 1/3 cup sugar and vanilla. Spread over baked layer. Arrange fruit in concentric circles over cream cheese layer. May substitute fruit of your choice.

Approx Per Serving: Cal 239; Prot 3 g; Carbo 29 g; T Fat 13 g; 48% Calories from Fat; Chol 37 mg; Fiber 1 g; Sod 252 mg

Jo Ann Buck, Flager HFH Inc., Palm Coast, FL

Fruit Sheet Pie

Yield: 25 servings

7 cups flour
2 cups sugar
1 teaspoon baking soda
2 teaspoons baking powder
1/8 teaspoon salt

2 eggs, beaten
1/2 cup milk
3 (21-ounce) cans cherry or
   blueberry pie filling

Combine flour, sugar, baking soda, baking powder and salt in bowl; mix well. Add eggs and milk, stirring until mixture forms a ball. Divide into 2 portions. Crumble 1 portion onto large baking sheet; cover with waxed paper. Roll with rolling pin until dough covers bottom of baking sheet; discard waxed paper. Spread with pie filling. Crumble desired amount of remaining dough over pie filling. Bake at 350 degrees for 20 to 30 minutes or until brown and bubbly.

Approx Per Serving: Cal 283; Prot 5 g; Carbo 63 g; T Fat 2 g; 5% Calories from Fat; Chol 18 mg; Fiber 1 g; Sod 115 mg

Audrey Costa, HFH of Carlisle PA, Mechanicsburg, PA

Icebox Cookies

Yield: 96 servings

1 cup melted butter or
   margarine
2 cups sugar
3 to 4 cups flour, sifted
1 teaspoon nutmeg
1 teaspoon cinnamon

1 teaspoon baking soda
2 teaspoons baking powder
3 eggs
1 to 2 cups pecan pieces
1 (15-ounce) package golden
   raisins

Combine butter and sugar in bowl; mix well. Add sifted mixture of flour, nutmeg, cinnamon, baking soda and baking powder; mix well. Add eggs 1 at a time, mixing well after each addition. Stir in pecans and raisins. Shape dough into balls or roll into log and slice. Arrange on cookie sheet. Bake at 250 degrees for 20 minutes; do not overbake. Remove to wire rack to cool. May store dough, wrapped in waxed paper, in refrigerator for several days.

Approx Per Serving: Cal 84; Prot 1 g; Carbo 12 g; T Fat 4 g; 39% Calories from Fat; Chol 12 mg; Fiber 1 g; Sod 38 mg

Sara Wingard, Wythe County HFH, Wytheville, VA

Lemon Cake Squares

Yield: 24 servings

6 tablespoons butter, softened
1 cup sugar
2 eggs, beaten
1¹/₂ cups sifted flour
1¹/₂ teaspoons baking powder

¹/₄ teaspoon salt
¹/₂ cup milk
¹/₂ teaspoon almond extract
Juice of 1 lemon
²/₃ cup sugar

Cream butter and 1 cup sugar in mixer bowl until light and fluffy. Add eggs, flour, baking powder, salt, milk and almond extract; mix well. Spread in greased 9x13-inch baking pan. Bake at 350 degrees for 25 minutes. Spoon mixture of lemon juice and ²/₃ cup sugar over baked layer. Bake for 5 minutes longer. Let stand until cool. Cut into squares. May substitute grated rind of 1 lemon for almond extract.

Approx Per Serving: Cal 115; Prot 1 g; Carbo 20 g; T Fat 4 g; 27% Calories from Fat; Chol 26 mg; Fiber <1 g; Sod 80 mg

Ellen S. Goodwin, Pioneer Valley HFH, Amherst, MA

Iced Lemon Cookies

Yield: 144 servings

7 cups flour
2 cups sugar
2 tablespoons (heaping) baking
  powder
1 teaspoon salt
2 cups butter-flavor shortening

12 eggs
1 tablespoon lemon extract
2 egg whites
1 (1-pound) package
  confectioners' sugar
1 tablespoon lemon juice

Combine flour, sugar, baking powder and salt in bowl; mix well. Cut in shortening until crumbly. Mix in eggs and lemon extract; dough should be moist but not sticky. Add additional flour if dough is too moist or add milk if too dry. Shape dough into 1-inch balls. Arrange on cookie sheet. Bake at 350 degrees for 10 minutes. May freeze cookies at this point for future use. Beat egg whites in mixer bowl until frothy. Add confectioners' sugar and lemon juice, beating until of desired consistency. Dip cookies in lemon mixture. Remove to wire rack. Let stand until set.

Approx Per Serving: Cal 77; Prot 1 g; Carbo 11 g; T Fat 3 g; 39% Calories from Fat; Chol 18 mg; Fiber <1 g; Sod 35 mg

Sylvia LaFalce, HFH of South Dutchess, Hopewell Junction, NY

Lemon Dessert

Yield: 12 servings

1 cup flour
1/2 cup melted margarine
1/2 cup finely chopped pecans
8 ounces cream cheese, softened
1 cup confectioners' sugar

8 ounces whipped topping
2 (4-ounce) packages lemon instant pudding mix
3 tablespoons lemon juice
2 1/2 cups milk
16 ounces whipped topping

Combine flour, margarine and pecans in bowl; mix well. Pat into bottom of 9x13-inch baking pan. Bake at 350 degrees for 15 minutes. Let stand until cool. Beat cream cheese, confectioners' sugar and 8 ounces whipped topping in mixer bowl until smooth. Spread over baked layer. Let stand for several minutes. Combine pudding mix, lemon juice and milk in mixer bowl; mix well. Spoon over prepared layers. Top with 16 ounces whipped topping. Chill until set. May substitute chocolate or butterscotch pudding mix for lemon pudding mix.

Approx Per Serving: Cal 527; Prot 5 g; Carbo 53 g; T Fat 34 g; 57% Calories from Fat; Chol 28 mg; Fiber 1 g; Sod 436 mg

Lydia Berger, Knox County HFH, Freelandville, IN

Frozen Lemon Dessert

Yield: 30 servings

1 (16-ounce) package vanilla wafers, crushed
1/3 cup melted butter or margarine
6 egg yolks
2 (14-ounce) cans sweetened condensed milk

1 (12-ounce) can frozen lemonade concentrate, thawed
1 cup whipping cream, whipped
6 egg whites
3/4 cup sugar

Combine vanilla wafer crumbs and butter in bowl; mix well. Pat into one 9x13-inch baking pan and one 8x8-inch baking pan. Beat egg yolks in mixer bowl. Add condensed milk and lemonade concentrate, beating until thickened. Fold in whipped cream. Spread over prepared layer. Beat egg whites in mixer bowl until soft peaks form. Add sugar, beating until stiff peaks form. Spread over prepared layers. Broil until light brown. Freeze until serving time. May substitute 8 ounces whipped topping for the whipping cream.

Approx Per Serving: Cal 252; Prot 4 g; Carbo 36 g; T Fat 11 g; 37% Calories from Fat; Chol 77 mg; Fiber <1 g; Sod 118 mg

Nancy B. Beilfuss, Flower City HFH, Macedon, NY

Lemon Pecan Tarts

Yield: 66 servings

1 cup margarine, softened
3 eggs
1 1/4 cups sugar
2 tablespoons lemon extract

2 cups flour
1 1/2 teaspoons baking powder
2 cups chopped pecans
8 ounces golden raisins

Cream margarine in mixer bowl until light and fluffy. Add eggs, beating until blended. Add sugar and lemon flavoring; mix well. Stir in sifted mixture of flour and baking powder. Fold in chopped pecans and raisins. Spoon into miniature muffin cups sprayed with nonstick cooking spray or lined with paper liners. Bake at 350 degrees for 12 minutes or just until light brown.

Approx Per Serving: Cal 92; Prot 1 g; Carbo 10 g; T Fat 5 g; 52% Calories from Fat; Chol 10 mg; Fiber 1 g; Sod 43 mg

Cathie Wilbourne, Barbour County HFH, Eufaula, AL

Grandma's Molasses Cookies

Yield: 84 servings

1 egg, beaten
2 cups baking molasses
1 cup sugar
1 cup butter, softened
1 cup buttermilk

2 teaspoons baking soda
1 tablespoon baking powder
1 teaspoon cinnamon
6 cups flour
1 cup sugar

Combine egg, molasses, 1 cup sugar, butter and buttermilk in bowl; mix well. Add mixture of baking soda, baking powder, cinnamon and flour gradually, mixing well after each addition. Drop by rounded tablespoonfuls onto greased cookie sheet; sprinkle with 1 cup sugar. Bake at 350 degrees for 10 minutes or until light brown. Remove to wire rack to cool.

Approx Per Serving: Cal 93; Prot 1 g; Carbo 17 g; T Fat 2 g; 23% Calories from Fat; Chol 9 mg; Fiber <1 g; Sod 61 mg

Karen Kapp, Cumberland Valley HFH, Mechanicsburg, PA

Standing in the background looking at a Habitat work site is something like gazing at an anthill. All that business and motion, yet purposeful and coordinated. Every worker has a job to do for the good of the whole colony. Progress in motion, goal just ahead.

KAREN KAPP
CUMBERLAND VALLEY HFH

*When I first saw a copy of **From Our House to Yours** cookbook, I piped up, "That sure is something I could get excited about promoting! I love cookbooks." Thus began my active involvement in our affiliate. I have chaired this fund-raising event for us and we have sold 1,000 copies. It will be even more exciting to promote the **Home Sweet Habitat** cookbook which includes recipes we have submitted.*

RITA M. GOEBERT
HFH OF WAYNE COUNTY NY INC.

Orange Scotch Cake

Yield: 16 servings

1/2 cup shortening
1 cup sugar
2 eggs
Grated rind of 1 orange
2 cups flour
1/2 teaspoon baking soda
1/2 teaspoon salt
2/3 cup buttermilk or sour milk
1 teaspoon vanilla extract
1 cup raisins
1/2 cup chopped walnuts
Juice of 1 orange
1/2 cup sugar

Cream shortening and 1 cup sugar in mixer bowl until light and fluffy. Add eggs 1 at a time, mixing well after each addition. Add orange rind; mix well. Add sifted mixture of flour, baking soda and salt alternately with buttermilk, mixing well after each addition. Stir in vanilla, raisins and walnuts. Spoon into greased and floured tube pan. Bake at 325 degrees for 1 hour. Pour mixture of orange juice and 1/2 cup sugar over hot cake. Cool in pan. Invert onto serving platter.

Approx Per Serving: Cal 257; Prot 4 g; Carbo 41 g; T Fat 10 g; 33% Calories from Fat; Chol 27 mg; Fiber 1 g; Sod 113 mg

Rita M. Goebert, HFH of Wayne County NY Inc., Palmyra, NY

Divine Peach Cobbler

Yield: 24 servings

6 cups sliced fresh peaches
1 cup sugar
1 teaspoon cinnamon
1 teaspoon nutmeg or mace
2 cups chopped walnuts
3 cups flour
2 cups sugar
2 teaspoons baking powder
1/2 teaspoon salt
2 eggs, beaten
1 cup milk
2/3 cup melted butter

Arrange peaches in greased 13x18-inch baking pan. Combine 1 cup sugar, cinnamon, nutmeg and walnuts in bowl; mix well. Sprinkle 3/4 of the sugar mixture over peaches. Combine flour, 2 cups sugar, baking powder and salt in bowl; mix well. Stir in eggs, milk and butter until blended. Pour over prepared layers; sprinkle with remaining sugar mixture. Place pan on middle rack in oven. Bake at 350 degrees for 1 hour or until brown and bubbly. Serve with whipped cream or whipped topping. May substitute any fresh fruit or four 16-ounce cans drained fruit for the peaches.

Approx Per Serving: Cal 294; Prot 4 g; Carbo 44 g; T Fat 12 g; 36% Calories from Fat; Chol 33 mg; Fiber 2 g; Sod 136 mg

Billie Kay Gross, Albany County HFH, Laramie, WY

Peanut Butter Balls

Yield: 144 servings

2 (1-pound) packages
   confectioners' sugar
1 (16-ounce) jar creamy peanut
   butter

1¹/₂ cups (or less) melted
   margarine
2 cups chocolate chips
1 (2-ounce) bar paraffin

Combine confectioners' sugar and peanut butter in bowl. Add enough margarine to make an easily handled mixture; mix well. Shape into 1-inch balls. Combine chocolate chips and paraffin in double boiler. Cook over hot water until smooth, stirring frequently. Dip candy balls in chocolate mixture; drain excess chocolate. Let stand on waxed paper until set.

Approx Per Serving: Cal 71; Prot 1 g; Carbo 8 g; T Fat 4 g; 50% Calories from Fat; Chol 0 mg; Fiber <1 g; Sod 38 mg

Norma C. Branch, Charlotte HFH, Charlotte, NC

Peanut Butter Cheesecake *Yield: 10 servings*

1¹/₄ cups chocolate graham
   cracker crumbs
¹/₄ cup sugar
¹/₄ cup melted butter
8 ounces cream cheese,
   softened

1 cup crunchy peanut butter
1 cup sugar
1 teaspoon vanilla extract
8 ounces whipped topping

Combine graham cracker crumbs, ¹/₄ cup sugar and butter in bowl; mix well. Press into 9-inch round baking dish. Bake at 375 degrees for 10 minutes. Let stand until cool. Beat cream cheese, peanut butter, 1 cup sugar and vanilla in mixer bowl until smooth. Fold in whipped topping. Spread over baked layer. Garnish with grated chocolate or chocolate graham cracker crumbs. Chill or freeze until serving time. Decrease fat grams by using light whipped topping and reduced-fat peanut butter.

Approx Per Serving: Cal 511; Prot 9 g; Carbo 47 g; T Fat 34 g; 58% Calories from Fat; Chol 37 mg; Fiber 2 g; Sod 344 mg

Nancy Konrad, HFH of Oshkosh Inc., Oshkosh, WI

Peanut Butter Crisps

Yield: 60 servings

12 slices sandwich bread
1 cup smooth peanut butter

1 cup corn or soy oil

Trim crusts from bread, reserving crusts. Cut each slice into 5 strips. Arrange strips and crusts on separate baking sheets. Bake at 200 degrees for 1 to 1½ hours or until crisp. Process crusts in blender until of crumb consistency. Combine peanut butter and corn oil in bowl; mix well. Dip bread strips into peanut butter mixture; roll in crumbs. Remove to wire rack to dry. Store in airtight container.

Approx Per Serving: Cal 73; Prot 2 g; Carbo 4 g; T Fat 6 g; 72% Calories from Fat; Chol <1 mg; Fiber <1 g; Sod 49 mg

Marjorie Rowland, HFH of Grayson County, Denison, TX

Peanut Chocolate Dessert

Yield: 18 servings

½ cup butter, softened
1 cup flour
⅔ cup chopped peanuts
8 ounces cream cheese, softened
⅓ cup peanut butter
1 cup confectioners' sugar
12 ounces whipped topping

1 (4-ounce) package vanilla instant pudding mix
1 (4-ounce) package chocolate instant pudding mix
2¾ cups milk
1 (2-ounce) chocolate candy bar
⅓ cup chopped peanuts

Cut butter into flour in bowl until crumbly. Stir in ⅔ cup peanuts. Press into 9x13-inch baking pan. Bake at 350 degrees for 20 minutes. Let stand until cool. Beat cream cheese, peanut butter and confectioners' sugar in mixer bowl until light and fluffy. Fold in 1 cup of the whipped topping. Spread over baked layer. Combine pudding mixes and milk in mixer bowl. Beat at medium speed for 2 minutes, scraping bowl occasionally. Spoon over prepared layers. Top with remaining whipped topping. Shave candy bar into curls; sprinkle over whipped topping. Sprinkle with ⅓ cup peanuts. Chill until set.

Approx Per Serving: Cal 351; Prot 6 g; Carbo 34 g; T Fat 22 g; 56% Calories from Fat; Chol 34 mg; Fiber 1 g; Sod 319 mg

Janet Love, Genesee Valley HFH, Alfred Station, NY

Pecan Pie Bars

Yield: 48 servings

A cookie version of a favorite southern pie contributed by a born-and-bred Yankee.

2¹/₂ cups flour
1 cup chilled butter
¹/₂ cup sugar
1 teaspoon salt
4 eggs
1¹/₂ cups corn syrup

1¹/₂ cups sugar
¹/₄ cup melted butter
2 teaspoons vanilla extract
2¹/₂ cups coarsely chopped
    pecans

Beat flour, 1 cup butter, ¹/₂ cup sugar and salt in mixer bowl until crumbly. Press into greased 10x15-inch baking pan. Bake at 350 degrees for 20 minutes or until golden brown. Beat eggs, corn syrup, 1¹/₂ cups sugar, ¹/₄ cup butter and vanilla in mixer bowl until blended. Stir in pecans. Spread over hot baked layer. Bake for 25 minutes or until set. Let stand until cool. Cut into 1¹/₂x2-inch bars.

Approx Per Serving: Cal 175; Prot 2 g; Carbo 22 g; T Fat 9 g; 47% Calories from Fat; Chol 31 mg; Fiber 1 g; Sod 111 mg

Jim Donovan, HFH Lake County IL, Waukegan, IL

Pineapple and Cherry Dump Cake

Yield: 16 servings

1 (20-ounce) can juice-pack
    crushed pineapple
1 (21-ounce) can cherry or
    blueberry pie filling

1 (2-layer) package yellow or
    white cake mix
¹/₂ cup butter
¹/₂ cup chopped pecans

Spread the undrained pineapple in bottom of ungreased 9x13-inch baking pan. Spoon cherry pie filling in mounds over pineapple. Sprinkle with cake mix; dot with butter. Top with pecans. Bake at 325 degrees for 15 minutes. Serve warm or cold with a dollop of whipped cream. Do not use pudding-recipe cake mix in this dessert.

Approx Per Serving: Cal 279; Prot 2 g; Carbo 42 g; T Fat 12 g; 39% Calories from Fat; Chol 16 mg; Fiber 1 g; Sod 288 mg

June A. Glennon, HFH of the Coachella Valley, Palm Springs, CA

The minister of my church asked me to attend a meeting of a group of people interested in starting an HFH affiliate. I said yes, thinking it was a one-time commitment. How naive of me. Six years later, I am still on the board of directors and have served three years as president. I am still very excited about our HFH service to the community.

JUNE A. GLENNON
HFH OF THE COACHELLA VALLEY

Great Pineapple Dessert
Yield: 15 servings

1 cup melted butter or
  margarine
1¹/₂ cups flour
1 (20-ounce) can crushed
  pineapple

1 cup sugar
2 tablespoons cornstarch
4 egg whites
1 cup sugar

Combine butter and flour in bowl; mix well. Press into 9x13-inch baking pan. Bake at 350 degrees for 15 minutes or until brown. Combine undrained pineapple, 1 cup sugar and cornstarch in saucepan; mix well. Cook until thickened, stirring constantly. Spread over hot baked layer. Beat egg whites in mixer bowl until soft peaks form. Add 1 cup sugar, beating constantly until stiff peaks form. Spread over prepared layers. Bake for 1 hour. Serve with whipped cream.

Approx Per Serving: Cal 295; Prot 2 g; Carbo 45 g; T Fat 12 g; 37% Calories from Fat; Chol 33 mg; Fiber 1 g; Sod 141 mg

Suzanne Browne, Mankato HFH, Mankato, MN

Praline Graham Yummies
Yield: 40 servings

40 graham cracker singles
¹/₂ cup butter
¹/₂ cup margarine

¹/₂ cup sugar
¹/₂ cup packed brown sugar
1 cup chopped pecans

Arrange graham crackers in single layer in ungreased 10x15-inch baking pan. Bring butter, margarine, sugar and brown sugar to a boil in saucepan. Boil for 3 minutes, stirring occasionally. Stir in pecans. Spread evenly over graham crackers. Bake at 350 degrees for 10 minutes. Let stand until cool. Break apart. Store in airtight container.

Approx Per Serving: Cal 108; Prot 1 g; Carbo 11 g; T Fat 7 g; 59% Calories from Fat; Chol 6 mg; Fiber <1 g; Sod 94 mg

Gloria G. Lacy, HFH/St. Joseph County IN, South Bend, IN

I helped hang sheetrock in a Habitat house, which was a new experience. It seemed as if I brought treats all the time and they were rapidly consumed by the "Old Fuds," as the guys called themselves. Just a great group doing a great job! We had many noon lunches at a fast-foods restaurant—dirty jeans and all.

SUZANNE BROWNE
MANKATO HFH

Pumpkin Gingerbread

Yield: 16 servings

1 (16-ounce) can pumpkin
4 eggs
3¹/2 cups flour
2 cups sugar
1 cup butter or margarine,
  softened
¹/2 cup light molasses
¹/3 cup water

2 teaspoons baking soda
1 teaspoon salt
1 teaspoon cinnamon
1 teaspoon ginger
¹/2 teaspoon baking powder
¹/4 teaspoon nutmeg
¹/4 teaspoon ground cloves

Combine pumpkin, eggs, flour, sugar, butter, molasses, water, baking soda, salt, cinnamon, ginger, baking powder, nutmeg and cloves in mixer bowl. Beat at low speed for 30 seconds, scraping bowl constantly. Beat at medium speed for 3 minutes, scraping bowl occasionally. Spoon into greased and floured 9x13-inch baking pan. Bake at 350 degrees for 50 minutes or until edges pull from sides of pan. Serve with whipped topping or warm applesauce.

Approx Per Serving: Cal 354; Prot 5 g; Carbo 55 g; T Fat 13 g; 33% Calories from Fat; Chol 84 mg; Fiber 2 g; Sod 385 mg

Kathy Bangasser, HFH of Greater Sioux Falls, Sioux Falls, SD

Punch Bowl Cake

Yield: 30 servings

1 (2-layer) package yellow cake
  mix
1 (4-ounce) package vanilla
  instant pudding mix,
  prepared
1 (6-ounce) package vanilla
  instant pudding mix,
  prepared

1 (20-ounce) can juice-pack
  crushed pineapple
2 (21-ounce) cans cherry pie
  filling
16 ounces whipped topping
¹/2 cup chopped pecans

Prepare and bake cake using package directions. Let stand until cool. Crumble cake. Layer cake, pudding, undrained pineapple, cherry pie filling, whipped topping and pecans ¹/2 at a time in punch bowl. Chill until serving time.

Approx Per Serving: Cal 262; Prot 3 g; Carbo 42 g; T Fat 9 g; 32% Calories from Fat; Chol 21 mg; Fiber 1 g; Sod 291 mg

Carrie Martin, HFH of Moore County, Pinehurst, NC

Working at Habitat is truly addictive. My husband volunteered for a week during the "BLITZ" in August of 1994, and is now working four to five days a week as part of the support group in the St. Joseph County HFH. He is constantly talking about Habitat with friends, Sunday school classes, service clubs, and other organizations. Sometimes if I want to see him during daytime hours, I have to make an appointment.

GLORIA G. LACY
HFH/ST. JOSEPH COUNTY IN

Company Punch Bowl Cake

Yield: 30 servings

1 (2-layer) package yellow cake mix
2 (21-ounce) cans strawberry pie filling
2 (6-ounce) packages vanilla instant pudding mix, prepared

1 (20-ounce) can juice-pack crushed pineapple
32 ounces whipped topping

Prepare and bake cake using package directions. Let stand until cool. Crumble cake. Layer cake, pie filling, pudding, undrained pineapple and whipped topping 1/2 at a time in punch bowl. Chill until serving time. May substitute cherry pie filling for strawberry pie filling and banana pudding for vanilla pudding.

Approx Per Serving: Cal 302; Prot 4 g; Carbo 46 g; T Fat 12 g; 35% Calories from Fat; Chol 22 mg; Fiber 1 g; Sod 311 mg

Eileen Hartzog, HFH of Spokane, Spokane, WA

Kahlúa Punch Bowl Cake

Yield: 30 servings

1 (2-layer) package pudding-recipe chocolate cake mix
1/2 cup Kahlúa
1 (6-ounce) package chocolate instant pudding mix, prepared

16 ounces whipped topping
6 Heath candy bars, crushed

Prepare and bake cake using package directions for 9x13-inch cake pan. Let stand until cool. Cut cake into 1-inch cubes. Layer cake, Kahlúa, pudding, whipped topping and candy 1/2 at a time in punch bowl. Chill until serving time. Prepare 1 day in advance to enhance flavor.

Approx Per Serving: Cal 232; Prot 3 g; Carbo 27 g; T Fat 13 g; 47% Calories from Fat; Chol 27 mg; Fiber 1 g; Sod 249 mg

Jane A. Brewer, Lakes Region HFH, Center Sandwich, NH

At our monthly Habitat board meeting, a decision was made to stop construction on the home we were building because of the lack of funds. Prayers were said and the next day checks arrived in the mail that allowed us to continue construction. This brings goose bumps when I think about the part God plays in our work!

**JANE A. BREWER
LAKES REGION HFH**

Strawberry Delight

Yield: 15 servings

1 cup flour
¹/₄ cup packed brown sugar
¹/₂ cup margarine or butter, softened
³/₄ cup chopped pecans
3 cups marshmallows
¹/₂ cup milk

1 (6-ounce) package strawberry gelatin
2 cups boiling water
1 (10-ounce) package frozen strawberries
8 ounces whipped topping

Combine flour and brown sugar in bowl; mix well. Cut in margarine until crumbly. Stir in pecans. Pat into bottom of 9x13-inch baking pan. Bake at 350 degrees for 15 minutes. Let stand until cool. Combine marshmallows and milk in double boiler. Cook over hot water until smooth, stirring frequently. Let stand until cool. Spread over baked layer. Dissolve gelatin in boiling water in bowl; mix well. Add strawberries, stirring until thawed. Let stand until cool. Pour over prepared layers. Chill for several hours or until set. Spread with whipped topping. Chill until serving time.

Approx Per Serving: Cal 268; Prot 3 g; Carbo 34 g; T Fat 14 g; 47% Calories from Fat; Chol 1 mg; Fiber 1 g; Sod 114 mg

Connie M. Garrison, Barbour County HFH, Eufaula, AL

Old-Fashioned Sugar Cookies

Yield: 144 servings

1 cup margarine, softened
1 cup canola oil
1 cup confectioners' sugar
1 cup sugar
2 eggs

4¹/₂ cups unbleached flour
1 teaspoon baking soda
1 teaspoon cream of tartar
1¹/₄ cups sugar

Beat margarine, canola oil, confectioners' sugar and 1 cup sugar in mixer bowl until blended. Add eggs, flour, baking soda and cream of tartar; mix well. Chill, covered, until firm. Shape dough into balls. Arrange on cookie sheet. Flatten with fork; sprinkle with 1¹/₄ cups sugar. Bake at 350 degrees for 12 minutes or until light brown. Remove to wire rack to cool.

Approx Per Serving: Cal 54; Prot <1 g; Carbo 7 g; T Fat 3 g; 48% Calories from Fat; Chol 3 mg; Fiber 0 g; Sod 22 mg

Sarah Hardy, Louisville KY HFH, Pewee Valley, KY

Santa Ynez Valley Toffee Bars

Yield: 50 servings

1 cup butter, softened
1 cup sugar
2 cups flour
1 egg yolk

1 teaspoon vanilla extract
1 egg white, lightly beaten
1/2 cup finely chopped pecans

Cream butter and sugar in mixer bowl until light and fluffy. Add flour, egg yolk and vanilla, beating until blended. Press evenly in greased 10x15-inch baking pan. Brush with egg white; sprinkle with pecans. Bake at 275 degrees for 1 hour and 10 minutes or until golden brown. Cut into bars immediately. Remove to wire rack to cool. Store in airtight container for up to 3 days. May freeze for future use.

Approx Per Serving: Cal 76; Prot 1 g; Carbo 8 g; T Fat 5 g; 54% Calories from Fat; Chol 14 mg; Fiber <1 g; Sod 39 mg

Aileen Houghton, Coachella Valley HFH, Thousand Palms, CA

Zucchini Bread

Yield: 24 servings

1 1/2 cups sugar
3 eggs
1 tablespoon vanilla extract
3/4 cup vegetable oil
2 cups grated zucchini

3 cups flour
1 teaspoon baking soda
1 teaspoon salt
1 1/2 teaspoons cinnamon
3/4 cup raisins

Beat sugar, eggs, vanilla and oil in mixer bowl until light and fluffy. Add zucchini; mix well. Stir in mixture of flour, baking soda, salt and cinnamon just until moistened. Fold in raisins. Spoon into 2 loaf pans. Bake at 325 degrees for 1 hour. Cool in pans for 15 minutes. Remove to wire rack to cool completely.

Approx Per Serving: Cal 195; Prot 3 g; Carbo 29 g; T Fat 8 g; 35% Calories from Fat; Chol 27 mg; Fiber 1 g; Sod 133 mg

Muriel C. Berry, Lakes Region HFH, Laconia, NH

Best-Ever Zucchini Bread

Yield: 24 servings

3 eggs
2 cups sugar
1 cup vegetable oil
1 tablespoon vanilla extract
1 teaspoon salt
2 cups grated peeled zucchini

2 cups flour
1 teaspoon baking soda
1/4 teaspoon baking powder
1 tablespoon cinnamon
1 cup chopped walnuts

Cream eggs, sugar, oil, vanilla and salt in mixer bowl until light and fluffy. Add zucchini; mix well. Add flour 1 cup at a time, mixing after each addition. Stir in baking soda, baking powder, cinnamon and walnuts. Spoon into greased and floured bundt pan, tube pan or 2 loaf pans. Bake at 325 degrees for 1 hour.

Approx Per Serving: Cal 230; Prot 3 g; Carbo 27 g; T Fat 13 g; 50% Calories from Fat; Chol 27 mg; Fiber 1 g; Sod 136 mg

Autrice Thomas, HFH of Harrison County Inc., Clarksburg, WV

Zucchini Brownies

Yield: 36 servings

2 1/2 cups flour
2 teaspoons baking powder
1 teaspoon baking soda
2 cups packed brown sugar
2 eggs, beaten
2 cups grated zucchini

1 teaspoon vanilla extract
1 cup melted butter or
 margarine
1 cup chocolate chips
3/4 cup chopped pecans

Combine flour, baking powder, baking soda and brown sugar in bowl; mix well. Stir in eggs, zucchini, vanilla and butter. Spread in greased 9x13-inch baking pan. Sprinkle with chocolate chips and pecans. Bake at 350 degrees for 30 minutes. Let stand until cool. Cut into squares.

Approx Per Serving: Cal 160; Prot 2 g; Carbo 20 g; T Fat 9 g; 46% Calories from Fat; Chol 26 mg; Fiber 1 g; Sod 102 mg

Donna Holter, Mercer County HFH, West Middlesex, PA

After the work of building a house comes the joy of seeing a family in need moving in. The dedication ceremony is so impressive. It makes everyone cry tears of joy.

BETTY HEER
HFH OF GREEN COUNTY WI

Zucchini Cookies

Yield: 60 servings

1/2 cup margarine, softened
1/2 cup sugar
1 cup packed brown sugar
2 eggs
2 teaspoons vanilla extract
2 cups grated zucchini
3 cups flour
1 teaspoon baking powder
1 1/2 teaspoons baking soda
1 1/2 teaspoons salt
1 teaspoon cinnamon
1 teaspoon ground cloves
1/2 teaspoon nutmeg
3/4 cup raisins
3/4 cup chocolate chips
1/2 cup chopped pecans

Cream margarine, sugar, brown sugar, eggs and vanilla in mixer bowl until smooth. Stir in zucchini. Add mixture of flour, baking powder, baking soda, salt, cinnamon, cloves and nutmeg; mix well. Stir in raisins, chocolate chips and pecans. Drop by teaspoonfuls onto cookie sheet. Bake at 375 degrees for 10 to 12 minutes or until light brown. Remove to wire rack to cool.

Approx Per Serving: Cal 81; Prot 1 g; Carbo 13 g; T Fat 3 g; 33% Calories from Fat; Chol 7 mg; Fiber 1 g; Sod 101 mg

Muriel C. Berry, Lakes Region HFH, Laconia, NH

My fondest memory is of helping to finish the roof on our first Habitat house in 1983. It was the day after Thanksgiving during a snowstorm. I brushed the snow off the tar paper and shingles. Another volunteer put the shingles on quickly. We got the job done.

MURIEL C. BERRY
LAKES REGION HFH

Play Dough

Great recipe for making nontoxic modeling clay.

1/2 cup salt
2 cups flour
1 tablespoon alum powder
1 1/2 cups boiling water
Food coloring of choice
1 tablespoon salad oil

Combine salt, flour and alum in bowl; mix well. Stir in mixture of boiling water, food coloring and oil. Knead until smooth. May store, tightly covered, in refrigerator for several weeks.

Betty Heer, HFH of Green County WI, Monroe, WI

Photograph at right by Julie A. Lopez

$\mathcal{L}$IGHT
$\mathcal{L}$DELIGHTS

"LORD, I have loved the habitation of Your house, and the place where Your glory dwells."

-Psalm 26:8

All-Season Sweet Bread
Yield: 24 servings

3 cups flour
2 teaspoons baking soda
1 teaspoon salt
1/2 teaspoon baking powder
1 1/2 teaspoons cinnamon
3/4 cup chopped walnuts
3 or 4 egg whites

2 cups sugar
1 large banana, mashed
2 teaspoons vanilla extract
1 (8-ounce) can crushed
   pineapple, drained
2 cups shredded or finely
   chopped apples

Mix flour, baking soda, salt, baking powder, cinnamon and walnuts together in bowl; set aside. Beat egg whites lightly in large mixer bowl. Add sugar, bananas and vanilla; beat until creamy. Stir in pineapple and apples; mix well. Add flour mixture, stirring just until moistened. Spoon into 2 greased and floured loaf pans. Bake at 350 to 375 degrees for 1 hour or until loaf tests done. Cool in pan for 10 minutes; remove to wire rack to cool completely. May substitute pumpkin, zucchini, pears, peaches or carrots for apples.

Approx Per Serving: Cal 165; Prot 3 g; Carbo 34 g; T Fat 3 g; 14% Calories from Fat; Chol 0 mg; Fiber 1 g; Sod 174 mg

Billie Kay Gross, Albany County HFH, Laramie, WY

Ambrosia
Yield: 4 servings

2 grapefruit
4 oranges

1/2 cup flaked coconut

Section grapefruit and oranges into serving bowl. Stir in coconut; toss gently. Chill until serving time.

Approx Per Serving: Cal 143; Prot 2 g; Carbo 29 g; T Fat 3 g; 19% Calories from Fat; Chol 0 mg; Fiber 6 g; Sod 2 mg

Gray Dinwiddie, Augusta/CSRA HFH, Augusta, GA

Mother's Ambrosia
Yield: 12 servings

Sections of 10 large seedless
   oranges, drained
1 (20-ounce) can crushed
   pineapple, drained

1 (14-ounce) package frozen
   grated coconut, thawed or 4
   cups freshly shredded
   coconut

Combine oranges, pineapple and coconut in bowl; mix well. Chill for up to 24 hours. Serve from clear glass or crystal bowl or in individual dessert dishes with slice of pound cake.

Approx Per Serving: Cal 230; Prot 3 g; Carbo 33 g; T Fat 11 g; 41% Calories from Fat; Chol 0 mg; Fiber 9 g; Sod 7 mg

Linda Fuller, Co-Founder HFHI, Americus, GA

No-Added-Sugar Apple Pie

Yield: 6 servings

1 (6-ounce) can frozen apple
   juice concentrate
1/2 juice can water
2 tablespoons cornstarch

1/2 teaspoon apple pie spices
4 large or 5 medium apples,
   peeled, sliced
1 recipe (2-crust) pie pastry

Combine apple juice concentrate, water, cornstarch and apple pie spices in saucepan; mix well. Cook until thickened, stirring constantly. Stir apples into apple juice mixture gently. Pour into pastry-lined pie plate. Top with remaining pastry, sealing edge and cutting vents. Bake at 350 degrees for 45 minutes. May add 1 envelope artificial sweetener to ingredients for sweeter taste.

Approx Per Serving: Cal 399; Prot 4 g; Carbo 55 g; T Fat 19 g; 42% Calories from Fat; Chol 0 mg; Fiber 3 g; Sod 296 mg

Marlene Woodfield, Michigan City HFH, La Porte, IN

Apple Turnovers

Yield: 12 servings

2 Granny Smith apples, peeled,
   chopped
1 teaspoon lemon juice
3 tablespoons sugar
1 tablespoon flour

1/2 teaspoon ground cinnamon
1/4 teaspoon ground nutmeg
8 sheets phyllo dough, thawed
2 tablespoons cinnamon
2 tablespoons sugar

Combine apples, lemon juice, 3 tablespoons sugar, flour, cinnamon and nutmeg in bowl; mix well. Place 2 phyllo sheets on work surface. Cover remaining phyllo dough with plastic wrap to prevent drying out. Spray butter-flavored nonstick cooking spray between sheets. Cut into three 4-inch wide strips. Spoon 1 heaping tablespoon of apple mixture 1 inch from corner. Fold to form triangle. Place turnovers seam side down on baking sheet lightly sprayed with butter-flavor nonstick cooking spray. Spray tops of turnovers with butter-flavor nonstick cooking spray. Sprinkle with mixture of cinnamon and 2 tablespoons sugar. Bake at 400 degrees for 15 to 17 minutes or until golden brown.

Approx Per Serving: Cal 80; Prot 1 g; Carbo 17 g; T Fat 1 g; 11% Calories from Fat; Chol 0 mg; Fiber 1 g; Sod 69 mg

Samantha Adams, HFHI, Americus, GA

Before I became a volunteer, I was visiting my parents who were in the International Partner training course at the time. One day, while my mother and I were walking, we met Millard Fuller, and he stopped and talked to us for about 15 minutes. After he left, I asked Mom who he was (I was not familiar with Habitat at the time). She told me that he was the head of Habitat. I thought to myself that any organization with a president that personable and unassuming must be doing a tremendous amount of good for the world. I then decided to become a volunteer.

**SAMANTHA ADAMS
HFHI**

Banana Muffins

Yield: 12 servings

3 cups flour
1 cup sugar
4 teaspoons baking powder
1/2 teaspoon salt
1 cup skim milk
Egg substitute equal to 2 eggs

2 tablespoons canola oil
3 tablespoons plain nonfat
  yogurt
3 bananas, mashed
1/2 to 1 cup chopped pecans

Mix flour, sugar, baking powder and salt in large bowl. Combine milk, egg substitute, canola oil, yogurt and bananas in mixer bowl. Add to dry ingredients; mix well. Stir in pecans. Fill muffin cups sprayed with nonstick cooking spray 2/3 full. Bake at 400 degrees for 20 to 25 minutes or until muffins test done. May substitute canned pumpkin with pumpkin spices, applesauce, grated apples, grated oranges with rind, or blueberries for bananas.

Approx Per Serving: Cal 309; Prot 6 g; Carbo 51 g; T Fat 10 g; 28% Calories from Fat; Chol 1 mg; Fiber 2 g; Sod 230 mg

Rosemary Delaney, Jubilee HFH, Jacksonville, IL

A key to Habitat's success has been its ability to adapt and change to the culture instead of the culture changing and adapting to Habitat. Habitat cannot be paternalistic in its approach.

Banana Snack Cake

Yield: 9 servings

1 1/4 cups mashed bananas
3/4 cup egg substitute
1/2 cup buttermilk or plain
  nonfat yogurt
1/2 cup packed brown sugar
1/3 cup applesauce

1 teaspoon vanilla extract
2 cups whole wheat flour
2 teaspoons baking powder
1 teaspoon baking soda
2 tablespoons brown sugar
1/4 teaspoon ground cinnamon

Combine bananas, egg substitute, buttermilk, 1/2 cup brown sugar, applesauce and vanilla together in mixer bowl. Mix whole wheat flour, baking powder and baking soda in bowl. Add to banana mixture; mix until smooth. Pour into lightly greased 9x9-inch baking pan. Sprinkle with mixture of 2 tablespoons brown sugar and cinnamon. Bake at 375 degrees for 20 to 25 minutes or until cake tests done. Remove to wire rack to cool. Cut into 3-inch squares.

Approx Per Serving: Cal 195; Prot 7 g; Carbo 41 g; T Fat 1 g; 6% Calories from Fat; Chol 1 mg; Fiber 4 g; Sod 222 mg

Samantha Adams, HFHI, Americus, GA

Banana Raisin Date Bread

Yield: 36 servings

1 cup rolled oats
3 eggs, beaten
1 cup raisins
1 cup chopped dates
1/2 cup milk
3/4 cup butter, melted
1/4 cup molasses
2 teaspoons lemon juice
3/4 cup honey
1 cup whole wheat flour
1 cup cake flour
3/4 teaspoon salt
2 teaspoons baking soda
2 teaspoons cinnamon
4 ripe bananas, mashed
1/2 cup chopped walnuts

Mix oats and eggs in bowl; set aside. Combine raisins and dates with milk in bowl; set aside. Combine butter, molasses, lemon juice and honey in bowl; mix well. Add oats mixture and raisin mixture, mixing well after each addition. Combine whole wheat flour, cake flour, salt, baking soda and cinnamon in bowl; mix well. Stir into oats mixture. Add bananas and walnuts; mix well. Spoon into 3 greased miniature loaf pans. Bake at 350 degrees for 1 hour or until bread tests done.

Approx Per Serving: Cal 150; Prot 2 g; Carbo 24 g; T Fat 6 g; 34% Calories from Fat; Chol 29 mg; Fiber 2 g; Sod 148 mg

Dave Carpenter, Morris HFH, Kinnelon, NJ

Berry Torte

Yield: 8 servings

1 cup low-fat sour cream
1 egg, lightly beaten
2 tablespoons sugar
1 tablespoon plus 1 teaspoon
   lemon juice
1/4 teaspoon vanilla extract
1 (9-inch) graham cracker pie
   shell
1 cup sliced strawberries
1 cup blueberries or raspberries
2 or 3 kiwifruit, sliced
1/3 cup raspberry jam
Lemon juice or water to taste

Whisk sour cream, egg, sugar, lemon juice and vanilla together in bowl. Pour into pie shell. Bake at 325 degrees for 15 to 20 minutes or until set. Chill, covered, for 20 to 30 minutes. Arrange strawberries around outer edge. Place blueberries in center. Arrange kiwifruit in between. Combine raspberry jam and lemon juice in saucepan; mix well. Cook until of honey consistency, stirring constantly. Brush over fruit. Chill, covered, until serving time. May substitute fat-free sour cream for low-fat sour cream.

Approx Per Serving: Cal 329; Prot 4 g; Carbo 48 g; T Fat 15 g; 39% Calories from Fat; Chol 38 mg; Fiber 3 g; Sod 260 mg

Paula Schmidt Weber, Las Vegas NM HFH, Las Vegas, NM

Good Old Brown Betty

Yield: 8 servings

8 Granny Smith apples, sliced
1/2 cup raisins
3 tablespoons flour
1 teaspoon cinnamon
1/2 teaspoon nutmeg
1/4 cup packed brown sugar
3/4 cup apple juice
1/2 cup honey
3/4 cup quick-cooking oats
1/2 cup flour
1/2 cup wheat germ
1/2 cup chopped walnuts
5 tablespoons butter or
    margarine
1/4 cup honey

Combine apples, raisins, flour, cinnamon, nutmeg, brown sugar and apple juice in large bowl; mix gently. Stir in 1/2 cup honey. Spread evenly in greased 7x11-inch baking pan. Combine oats, flour, wheat germ, walnuts and butter in bowl. Add 1/4 cup honey; mix well. Spread over apples. Bake at 350 degrees for 45 to 50 minutes or until brown. May substitute orange juice for apple juice.

Approx Per Serving: Cal 435; Prot 6 g; Carbo 79 g; T Fat 14 g; 26% Calories from Fat; Chol 19 mg; Fiber 5 g; Sod 81 mg

Dale Rasmussen, Southeast New Hampshire HFH, Dover, NH

Low-Fat Brownies

Yield: 42 servings

1/2 cup diet margarine
1 1/2 cups sugar
1 cup frozen egg substitute,
    thawed
1 teaspoon vanilla extract
1 1/4 cups flour
1 teaspoon baking powder
3/4 cup baking cocoa

Beat diet margarine, sugar, egg substitute and vanilla in bowl until well blended. Add flour, baking powder and baking cocoa; mix well. Spread evenly in foil-lined 9x13-inch baking pan sprayed with nonstick cooking spray. Bake at 350 degrees for 18 to 20 minutes or until edges pull from sides of pan. Let stand until cool. Cut into squares.

Approx Per Serving: Cal 66; Prot 1 g; Carbo 11 g; T Fat 2 g; 29% Calories from Fat; Chol <1 mg; Fiber 1 g; Sod 33 mg

Donna Rossman, Northwest Indiana-Hammond HFH, Griffith, IN

Chocolate Cocoa Cake

Yield: 12 servings

1¹/4 cups cake flour
¹/2 cup baking cocoa
1 teaspoon baking powder
¹/2 teaspoon baking soda
¹/2 teaspoon Lite salt
1¹/4 cups sugar
²/3 cup water
1¹/2 egg whites

1 (4-ounce) jar baby food prunes
1 cup baking cocoa
1³/4 cups sugar
¹/2 cup hot water
¹/2 cup reconstituted powdered milk
1 teaspoon vanilla extract

Combine cake flour, ¹/2 cup baking cocoa, baking powder, baking soda and Lite salt in bowl; mix well. Whisk 1¹/4 cups sugar and ²/3 cup water in large bowl. Add egg whites and prunes; whisk until blended. Add flour mixture gradually, stirring until smooth. Pour into lightly greased 9x9-inch baking pan. Bake at 350 degrees for 30 to 35 minutes or until cake tests done. Remove to wire rack to cool. Blend 1 cup baking cocoa and 1³/4 cups sugar in saucepan. Stir in ¹/2 cup hot water; mix until smooth. Add milk. Bring to a boil. Cook for 2 minutes, stirring occasionally. Remove from heat. Let stand until cool. Stir in vanilla. Drizzle over cake.

Approx Per Serving: Cal 271; Prot 4 g; Carbo 65 g; T Fat 3 g; 9% Calories from Fat; Chol <1 mg; Fiber 3 g; Sod 160 mg

Jim Solomon, Clark County Community HFH, Springfield, OH

Chocolate Tofu Cheesecake

Yield: 12 servings

2¹/2 cups water
¹/4 cup baking cocoa
1 cup couscous
1¹/2 cups honey
1 tablespoon vanilla extract

³/4 cup pecans, toasted, ground
2 (10-ounce) packages firm tofu
2 cups semisweet chocolate chips, melted

Mix water, baking cocoa and couscous in saucepan. Add honey in fine stream; mix well. Bring to a simmer. Cook for 5 to 10 minutes or until thickened, stirring constantly. Stir in vanilla. Pour into 9-inch round baking dish or springform pan. Sprinkle ¹/2 cup of pecans over top. Process tofu in blender until smooth. Add chocolate chips; mix well. Pour over prepared layer. Sprinkle with remaining pecans. Chill, covered, for 2 hours.

Approx Per Serving: Cal 405; Prot 8 g; Carbo 67 g; T Fat 16 g; 33% Calories from Fat; Chol 0 mg; Fiber 4 g; Sod 10 mg

Lori Giese, Green County HFH, Monroe, WI

Hearing the words of gratitude expressed by one of our partner families for a group get-well card we sent him was truly uplifting and made all of our work all the more meaningful.

LORI GIESE
GREEN COUNTY HFH

No-Flour Chocolate Cake   *Yield: 10 servings*

3/4 cup water
6 whole dried apricots
2 egg whites
1 cup sugar
1/2 cup baking cocoa

1 cup Grape-Nuts cereal
6 egg whites
2 tablespoons confectioners'
   sugar

Simmer water and apricots in saucepan for 20 minutes. Process in blender until puréed. Whisk 2 egg whites into apricot mixture in bowl. Whisk in all but 2 tablespoons of sugar. Add baking cocoa and cereal, mixing well after each addition. Beat 6 egg whites in mixer bowl until soft peaks form. Add remaining sugar gradually, beating constantly until stiff peaks form. Stir 1/3 of the meringue into cocoa mixture. Fold in remaining meringue just until blended. Spoon into 8-inch springform pan lightly sprayed with nonstick cooking spray. Bake at 350 degrees for 25 to 35 minutes or until cake begins to pull from side of pan. Cool in pan on wire rack. Dust with confectioners' sugar. Cut into wedges.

Approx Per Serving: Cal 155; Prot 5 g; Carbo 36 g; T Fat 1 g; 3% Calories from Fat; Chol 0 mg; Fiber 3 g; Sod 121 mg

Samantha Adams, HFHI, Americus, GA

Low-Fat Cinnamon and Oatmeal Muffins   *Yield: 12 servings*

1 cup rolled oats
1 cup buttermilk
1 cup flour
1 1/2 teaspoons baking powder

1/2 teaspoon baking soda
1 teaspoon cinnamon
1/3 cup packed brown sugar
2 egg whites, lightly beaten

Combine oats and buttermilk in bowl; mix well. Let stand for 5 minutes. Sift flour, baking powder, baking soda and cinnamon into bowl; mix well. Make well in center of dry ingredients. Stir brown sugar and egg white into oat mixture. Spoon into well, stirring just until moistened. Fill nonstick muffin cups 2/3 full. Bake at 400 degrees for 18 minutes.

Approx Per Serving: Cal 94; Prot 3 g; Carbo 19 g; T Fat 1 g; 7% Calories from Fat; Chol 1 mg; Fiber 1 g; Sod 108 mg

Rhonda Koser, Partner Family HFH, Mercer, PA

'The theology of the hammer' proclaims that, with God, all things are possible, and that certainly includes a world without shacks and homeless people.

MILLARD FULLER
PRESIDENT AND
CO-FOUNDER OF HFHI

Crazy Cake

Yield: 16 servings

1¹/₂ cups sifted flour
1 cup sugar
3 tablespoons baking cocoa
¹/₄ teaspoon salt
1 tablespoon baking soda

1 cup water
1 teaspoon vanilla extract
1 tablespoon vinegar
¹/₃ cup salad oil

Sift flour, sugar, baking cocoa, salt and baking soda into bowl. Add water, vanilla, vinegar and oil, mixing well. Pour into greased 8x8-inch baking pan. Bake at 350 degrees for 30 minutes or until cake tests done. Frost with favorite frosting or serve with whipped cream. May double recipe for layer cake or 9x13-inch cake.

Approx Per Serving: Cal 130; Prot 1 g; Carbo 21 g; T Fat 5 g; 32% Calories from Fat; Chol 0 mg; Fiber 1 g; Sod 34 mg

Della Lindsay, Oregon Trail HFH, Hermiston, OR

Fruit Delight

Yield: 4 servings

Sections of 2 oranges
2 bananas, sliced
1¹/₂ cups juice-pack crushed
**   pineapple**

¹/₃ cup chopped pecans

Cut oranges into bite-size pieces. Combine oranges, bananas, pineapple and pecans in bowl; mix well. Let stand at room temperature. Serve with vanilla wafers.

Approx Per Serving: Cal 217; Prot 3 g; Carbo 41 g; T Fat 7 g; 27% Calories from Fat; Chol 0 mg; Fiber 5 g; Sod 2 mg

Wade R. Collier, HFH of Sarasota, Sarasota, FL

Photo by Julie A. Lopez

JANE FONDA

Fruit Parfait

Yield: 1 serving

Serve after a heavy meal, as an appetizer or as an accompaniment with sweet rolls or toast at breakfast.

1/4 **cup chopped apple**	2 **tablespoons plain nonfat**
1/4 **cup sliced banana**	**yogurt**
1/4 **cup grape halves**	1/4 **teaspoon ginger, optional**
2 **tablespoons orange juice**	1 **sprig of fresh mint**

Combine apple, banana and grapes in bowl; mix gently. Pour mixture of orange juice, yogurt and ginger over fruit. Top with fresh mint sprig, if available.

Approx Per Serving: Cal 140; Prot 3 g; Carbo 33 g; T Fat 1 g; 5% Calories from Fat; Chol 1 mg; Fiber 3 g; Sod 26 mg

Linda Fuller, Co-Founder HFHI, Americus, GA

Mixed Fruit Dessert

Yield: 8 servings

1 **(4-ounce) package vanilla**	1 **(11-ounce) can mandarin**
instant pudding mix	**oranges, drained**
1 **(8-ounce) can juice-pack**	1 **cup miniature marshmallows**
crushed pineapple	1 **cup whipped topping**
1 **(16-ounce) can fruit cocktail,**	
drained	

Combine pudding mix and undrained pineapple in 2-quart bowl; mix well. Stir in fruit cocktail and mandarin oranges. Fold in marshmallows and whipped topping. Chill, covered, for 4 hours.

Approx Per Serving: Cal 166; Prot 1 g; Carbo 38 g; T Fat 3 g; 13% Calories from Fat; Chol 0 mg; Fiber 1 g; Sod 189 mg

Verna Rhodes, Show-Me Central HFH, Columbia, MO

Grapes Juanita

Yield: 6 servings

2 pounds seedless green grapes
1 cup sour cream
1/2 cup packed light brown
    sugar

2 tablespoons grated orange
    rind

Combine grapes and sour cream in bowl; mix gently. Sprinkle with brown sugar. Chill, covered, for 2 hours. Sprinkle orange rind over top before serving.

Approx Per Serving: Cal 247; Prot 2 g; Carbo 44 g; T Fat 9 g; 30% Calories from Fat; Chol 17 mg; Fiber 2 g; Sod 29 mg

Margaret Cook, Bergen County HFH, Westwood, NJ

Heavenly Light Dessert

Yield: 12 servings

1 package angel food cake mix
1/3 cup slivered almonds
2 small packages sugar-free
    vanilla instant pudding and
    pie filling mix

2 teaspoons almond extract
2 pounds fresh peaches, sliced

Prepare and bake cake using package directions. Toast almonds on ungreased baking sheet at 350 degrees for 10 minutes or until brown, stirring occasionally. Prepare pudding mix according to package directions using skim milk. Stir in almond extract. Let stand for 5 minutes or just until set. Cut cake into 12 slices. Place each slice on dessert plate. Top each slice with pudding mixture, peaches and almonds. May substitute 2 (12-ounce) packages frozen peaches, thawed, drained or 3 (16-ounce) cans sliced peaches, drained for fresh peaches.

Approx Per Serving: Cal 227; Prot 7 g; Carbo 46 g; T Fat 2 g; 9% Calories from Fat; Chol 1 mg; Fiber 2 g; Sod 401 mg

Tommie Lou Hunter, Page HFH, Luray, VA

No organization in America has done more to promote the cause of decent shelter for all people than Habitat for Humanity. But this vital organization is not only an energetic voice for housing as a human right; it is building more than 20 houses every day in more than 40 nations. Under Millard Fuller's leadership, Habitat for Humanity has provided a vibrant testament to the power of love in action to those in need around the world.

CORETTA SCOTT KING
FOUNDING PRESIDENT OF
THE MARTIN LUTHER KING, JR.
CENTER FOR NONVIOLENT
SOCIAL CHANGE

Lemon Snow

Yield: 8 servings

Lemon Snow is a light dessert after a heavy meal. The lemon sauce is good served over angel food cake.

2 envelopes unflavored gelatin	1 tablespoon cornstarch
1/2 cup cold water	1/2 cup sugar
1/2 cup boiling water	1/4 teaspoon salt
1 cup sugar	1 cup water
2 cups ice water	1 teaspoon grated lemon rind
3/4 cup lemon juice	3 tablespoons lemon juice
1 tablespoon grated lemon rind	1 tablespoon butter or
4 egg whites, stiffly beaten	margarine

Soften gelatin in 1/2 cup cold water in double boiler. Stir in 1/2 cup boiling water. Cook over low heat until gelatin is dissolved, stirring constantly. Add 1 cup sugar. Cook until dissolved, stirring constantly. Remove from heat. Add ice water, 3/4 cup lemon juice and 1 tablespoon lemon rind; mix well. Let stand until partially set. Beat until frothy; fold in egg whites. Chill for 2 to 4 hours. Combine cornstarch, sugar, salt and 1 cup water in saucepan. Add 1 teaspoon lemon rind, 3 tablespoons lemon juice and butter; mix well. Bring to a boil, stirring constantly until smooth. Let stand until cool. Spoon Lemon Snow into dessert bowls; drizzle with lemon sauce.

Approx Per Serving: Cal 183; Prot 3 g; Carbo 41 g; T Fat 1 g; 7% Calories from Fat; Chol 4 mg; Fiber <1 g; Sod 113 mg

Carrol Gensert, Greater Cleveland HFH, Cleveland Heights, OH

Lentil Oatmeal Cookies

Yield: 72 servings

2/3 cup lentils	33/4 cups flour
11/2 cups boiling water	1 teaspoon salt
2 cups packed brown sugar	2 teaspoons baking soda
11/2 cups margarine, softened	5 cups quick-cooking oats
2 eggs	2 cups chocolate chips
2 teaspoons vanilla extract	2 cups finely chopped walnuts

Rinse lentils. Mix with boiling water in saucepan. Simmer, covered, for 35 minutes or until tender. Purée in blender. Cream brown sugar and margarine in mixer bowl at medium speed. Add eggs. Beat at low speed just until blended. Add vanilla and lentil purée; mix well. Combine flour, salt and baking soda in bowl; mix well. Add flour mixture 1/3 at a time, mixing a low speed just until blended. Stir in oats, chocolate chips and walnuts. Drop by teaspoonfuls onto greased cookie sheet. Bake at 375 degrees for 12 to 15 minutes or until light brown. May substitute butterscotch chips or peanut butter chips for chocolate chips.

Approx Per Serving: Cal 150; Prot 3 g; Carbo 18 g; T Fat 8 g; 45% Calories from Fat; Chol 6 mg; Fiber 1 g; Sod 102 mg

Pamela Peterson, Palouse HFH, Moscow, ID

Individual Lime Cheesecakes

Yield: 12 servings

12 vanilla wafers
6 ounces low-fat cottage cheese
8 ounces Neufchâtel cheese, softened
¹/₄ cup plus 2 tablespoons sugar
2 eggs
1 tablespoon grated lime rind

1 tablespoon lime juice
1 teaspoon vanilla extract
¹/₄ cup vanilla low-fat yogurt
2 medium kiwifruit, peeled, sliced, cut into halves, drained

Place 1 vanilla wafer into each of 12 paper-lined muffin cups. Process cottage cheese in food processor until smooth. Combine with Neufchâtel cheese in mixer bowl. Beat at medium speed until creamy. Add sugar gradually; mix well. Add eggs, lime rind, lime juice and vanilla; mix well. Spoon evenly over vanilla wafers. Bake at 350 degrees for 20 minutes or until almost set. Cool in muffin cups on wire racks. Remove from pans. Chill in refrigerator. Spread yogurt evenly over cheesecakes; top with kiwifruit.

Approx Per Serving: Cal 129; Prot 5 g; Carbo 13 g; T Fat 6 g; 43% Calories from Fat; Chol 54 mg; Fiber <1 g; Sod 160 mg

Judi Dilworth, Norristown HFH, Roslyn, PA

Meringue Puffs

Yield: 50 servings

4 egg whites
1 cup sugar

Red food coloring
1 teaspoon vanilla extract

Beat egg whites in mixer bowl until stiff peaks form. Add sugar gradually, beating after each addition until smooth. Add food coloring and vanilla; beat until blended. Spoon into decorator tube fitted with star tip. Pipe 1¹/₂-inch rosettes onto 2 foil-lined baking sheets. Bake at 200 degrees for 1¹/₂ to 2 hours or until firm. May substitute peppermint extract for vanilla extract.

Approx Per Serving: Cal 17; Prot <1 g; Carbo 4 g; T Fat 0 g; 0% Calories from Fat; Chol 0 mg; Fiber 0 g; Sod 4 mg

Pat Harper, Mon County HFH, Morgantown, WV

Creamy Orange Dessert

Yield: 12 servings

1 (6-ounce) package orange
    gelatin
3 cups boiling water
8 ounces cream cheese,
    softened
1/2 cup frozen orange juice
    concentrate, thawed

2 tablespoons frozen lemonade
    concentrate, thawed
1 (11-ounce) can mandarin
    oranges, drained
1 (16-ounce) can crushed
    pineapple, drained

Combine orange gelatin and boiling water in mixer bowl, stirring until dissolved. Add cream cheese, orange juice concentrate and lemonade concentrate; beat until smooth. Spoon into 9x9-inch dish. Chill for 1 hour. Stir in mandarin oranges and crushed pineapple. Chill for 4 hours or until set.

Approx Per Serving: Cal 180; Prot 3 g; Carbo 29 g; T Fat 7 g; 32% Calories from Fat; Chol 21 mg; Fiber <1 g; Sod 94 mg

Allison Timm, Bay Area/Houston HFH, Webster, TX

Orange Juice Ice Cream

Yield: 16 servings

1 (14-ounce) can evaporated
    skim milk
1 (6-ounce) can frozen orange
    juice concentrate, thawed

1/2 teaspoon vanilla extract
6 envelopes artificial sweetener

Chill evaporated milk, mixer bowl and electric mixer beaters for 24 hours. Beat evaporated milk in chilled mixer bowl until soft peaks form. Fold in orange juice concentrate, vanilla and artificial sweetener. Beat until blended. Freeze for 2 to 4 hours.

Approx Per Serving: Cal 38; Prot 2 g; Carbo 7 g; T Fat <1 g; 2% Calories from Fat; Chol <1 mg; Fiber <1 g; Sod 30 mg

Mrs. Jackie Turk, HFH of Sumter County FL, Wildwood, FL

Photo by Julie A. Lopez

Frozen Fresh Peaches in Orange Juice

Yield: 10 servings

Juice of 1 orange
1/2 cup sugar

12 fresh peaches, peeled, cut
into quarters

Combine orange juice and sugar in bowl; mix well. Stir in peaches. Pour in 9x12-inch dish. Let stand at room temperature for 2 hours, stirring occasionally. Freeze, covered, until firm. Thaw partially before serving.

Approx Per Serving: Cal 87; Prot 1 g; Carbo 22 g; T Fat <1 g; 1% Calories from Fat; Chol 0 mg; Fiber 2 g; Sod <1 mg

Lynn Haviland-Samuelson, S.W. Iowa HFH, Shenandoah, IA

Hawaiian Pineapple Dessert

Yield: 12 servings

1 tablespoon unflavored gelatin
2 (3-ounce) packages lime
   gelatin
3 cups boiling water

1 cup drained crushed
   pineapple
1 cup whipped topping

Soften unflavored gelatin in a small amount of cold water in bowl; mix well. Combine softened gelatin, lime gelatin and boiling water in bowl, stirring until dissolved. Let stand until cool. Stir in pineapple. Chill until partially set. Fold in whipped topping. Spoon into 1-quart mold. Chill until set. Unmold onto serving plate. Garnish with assorted fruit.

Approx Per Serving: Cal 87; Prot 2 g; Carbo 17 g; T Fat 2 g; 16% Calories from Fat; Chol 0 mg; Fiber <1 g; Sod 39 mg

Ellen T. Watanabe, Hale Aloha O Hilo HFH, Hilo, HI

I am filled with joy every time I think about the man who sat by the window of his Habitat house and watched happily as the rain ran down on the OUTSIDE of his house.

FRAN COLLIER
HFH OF SARASOTA

Mock Pineapple Cheese Pie

Yield: 6 servings

1 small package lemon
   sugar-free gelatin
1 cup boiling water
2 cups low-fat cottage cheese

2 envelopes artificial sweetener
1 (9-inch) graham cracker pie
   shell

Dissolve gelatin in boiling water in mixer bowl. Add cottage cheese and artificial sweetener; beat until smooth. Spoon into pie shell. Chill for 1 hour or longer.

Approx Per Serving: Cal 342; Prot 14 g; Carbo 39 g; T Fat 15 g; 39% Calories from Fat; Chol 6 mg; Fiber 1 g; Sod 653 mg

Donna Holter, Mercer County HFH, West Middlesex, PA

Pumpkin Pie

Yield: 8 servings

1 (16-ounce) can pumpkin
1 (12-ounce) can evaporated
  skim milk
1 egg
2 egg whites
1/2 cup baking mix

8 envelopes artificial sweetener
2 tablespoons brown sugar
  substitute
2 teaspoons pumpkin pie spice
2 teaspoons vanilla extract

Process pumpkin, evaporated milk, egg, egg whites, baking mix, artificial sweetener, brown sugar substitute, pumpkin pie spice and vanilla in blender until smooth. Pour into pie plate sprayed with nonstick cooking spray. Bake at 350 degrees for 45 to 55 minutes or until center is puffed.

Approx Per Serving: Cal 141; Prot 6 g; Carbo 26 g; T Fat 2 g; 12% Calories from Fat; Chol 28 mg; Fiber <1 g; Sod 285 mg

Sherry Baker, Southern Crescent HFH–Jonesboro, Rex, GA

Rosalynn Carter's Raisin Oatmeal Cookies

Yield: 36 servings

1 cup flour, sifted
1/2 teaspoon baking soda
1/4 teaspoon cinnamon
1 1/2 cups quick-cooking oats
2 egg whites, lightly beaten

1 cup packed brown sugar
1/3 cup vegetable oil
1/2 cup skim milk
1 teaspoon vanilla extract
1 cup seedless raisins

Sift flour, baking soda and cinnamon into bowl. Stir in oats. Combine egg whites, brown sugar, oil, milk, vanilla and raisins in bowl; mix well. Add to flour mixture; mix well. Drop by teaspoonfuls onto greased cookie sheet. Bake at 375 degrees for 12 to 15 minutes or until light brown. Increase baking time for crisp cookies or decrease baking time for chewy cookies.

Approx Per Serving: Cal 78; Prot 1 g; Carbo 14 g; T Fat 2 g; 26% Calories from Fat; Chol <1 mg; Fiber 1 g; Sod 19 mg

Rosalynn Carter,
Former First Lady, Plains, GA

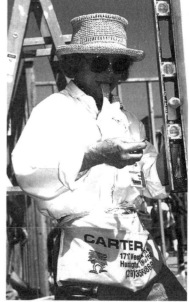

Photo by Robert Baker

Old-Fashioned Rice Pudding

Yield: 10 servings

1/2 cup uncooked rice
1/2 cup sugar
1/2 teaspoon salt

1/2 teaspoon nutmeg
8 cups 1% milk
3/4 cup raisins

Combine rice, sugar, salt, nutmeg and milk in bowl; mix well. Pour into 2 1/2-quart baking dish. Bake at 325 degrees for 1 1/2 hours, stirring 2 times. Add raisins. Bake for 1 hour longer or until brown. Serve warm or chilled. Do not use skim milk; it will affect consistency of pudding. May omit raisins.

Approx Per Serving: Cal 191; Prot 7 g; Carbo 36 g; T Fat 2 g; 10% Calories from Fat; Chol 8 mg; Fiber 1 g; Sod 207 mg

Rose Tillinghast, HFH of South Dutchess, Wappinger Falls, NY

Three-In-One Sherbet

Yield: 6 servings

Juice of 1 lemon
Juice of 1 orange
1 cup water

1 cup sugar
1 banana, mashed

Combine lemon juice, orange juice, water and sugar in bowl; mix well. Stir in banana. Pour into 5x9-inch dish. Freeze, stirring every hour until mixture is of slushy consistency. Freeze until set.

Approx Per Serving: Cal 154; Prot <1 g; Carbo 40 g; T Fat <1 g; 1% Calories from Fat; Chol 0 mg; Fiber <1 g; Sod 1 mg

Carl W. Umland, Houston HFH, Houston, TX

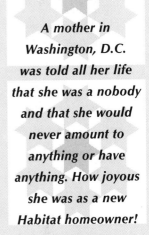

A mother in Washington, D.C. was told all her life that she was a nobody and that she would never amount to anything or have anything. How joyous she was as a new Habitat homeowner!

CARL W. UMLAND
HOUSTON HFH

Sponge Cake

Yield: 18 servings

6 egg whites
1 cup sugar
6 egg yolks, beaten
1 cup cake flour
1 teaspoon baking powder
¹/₄ teaspoon salt

¹/₂ teaspoon vanilla extract
1 large package sugar-free
   lemon instant pudding mix,
   prepared
2 to 3 tablespoons
   confectioners' sugar

Beat egg whites in mixer bowl until soft peaks form. Add sugar gradually, beating until stiff peaks form. Add egg yolks; mix well. Add flour, baking powder, salt and vanilla. Beat at low speed for 2 minutes, scraping bowl occasionally. Pour into greased and waxed paper-lined 9x13-inch baking pan. Bake at 350 degrees for 25 minutes or until cake tests done. Let stand until cool. Invert onto serving platter. Slice cake into halves horizontally. Spread cut side of bottom layer with pudding. Top with remaining layer. Sprinkle with confectioners' sugar.

Approx Per Serving: Cal 124; Prot 4 g; Carbo 19 g; T Fat 4 g; 28% Calories from Fat; Chol 76 mg; Fiber <1 g; Sod 153 mg

Elaine A. Huy, Mon County HFH, Morgantown, WV

Tapioca Pudding

Yield: 4 servings

¹/₂ cup small pearl tapioca
3 cups water
¹/₄ teaspoon salt
1 cup nonfat dry milk powder

¹/₄ cup sugar
2 eggs
2 teaspoons vanilla extract

Combine tapioca, water and salt in saucepan. Let stand for 1 to 8 hours. Stir in milk powder. Heat just to a boil, stirring constantly. Add sugar gradually; mix well. Beat eggs in mixer bowl. Stir 2 cups of hot mixture into eggs gradually; stir eggs into hot mixture. Cook until thickened, stirring constantly. Remove from heat. Cool for 15 minutes. Stir in vanilla. Serve warm or cold. Garnish with maraschino cherries, sliced bananas, plain nonfat yogurt or pecans.

Approx Per Serving: Cal 211; Prot 9 g; Carbo 38 g; T Fat 3 g; 11% Calories from Fat; Chol 109 mg; Fiber <1 g; Sod 258 mg

Fran Collier, HFH of Sarasota, Sarasota, FL

I organized all the volunteers for our first HFH home two years ago. We had reached a standstill with the siding and interior walls. A young man called saying he had some free time and construction experience. He worked for three weeks, then disappeared without a word. He was the answer to our prayers.

ELAINE A. HUY
MON COUNTY HFH

Photograph at right by Julie A. Lopez

NO-BAKE GOODIES

"Then God said, 'Let the earth bring forth grass,
the herb that yields seed, and the fruit tree that
yields fruit according to its kind, whose seed
is in itself, on the earth;' and it was so."

-Genesis 1:11

Angel Cake Dessert

Yield: 12 servings

8 ounces cream cheese,
  softened
1/2 cup sugar
1/2 cup evaporated milk
16 ounces whipped topping

1 angel food cake, torn into
  bite-size pieces
1 (21-ounce) can cherry pie
  filling

Beat cream cheese and sugar in mixer bowl until smooth. Add evaporated milk; mix well. Fold in whipped topping. Fold in angel food cake. Spread in 9x13-inch dish. Spread pie filling evenly over the top. Chill until serving time.

Approx Per Serving: Cal 428; Prot 6 g; Carbo 63 g; T Fat 18 g; 37% Calories from Fat; Chol 24 mg; Fiber 1 g; Sod 499 mg

Linda Blue Stanfield, Pilot Mountain Area HFH, Mt. Airy, NC

Angel Fluff

Yield: 9 servings

1 (16-ounce) can juice-pack
  fruit cocktail
1 angel food cake, torn into
  bite-size pieces

2 packages any flavor sugar-free
  gelatin
2 cups hot water
4 bananas, sliced

Drain fruit cocktail, reserving juice. Combine fruit cocktail with angel food cake in bowl; mix well. Spread evenly in 9x12-inch dish. Dissolve gelatin in hot water in bowl; mix well. Combine reserved juice with enough water to measure 1 1/2 cups. Stir into gelatin mixture. Combine bananas with a small portion of the gelatin mixture in blender container. Process until smooth. Let stand until partially set. Stir into remaining gelatin. Pour over prepared layer; press firmly. Chill until set. Serve with whipped topping.

Approx Per Serving: Cal 260; Prot 6 g; Carbo 59 g; T Fat 1 g; 3% Calories from Fat; Chol 0 mg; Fiber 2 g; Sod 580 mg

Jean Dyer, Ottumwa HFH, Ottumwa, IA

They came from as far away as Germany and as close as the next block over. They ranged from young to old, skilled and unskilled, male and female, organization-affiliated and loners, students, the employed, retirees, twenty different religious affiliations, from every walk of life. For a few hours, we forgot who we were. We found out something new about ourselves through our participation in a Habitat project.

WILLIAM GAVETT
HFH VOLUNTEER

Apricot Pies

Yield: 12 servings

1 (6-ounce) package apricot
gelatin
1 (20-ounce) can crushed
pineapple
1/2 cup sugar
8 ounces cream cheese,
softened

1 cup plus 6 tablespoons cold
water
8 ounces whipped topping
1/2 cup chopped pecans
2 (9-inch) graham cracker pie
shells

Combine gelatin, undrained pineapple and sugar in saucepan; mix well.
Stir in cream cheese. Bring to a boil, stirring constantly. Remove from
heat. Stir in cold water. Chill just until thickened, but not set. Fold in
whipped topping and pecans. Spoon into pie shells. Chill for 8 to 10
hours or until set.

Approx Per Serving: Cal 550; Prot 6 g; Carbo 72 g; T Fat 28 g;
45% Calories from Fat; Chol 21 mg; Fiber 2 g; Sod 406 mg

Dede Culverhouse, Greater Lynchburg HFH, Huddleston, VA

Banana Split Cake

Yield: 10 servings

1 (16-ounce) package vanilla
wafers, crushed
1 (3-ounce) can flaked coconut
1/2 cup butter, softened
1 (1-pound) package
confectioners' sugar
3 eggs

1 cup butter or margarine,
softened
3 or 4 bananas, sliced
1 (20-ounce) can crushed
pineapple, drained
12 ounces whipped topping

Combine vanilla wafer crumbs, coconut and 1/2 cup butter in bowl; mix
well. Press into bottom of 9x13-inch dish. Combine confectioners'
sugar, eggs and 1 cup butter in bowl; mix well. Spread in prepared dish.
Layer with bananas and pineapple. Spread with whipped topping.
Garnish with maraschino cherries and pecan or walnut pieces. May
substitute 1 package crushed coconut cookies for vanilla wafer and
coconut mixture.

Approx Per Serving: Cal 859; Prot 6 g; Carbo 108 g; T Fat 48 g;
48% Calories from Fat; Chol 164 mg; Fiber 2 g; Sod 454 mg

Linda C. Whelan, Meade City HFH, Vine Grove, KY

You see in the faces of the homeowners and the volunteers what Habitat for Humanity really means.

**FORMER PRESIDENT
JIMMY CARTER
HFH VOLUNTEER**

I would like to highlight three special events for me with Lebanon Area HFH. The first was our affiliation on October 1, 1993. The second was the evening the Family Selection Committee visited the first two families chosen, and the third is the ground-breaking for our first house on February 11, 1995.

PAT COX
LEBANON AREA HFH

Berry Delight

Yield: 15 servings

1¹/₂ teaspoons margarine, softened
1 quart fresh, frozen or canned boysenberries or loganberries
3 tablespoons cornstarch
1 cup sugar
¹/₂ cup margarine

¹/₄ cup sugar
4 ounces graham crackers, crushed
8 ounces marshmallows
1 cup milk
1 to 2 cups whipping cream, whipped

Grease sides and bottom of 9x13-inch dish with 1¹/₂ teaspoons margarine. Combine boysenberries with mixture of cornstarch and 1 cup sugar in saucepan; mix well. Cook over low heat until thickened, stirring frequently. Let stand until cool. Combine ¹/₂ cup margarine and ¹/₄ cup sugar in saucepan. Cook until margarine melts, stirring frequently. Reserve ¹/₂ cup of the graham cracker crumbs. Stir remaining graham cracker crumbs into margarine mixture. Pat mixture into prepared dish. Combine marshmallows and milk in saucepan. Cook over low heat until smooth, stirring constantly. Let stand until cool. Fold in whipped cream. Spread ¹/₂ of the marshmallow mixture over prepared layer. Top with berry mixture. Spread with remaining marshmallow mixture. Sprinkle with reserved crumbs. Chill until serving time. May substitute whipped topping for whipped cream.

Approx Per Serving: Cal 348; Prot 2 g; Carbo 43 g; T Fat 20 g; 50% Calories from Fat; Chol 46 mg; Fiber 2 g; Sod 149 mg

Pat Cox, Lebanon Area HFH, Lebanon, OR

Blueberry Delight

Yield: 15 servings

2 (3-ounce) packages grape gelatin
2 cups boiling water
1 (21-ounce) can blueberry pie filling
1 (8-ounce) can crushed pineapple, drained

1 cup sour cream, at room temperature
8 ounces cream cheese, softened
³/₄ cup sugar
1 tablespoon vanilla extract

Dissolve gelatin in boiling water in bowl; mix well. Stir in pie filling and pineapple. Pour into 9x13-inch dish. Chill until set. Beat sour cream, cream cheese and sugar in mixer bowl until smooth. Stir in vanilla. Spread over chilled layer. Chill until serving time.

Approx Per Serving: Cal 219; Prot 3 g; Carbo 34 g; T Fat 9 g; 35% Calories from Fat; Chol 23 mg; Fiber 1 g; Sod 92 mg

Jennifer Jones, Macon County HFH, Franklin, NC

Buckeye Balls

Yield: 48 servings

1/4 cup butter, softened
2 cups crunchy peanut butter
2 cups confectioners' sugar

3 1/2 cups crisp rice cereal
2 cups chocolate chips, melted

Combine butter, peanut butter, confectioners' sugar and cereal in bowl; mix well. Chill for 30 minutes. Shape into 1-inch balls. Chill for 1 hour. Melt chocolate chips in double boiler over hot water, stirring until smooth. Dip 1/2 of each ball into the chocolate. Arrange on waxed paper. Let stand until set. May freeze for future use.

Approx Per Serving: Cal 132; Prot 3 g; Carbo 14 g; T Fat 8 g; 53% Calories from Fat; Chol 3 mg; Fiber 1 g; Sod 87 mg

Thelma Battershell, Painesville Area HFH, Painesville, OH

Cherries-in-the-Snow

Yield: 12 servings

1 (8-ounce) angel food cake
8 ounces cream cheese,
   softened
1/2 cup sugar
3/4 cup milk

8 ounces whipped topping
1 (21-ounce) can cherry pie
   filling
1/2 teaspoon almond extract

Remove brown crust from cake; tear cake into bite-size pieces. Beat cream cheese and sugar in mixer bowl until creamy. Add milk; mix well. Fold in whipped topping. Fold in cake pieces. Swirl mixture of pie filling and almond extract into cake mixture. Spoon into 9x13-inch dish or crystal bowl. Chill, covered, for up to 2 days.

Approx Per Serving: Cal 275; Prot 4 g; Carbo 39 g; T Fat 13 g; 40% Calories from Fat; Chol 23 mg; Fiber <1 g; Sod 235 mg

Loretta M. Troyer, HFHI, Middlebury, IN

Photo by HFHI

Chocolate Cookies

Yield: 36 servings

2 cups sugar
1/2 cup butter or margarine
1/2 cup baking cocoa
1/2 cup milk

3 cups instant oats
1/2 cup flaked coconut
1 teaspoon vanilla extract
1/2 cup chopped pecans

Combine sugar, butter, baking cocoa and milk in saucepan. Cook until butter melts, stirring constantly. Remove from heat. Stir in oats, coconut, vanilla and pecans. Let stand until slightly cooled. Drop by teaspoonfuls onto waxed paper-lined sheet. Chill for 4 hours or until set. Increase oats by 1/4 cup on extremely humid days.

Approx Per Serving: Cal 112; Prot 2 g; Carbo 17 g; T Fat 5 g; 36% Calories from Fat; Chol 7 mg; Fiber 1 g; Sod 29 mg

Karen Wilke, Michigan City HFH, Michigan City, IN

Chocolate Cream Pie

Yield: 6 servings

1 (6-ounce) package chocolate instant pudding mix
1 (9-inch) graham cracker pie shell

12 ounces whipped topping

Prepare pudding mix using package directions. Spoon into pie shell. Chill for 1 hour or until set. Spread with whipped topping.

Approx Per Serving: Cal 610; Prot 8 g; Carbo 76 g; T Fat 32 g; 47% Calories from Fat; Chol 16 mg; Fiber 2 g; Sod 741 mg

Kathy Pevine, Lakes Region HFH, Franklin, NH

Chocolate Satin Pie

Yield: 6 servings

2 cups chocolate chips
1/4 cup milk
1/4 cup sugar
Dash of salt
4 egg yolks

1 teaspoon vanilla extract
4 egg whites, stiffly beaten
1 (9-inch) graham cracker pie shell

Combine chocolate chips, milk, sugar and salt in double boiler. Cook over hot water until smooth, stirring frequently. Cool slightly. Add egg yolks 1 at a time, mixing well after each addition. Stir in vanilla. Fold in egg whites. Spoon into pie shell. Chill for 2 to 3 hours or until set.

Approx Per Serving: Cal 627; Prot 9 g; Carbo 81 g; T Fat 34 g; 46% Calories from Fat; Chol 143 mg; Fiber 5 g; Sod 362 mg

Jennifer D. Jones, Macon County HFH, Franklin, NC

Simple, decent houses is the common phrase that describes Habitat houses and the approach to construction: namely, Habitat builds houses that are basic in design and construction and without frills—and built to last and withstand the batterings of climate.

Chocolate Eclair Cake

Yield: 15 servings

1 tablespoon butter
1 (16-ounce) package graham crackers
1 (6-ounce) package vanilla instant pudding mix
3 cups milk
8 ounces whipped topping

1 cup sugar
1/8 teaspoon salt
1/3 cup baking cocoa
1/4 cup milk
1/4 cup butter
1 teaspoon vanilla extract

Coat sides and bottom of 9x13-inch dish with 1 tablespoon butter. Line with graham crackers. Combine pudding mix and 3 cups milk in mixer bowl. Beat for 2 minutes, scraping bowl occasionally. Fold in whipped topping. Spread 1/2 of the pudding mixture in prepared dish. Repeat the layers. Top with remaining graham crackers. Bring sugar, salt, baking cocoa and milk to a boil in saucepan, stirring constantly. Boil for 1 minute, stirring frequently. Remove from heat. Stir in butter and vanilla. Beat for 10 minutes or until of spreading consistency. Spread over top layer. Chill for 12 to 24 hours.

Approx Per Serving: Cal 340; Prot 4 g; Carbo 54 g; T Fat 13 g; 33% Calories from Fat; Chol 18 mg; Fiber 1 g; Sod 433 mg

Margo D. Foust, Greater Lynchburg HFH, Rustburg, VA

Cookie Whip

Yield: 8 servings

2 cups crushed chocolate sandwich cookies
8 ounces whipped topping

1 cup miniature marshmallows
1/2 cup chopped walnuts

Combine cookie crumbs and whipped topping in bowl; mix well. Stir in marshmallows and walnuts. Chill, covered, for 1 hour. Spoon into dessert bowls. May substitute chocolate chip cookies, gingersnaps or oatmeal cookies for chocolate sandwich cookies.

Approx Per Serving: Cal 274; Prot 3 g; Carbo 30 g; T Fat 17 g; 54% Calories from Fat; Chol 0 mg; Fiber 1 g; Sod 162 mg

Mary Agnes Bloom, Rapid City HFH, Rapid City, SD

Crispy Rice Bars

Yield: 24 servings

1/4 cup margarine
1 (10-ounce) package
  marshmallows

6 cups crisp rice cereal

Heat margarine in saucepan until melted. Stir in marshmallows. Cook until blended, stirring constantly. Remove from heat. Stir in cereal. Press into buttered 9x13-inch dish with buttered spatula. Let stand until cool. Cut into bars.

Approx Per Serving: Cal 82; Prot 1 g; Carbo 16 g; T Fat 2 g; 21% Calories from Fat; Chol 0 mg; Fiber <1 g; Sod 112 mg

Eileen L. Oehler, Barry County HFH, Hastings, MI

Crunchy Cookies

Yield: 48 servings

20 to 22 ounces almond bark,
  melted
1/2 cup miniature marshmallows

1 cup mixed salted nuts
4 cups crisp rice cereal

Combine almond bark, marshmallows, salted nuts and cereal in bowl; mix well. Drop by teaspoonfuls onto cookie sheet lined with waxed paper. Chill until set.

Approx Per Serving: Cal 99; Prot 1 g; Carbo 12 g; T Fat 5 g; 48% Calories from Fat; Chol 0 mg; Fiber <1 g; Sod 48 mg

Jane Carter, Mesilla Valley HFH, Las Cruces, NM

Photo by Dennis E. Meola

Date Balls

Yield: 36 servings

1/4 cup butter
1 pound dates, chopped
1 cup sugar
1 egg, beaten
1 cup chopped pecans
2 cups crisp rice cereal
1 teaspoon vanilla extract
1 cup flaked coconut

Combine butter, dates, sugar and egg in saucepan; mix well. Cook over medium heat for 12 minutes, stirring frequently. Remove from heat. Stir in pecans, cereal and vanilla. Shape with buttered hands into small balls; roll in coconut.

Approx Per Serving: Cal 107; Prot 1 g; Carbo 18 g; T Fat 4 g; 35% Calories from Fat; Chol 9 mg; Fiber 2 g; Sod 34 mg

Ruth E. Lanham, Southeast New Hampshire HFH, New Castle, NH

Dirt Cake

Yield: 8 servings

Use as a centerpiece at a children's party or bridal shower.

8 ounces cream cheese,
   softened
1/4 cup margarine, softened
2 (3-ounce) packages French
   vanilla instant pudding mix
3 1/2 cups milk
16 ounces whipped topping
1 (1 1/4-pound) package
   chocolate sandwich cookies,
   crushed

Line new 8-inch flowerpot with plastic wrap. Beat cream cheese and margarine in mixer bowl until smooth. Stir in mixture of pudding mix and milk. Fold in whipped topping. Layer cookies and cream cheese mixture alternately in flowerpot until all ingredients are used, ending with cookies. Garnish with gummy worms, gummy spiders and artificial flowers. May substitute chocolate pudding for French vanilla pudding.

Approx Per Serving: Cal 808; Prot 10 g; Carbo 88 g; T Fat 48 g; 53% Calories from Fat; Chol 46 mg; Fiber 2 g; Sod 952 mg

Mary Evans, Blue Spruce HFH, Evergreen, CO
Debbie Walker, Southwest Butler County HFH, Wexford, PA

When I attended my first Habitat dedication for six units of a condominium complex, I was overwhelmed with the presence of so much hope and joy.

ARWEN GUSTAFSON
UPTOWN HFH

Dirt Dessert

Yield: 15 servings

1 envelope unflavored gelatin
¹/₄ cup cold water
3 egg yolks
³/₄ cup sugar
1 cup milk

1 teaspoon vanilla extract
3 egg whites, stiffly beaten
1 cup whipping cream, whipped
1 (11-ounce) package chocolate
    sandwich cookies, crushed

Soften gelatin in cold water; mix well. Combine egg yolks and sugar in double boiler; mix well. Stir in milk. Cook until thickened, stirring constantly. Remove from heat. Stir in vanilla and gelatin. Cool until thickened. Fold in egg whites and whipped cream. Sprinkle ¹/₂ of the cookie crumbs in 9x13-inch dish. Spread evenly with whipped cream mixture; sprinkle with remaining cookie crumbs. Chill until set.

Approx Per Serving: Cal 218; Prot 3 g; Carbo 26 g; T Fat 12 g; 47% Calories from Fat; Chol 66 mg; Fiber 1 g; Sod 153 mg

Arwen Gustafson, Uptown HFH, Chicago, IL

. . . my mind has been renewed by the volunteers. For our family, you have made a big difference in our lives—a change we will never forget.

MARK DORSEY
HFH HOMEOWNER

French Pudding

Yield: 15 servings

2 (4-ounce) packages pistachio
    instant pudding mix
3 cups milk
8 ounces whipped topping
1 (16-ounce) package graham
    crackers

3 tablespoons baking cocoa
1¹/₂ cups confectioners' sugar
3 tablespoons butter, softened
1 teaspoon vanilla extract
3 tablespoons hot water

Beat pudding mix and milk in mixer bowl until blended. Fold in whipped topping. Layer ¹/₃ of the graham crackers and ¹/₂ of the pudding mixture in 9x11-inch dish. Repeat layers. Top with remaining graham crackers. Beat baking cocoa, confectioners' sugar, butter, vanilla and hot water in mixer bowl until smooth. Spread over prepared layers. Chill until serving time.

Approx Per Serving: Cal 331; Prot 4 g; Carbo 56 g; T Fat 11 g; 29% Calories from Fat; Chol 13 mg; Fiber 1 g; Sod 452 mg

Carolyn Roberts, Central Oklahoma HFH, Edmond, OK

Fruitcakes

Yield: 25 servings

1 (14-ounce) package graham
    cracker crumbs
1 (12-ounce) can evaporated
    milk
4 cups chopped candied mixed
    fruit
4 cups chopped pecans

1¹/₂ cups raisins
1 cup chopped dates
¹/₂ cup candied whole red
    cherries
¹/₂ cup candied whole green
    cherries
¹/₂ cup English walnut halves

Combine graham cracker crumbs, evaporated milk, mixed fruit, pecans, raisins, dates, red cherries and green cherries in bowl; mix well. Press into 2 waxed paper-lined 4x8-inch pans or one 4x14-inch dish. Garnish with walnut halves or additional candied cherries. Chill for 24 hours. Store in refrigerator.

Approx Per Serving: Cal 419; Prot 4 g; Carbo 68 g; T Fat 17 g; 35% Calories from Fat; Chol 4 mg; Fiber 3 g; Sod 217 mg

Marie Richards, Southwest Iowa HFH, Farragut, IA

Easy Fruit Dessert

Yield: 8 servings

1¹/₂ cups cottage cheese,
    drained
1 (12-ounce) can crushed
    pineapple, drained
1 (16-ounce) can mandarin
    oranges, drained

1 (6-ounce) package orange
    gelatin
¹/₃ cup chopped pecans
8 ounces whipped topping

Combine cottage cheese, pineapple, mandarin oranges, gelatin and pecans in bowl; mix well. Fold in whipped topping. Chill, covered, until serving time.

Approx Per Serving: Cal 301; Prot 8 g; Carbo 43 g; T Fat 12 g; 36% Calories from Fat; Chol 6 mg; Fiber 1 g; Sod 225 mg

Myra Bright, Bryan/College Station HFH, College Station, TX

Biblical economics is defined by Habitat for Humanity Co-founder and President Millard Fuller: "In our dealings with poor people, we are to charge no interest and seek no profit." The Biblical foundation is Exodus 22:25.

Graham Cracker Cake Squares

Yield: 14 servings

2 (4-ounce) packages vanilla instant pudding mix
1 (16-ounce) package graham crackers

1 (16-ounce) can chocolate frosting

Prepare pudding mix using package directions. Layer graham crackers and pudding alternately in 9x13-inch dish until all ingredients are used, beginning and ending with graham crackers. Microwave frosting for 3 minutes or until melted. Spread evenly over top layer. Chill for 2 hours or until set. Cut into squares.

Approx Per Serving: Cal 358; Prot 5 g; Carbo 62 g; T Fat 11 g; 28% Calories from Fat; Chol 9 mg; Fiber 1 g; Sod 487 mg

Fayette Potter, Pemi-Valley HFH, Ashland, NH

Ladyfinger Delight

Yield: 12 servings

11 ounces cream cheese, softened
³/₄ cup sugar
1 teaspoon vanilla extract
2 cups whipping cream, whipped

3 (3-ounce) packages ladyfingers, split into halves
1 (21-ounce) can cherry pie filling, chilled

Beat cream cheese, sugar and vanilla in mixer bowl until smooth. Fold in whipped cream. Line bottom and side of 10-inch springform pan with ladyfinger halves. Spread ¹/₂ of cream cheese mixture over ladyfingers. Top with remaining ladyfinger halves; spread with remaining cream cheese mixture. Chill for 30 minutes. Spread with pie filling. Remove side of springform pan just before serving. May substitute blueberry or pineapple pie filling for cherry pie filling.

Approx Per Serving: Cal 411; Prot 5 g; Carbo 42 g; T Fat 26 g; 55% Calories from Fat; Chol 159 mg; Fiber <1 g; Sod 142 mg

Darlene Foley, Meridian Bank HFH, Sicklerville, NJ

Lemon Cream Angel Cake

Yield: 12 servings

6 egg yolks
1/2 cup fresh lemon juice
Grated lemon rind to taste
1/4 cup fresh orange juice
Grated orange rind to taste
1 envelope unflavored gelatin

1/4 cup cold water
6 egg whites
3/4 cup sugar
1 angel food cake, torn into bite-size pieces
1 cup whipped cream, whipped

Combine egg yolks, lemon juice, lemon rind, orange juice and orange rind in double boiler; mix well. Cook for 15 minutes or until thickened, stirring constantly. Cool in refrigerator. Soften gelatin in cold water in saucepan; mix well. Heat until gelatin dissolves, stirring constantly. Let stand until cool. Beat egg whites in mixer bowl until soft peaks form. Add sugar gradually, beating constantly until stiff peaks form. Fold in gelatin. Fold in lemon mixture. Alternate layers of lemon custard and angel food cake in bowl until all ingredients are used, ending with lemon custard. Chill for 24 hours. Spread with whipped cream.

Approx Per Serving: Cal 299; Prot 7 g; Carbo 45 g; T Fat 10 g; 31% Calories from Fat; Chol 133 mg; Fiber <1 g; Sod 437 mg

Patricia Richardson, Santa Monica, CA

Lemon Delight

Yield: 15 servings

1 envelope unflavored gelatin
1/4 cup cold water
24 graham crackers, crushed
6 tablespoons melted butter
4 egg yolks

1 cup sugar
Juice of 1 large lemon
4 egg whites
1/2 cup sugar
1 cup whipping cream, whipped

Soften gelatin in cold water; mix well. Combine graham cracker crumbs and butter in bowl; mix well. Reserve 1/4 cup of crumb mixture. Press remaining crumb mixture in 9x13-inch dish. Combine egg yolks and 1 cup sugar in saucepan. Cook until thickened, stirring constantly. Stir in lemon juice and gelatin. Let stand until cool. Beat egg whites in mixer bowl until soft peaks form. Add 1/2 cup sugar gradually, beating constantly until stiff peaks form. Fold in lemon custard. Fold in whipped cream. Spread in prepared dish. Sprinkle with reserved crumb mixture. Chill for 6 hours or longer. Serve with additional whipped cream.

Approx Per Serving: Cal 243; Prot 3 g; Carbo 30 g; T Fat 13 g; 47% Calories from Fat; Chol 91 mg; Fiber <1 g; Sod 138 mg

Ruth V. LaRue, Polk HFH, Dallas, OR

My favorite Habitat story is how Linda and Millard Fuller were able to solve their marriage difficulties and give their money to needy causes, eventually starting Habitat for Humanity.

RUTH V. LaRUE
POLK HFH

Lime Swirl

Yield: 9 servings

2 cups chocolate wafer crumbs
3 tablespoons melted butter
1 (3-ounce) package lime gelatin
1/2 cup hot water
1/4 cup lemon juice
1 1/2 teaspoons grated lemon
   rind
1/4 cup sugar
1 (12-ounce) can evaporated
   milk, chilled
1/2 cup chocolate wafer crumbs

Combine 2 cups chocolate wafer crumbs and butter in bowl; mix well. Press into 9x13-inch dish. Dissolve gelatin in hot water in bowl; mix well. Chill until partially set. Beat until fluffy. Stir in lemon juice, lemon rind and sugar. Beat evaporated milk in mixer bowl until soft peaks form. Fold into gelatin mixture. Spoon into prepared dish. Sprinkle with 1/2 cup chocolate wafer crumbs.

Approx Per Serving: Cal 250; Prot 5 g; Carbo 36 g; T Fat 10 g; 36% Calories from Fat; Chol 22 mg; Fiber <1 g; Sod 245 mg

Rose D. Gambill, Carteret County NC HFH, Morehead City, NC

Creamy Peanut Butter Pie

Yield: 6 servings

8 ounces cream cheese,
   softened
1 cup sugar
1 cup peanut butter
1 teaspoon vanilla extract
8 ounces whipped topping
1 (9-inch) graham cracker pie
   shell

Beat cream cheese, sugar and peanut butter in mixer bowl until smooth. Beat in vanilla until blended. Fold in whipped topping. Spoon into pie shell. Chill until serving time. May drizzle with chocolate syrup.

Approx Per Serving: Cal 899; Prot 16 g; Carbo 87 g; T Fat 58 g; 56% Calories from Fat; Chol 42 mg; Fiber 4 g; Sod 633 mg

Dede Black, Putnam County HFH, Greencastle, IN

Company Peanut Butter Pie

Yield: 6 servings

²/₃ cup sugar
1 tablespoon flour
2¹/₂ tablespoons cornstarch
¹/₂ teaspoon salt
3 cups milk

3 egg yolks, lightly beaten
³/₄ cup peanut butter
1 tablespoon butter
1 (9-inch) Oreo cookie pie shell
1 (2-ounce) chocolate candy bar

Combine sugar, flour, cornstarch and salt in saucepan; mix well. Stir in milk. Cook over low heat until thickened, stirring constantly. Remove from heat. Stir a small amount of hot mixture into egg yolks; stir egg yolks into hot mixture. Bring to a boil. Boil for 1 minute, stirring constantly. Stir in peanut butter and butter. Cool slightly. Spoon into pie shell. Heat candy bar in double boiler over boiling water until melted, stirring frequently. Drizzle over pie.

Approx Per Serving: Cal 621; Prot 15 g; Carbo 66 g; T Fat 34 g; 49% Calories from Fat; Chol 130 mg; Fiber 2 g; Sod 554 mg

Janet A. Means, Mountaineer HFH, Charleston, WV

Rich Peanut Butter Pie

Yield: 6 servings

²/₃ cup crunchy peanut butter
4 ounces cream cheese, softened
1 cup confectioners' sugar

16 ounces whipped topping
1 (9-inch) graham cracker pie shell

Cream peanut butter and cream cheese in mixer bowl until light and fluffy. Beat in confectioners' sugar. Fold in ¹/₂ of the whipped topping. Spoon into pie shell. Spread with remaining whipped topping. Garnish with chocolate curls. May substitute Oreo cookie pie shell for graham cracker pie shell.

Approx Per Serving: Cal 818; Prot 12 g; Carbo 79 g; T Fat 54 g; 57% Calories from Fat; Chol 21 mg; Fiber 3 g; Sod 522 mg

Martha Vandervoort, HFH of Calhoun County, Anniston, AL

Every house dedication is different, but each is very special. As the wife of the Executive Director of Mountaineer HFH, I have stood in ankle-deep snow and stood shoulder-to-shoulder in a gymnasium. It is always a pleasure to stand with my partners in Christ, no matter where we are, dedicating our efforts to Him.

**JANET A. MEANS
MOUNTAINEER HFH**

Peanut Butter Cream Pie

Yield: 6 servings

6 ounces cream cheese,
  softened
3/4 cup confectioners' sugar
1/2 cup crunchy peanut butter
2 tablespoons milk
1 envelope whipped topping mix
1/2 cup milk

1/2 teaspoon vanilla extract
1 (9-inch) graham cracker pie
  shell
1 envelope whipped topping mix
1/2 cup milk
1/2 teaspoon vanilla extract
1 cup chopped roasted peanuts

Beat cream cheese and confectioners' sugar in mixer bowl until light and fluffy. Add peanut butter and 2 tablespoons milk, beating until mixed. Prepare 1 envelope whipped topping mix according to package directions using 1/2 cup milk and 1/2 teaspoon vanilla. Fold into cream cheese mixture. Spoon into pie shell. Prepare 1 envelope whipping topping mix according to package directions using 1/2 cup milk and 1/2 teaspoon vanilla. Spread evenly over pie. Sprinkle with peanuts. Chill for 5 hours or longer.

Approx Per Serving: Cal 857; Prot 18 g; Carbo 76 g; T Fat 57 g; 58% Calories from Fat; Chol 37 mg; Fiber 5 g; Sod 554 mg

Cordella Faye Rice, HFH of Sumter County, Wildwood, FL

People Chow

Yield: 24 servings

1/2 cup butter
1 cup peanut butter
2 cups milk chocolate chips
1 (12-ounce) package Honey
  Graham cereal

3 cups sifted confectioners'
  sugar

Combine butter, peanut butter and chocolate chips in saucepan. Cook over low heat until smooth, stirring constantly. Remove from heat. Stir in cereal. Add 1/2 of the confectioners' sugar to sealable plastic storage bag. Add cereal mixture and remaining confectioners' sugar; seal tightly. Shake gently to coat. Pour mixture onto 2 cookie sheets. Let stand until cool; separate large pieces with fork.

Approx Per Serving: Cal 272; Prot 4 g; Carbo 35 g; T Fat 14 g; 44% Calories from Fat; Chol 14 mg; Fiber 2 g; Sod 241 mg

Christie Oliver, Somerset HFH, Somerset, KY

Evon Jackson could not believe she had been chosen as the recipient of the Habitat house sponsored by Channel 2. Her son was not convinced, even after the land had been cleared and the foundation poured. "Mom, they're just fooling us. We ain't gonna get no house." On Dedication day, with a look of amazement, he declared, "We got a house; I got my own bed, too."

**Cordella Faye Rice
HFH of Sumter County**

Pots de Crème

Yield: 6 servings

1 cup chocolate chips
2 eggs

2 tablespoons hot strong coffee
3/4 cup boiling milk

Combine chocolate chips, eggs, coffee and milk in blender container. Process at high speed for 2 minutes. Pour into 6 demitasse cups or 4 parfait glasses. Chill for 8 to 10 hours. Garnish with whipped cream and maraschino cherry or chocolate curls. May add 3 tablespoons rum or orange liqueur to mixture.

Approx Per Serving: Cal 179; Prot 4 g; Carbo 20 g; T Fat 11 g; 51% Calories from Fat; Chol 75 mg; Fiber 2 g; Sod 39 mg

Marilyn Veley, Charlotte County HFH, Port Charlotte, FL

Pudding Pie

Yield: 6 servings

1 (6-ounce) package any flavor instant pudding mix

1 (9-inch) graham cracker pie shell

Prepare pudding mix using package directions. Spoon into pie shell. Chill for 3 hours or until set.

Approx Per Serving: Cal 430; Prot 6 g; Carbo 63 g; T Fat 18 g; 36% Calories from Fat; Chol 16 mg; Fiber 2 g; Sod 715 mg

Steven Knowlton, Uptown HFH, Chicago, IL

Photo by Julie A. Lopez

JIMMY CARTER (FAR LEFT)

The Pollard family offered to help the Winter Park Presbyterian Church build a Habitat house. During the week of drywall installation, the Pollard family brought the entire congregation of the Leonards Chapel Church of God, Pentecostal to help. They also brought lunch for everyone!

SUE RUDOLPH
WINTER PARK-MAITLAND HFH

Rocky Road Bars

Yield: 50 servings

2 cups salted dry roasted
    peanuts
1 cup miniature marshmallows
2 cups semisweet chocolate
    chips

2 tablespoons margarine
1 (14-ounce) can sweetened
    condensed milk

Combine peanuts and marshmallows in bowl; mix well. Combine chocolate chips and margarine in double boiler. Cook over hot water until blended, stirring frequently. Combine chocolate mixture and condensed milk in bowl; mix well. Pour over peanut mixture; mix well. Spread in waxed paper-lined 9x13-inch dish. Chill for 2 to 10 hours. Cut into 1-inch bars. May substitute unsalted dry roasted peanuts for salted dry roasted peanuts.

Approx Per Serving: Cal 99; Prot 2 g; Carbo 11 g; T Fat 6 g; 51% Calories from Fat; Chol 3 mg; Fiber <1 g; Sod 64 mg

Sue Rudolph, Winter Park-Maitland HFH, Winter Park, FL

Yummy Dessert

Yield: 12 servings

1 cup milk chocolate chips
3 egg yolks, beaten
3 egg whites, stiffly beaten
1 teaspoon vanilla extract

2 cups whipped topping
1 angel food cake, torn into
    bite-size pieces
1 cup chopped pecans

Melt chocolate chips in double boiler over hot water, stirring until smooth. Cool slightly. Stir in egg yolks until blended. Fold in egg whites. Fold in vanilla and whipped topping. Pour over angel food cake in bowl; mix gently. Spread in 9x13-inch dish. Sprinkle with pecans. Chill for 2 hours or longer. May freeze for future use.

Approx Per Serving: Cal 335; Prot 7 g; Carbo 44 g; T Fat 16 g; 42% Calories from Fat; Chol 56 mg; Fiber 1 g; Sod 427 mg

Betty Warstler, Macon County HFH, Franklin, NC

Habitat is a program that has a lot of heart, rings a bell with our people and fits in with the Dow corporate culture. This is a commitment from our hearts, not just our pocketbooks. We really see what can happen when people give time and energy to help someone else realize the dream of homeownership.

KATHLEEN BADER
VICE PRESIDENT
FABRICATED PRODUCTS DIVISION
THE DOW CHEMICAL COMPANY

Photograph at right by HFHI

HOLIDAY TREATS

"Whoever keeps the fig tree will eat its fruit; so
he who waits on his master will be honored."

-Proverbs 27:18

Almond and Cherry Butter Cookies

Yield: 28 servings

1 cup butter, softened
1/4 cup sugar
1 teaspoon vanilla extract
2 cups flour, sifted
1 cup ground almonds
1 (8-ounce) jar red or green maraschino cherries, drained
3/4 to 1 cup confectioners' sugar

Beat butter and sugar in mixer bowl until light and fluffy. Add vanilla; mix well. Stir in flour and almonds until easily handled dough is formed. Shape into 1-inch balls using 2 tablespoons dough for each ball. Arrange on ungreased cookie sheet. Press cherry halfway into each ball. Bake on middle rack of oven at 325 degrees for 35 minutes. Remove to wire rack to cool. Dust with confectioners' sugar before serving.

Approx Per Serving: Cal 139; Prot 2 g; Carbo 16 g; T Fat 8 g; 51% Calories from Fat; Chol 18 mg; Fiber 1 g; Sod 68 mg

Vincent T. D'Amico, Norristown HFH, Norristown, PA

Brandy Alexander Soufflé

Yield: 8 servings

2 envelopes unflavored gelatin
2 cups water
3/4 cup sugar
4 egg yolks, beaten
8 ounces cream cheese, softened
3 tablespoons crème de cacao
3 tablespoons brandy
4 egg whites
1/4 cup sugar
1 cup whipping cream, whipped

Prepare a 1½-quart soufflé dish with a foil collar extending 3 inches above rim of dish; secure with tape. Soften gelatin in 1 cup of the water in saucepan; mix well. Cook over low heat until dissolved, stirring constantly. Stir in remaining water. Remove from heat. Stir in 3/4 cup sugar and egg yolks. Cook for 2 to 3 minutes or until slightly thickened, stirring constantly. Combine with cream cheese in bowl, stirring until blended. Stir in crème de cacao and brandy. Chill until slightly thickened. Beat egg whites in mixer bowl until soft peaks form. Add 1/4 cup sugar gradually, beating constantly until stiff peaks form. Fold egg whites and whipped cream into cream cheese mixture. Spoon into prepared dish. Chill for 8 to 10 hours. Garnish with chocolate shavings.

Approx Per Serving: Cal 377; Prot 7 g; Carbo 29 g; T Fat 24 g; 55% Calories from Fat; Chol 178 mg; Fiber 0 g; Sod 130 mg

Flo Grabay, Bay County FL HFH Inc., Panama City, FL

We had a group of girls from Gwynd Mercy College volunteer at the Habitat job site when we were doing demolition. We were hauling five-gallon buckets of plaster which weighed between fifty-five to sixty pounds. I asked one of the girls if she wanted me to take the bucket to the dumpster. She flatly said "No," so I went on my way.

VINCENT T. D'AMICO
NORRISTOWN HFH

Photo by Julie A. Lopez

Butterscotch Grahams

Yield: 20 servings

Great dessert for a Christmas Habitat house blessing.

10 to 12 whole graham crackers
1 cup butter

1 cup packed brown sugar
1 cup chopped pecans

Arrange graham crackers in single layer in 9x13-inch baking pan. Bring butter and brown sugar to a boil in saucepan, stirring occasionally. Boil for 3 minutes, stirring occasionally. Remove from heat. Stir in pecans. Pour over graham crackers. Bake at 325 degrees for 10 minutes. Cut into squares while warm.

Approx Per Serving: Cal 173; Prot 1 g; Carbo 13 g; T Fat 14 g; 69% Calories from Fat; Chol 25 mg; Fiber 1 g; Sod 123 mg

Kaye Crawford, Salina HFH, Salina, KS

Cheese Crisps

Yield: 48 servings

1 cup margarine, softened
8 ounces sharp Cheddar
  cheese, shredded

2 cups flour
$1/2$ teaspoon salt
2 cups crisp rice cereal

Cream margarine and Cheddar cheese in mixer bowl until smooth. Add flour, salt and cereal; mix well. Shape into 1-inch balls. Place 2 inches apart on baking sheet; flatten slightly. Bake at 350 degrees for 15 minutes. Serve with assorted fresh fruit. May add $1/2$ teaspoon cayenne for spicy flavor.

Approx Per Serving: Cal 77; Prot 2 g; Carbo 5 g; T Fat 5 g; 64% Calories from Fat; Chol 5 mg; Fiber <1 g; Sod 110 mg

Pat Trader, HFH of Harrison County Inc., Clarksburg, WV

Cherry Walnut Christmas Bars

Yield: 48 servings

1 (2-ounce) jar maraschino
    cherries
2¹/₄ cups sifted flour
¹/₂ cup sugar
1 cup butter, softened
2 eggs
1 cup packed brown sugar

¹/₂ teaspoon salt
¹/₂ teaspoon baking powder
¹/₂ teaspoon vanilla extract
¹/₂ cup chopped walnuts
1 tablespoon butter, softened
1 cup confectioners' sugar

Drain cherries, reserving juice. Chop cherries. Combine flour and sugar in bowl; mix well. Cut in butter until crumbly. Press into ungreased 9x13-inch baking pan. Bake at 350 degrees for 20 minutes or until light brown. Combine eggs, brown sugar, salt, baking powder and vanilla in bowl; mix well. Stir in cherries and walnuts. Spread over baked layer. Bake for 25 minutes. Let stand until cool. Combine 1 tablespoon butter and confectioners' sugar in mixer bowl. Add desired amount of reserved cherry juice, beating until of spreading consistency. Spread over baked layers. Let stand until set. Cut into 1x2-inch bars. May sprinkle ¹/₂ cup flaked coconut over icing.

Approx Per Serving: Cal 100; Prot 1 g; Carbo 13 g; T Fat 5 g; 45% Calories from Fat; Chol 20 mg; Fiber <1 g; Sod 72 mg

Pat Bollman, HFH of Wayne County NY Inc., Williamson, NY

Baked Chocolate-Covered Cherries

Yield: 42 servings

¹/₂ cup margarine, softened
1 cup sugar
1 egg
1¹/₂ teaspoons vanilla extract
1¹/₂ cups flour
¹/₄ teaspoon each salt, baking
    powder and baking soda

¹/₂ cup baking cocoa
42 maraschino cherries, drained
1 cup chocolate chips
¹/₂ cup sweetened condensed milk
¹/₄ teaspoon salt
1 teaspoon maraschino cherry
    juice

Preheat oven to 375 degrees. Cream margarine, sugar, egg and vanilla in mixer bowl until smooth. Add flour, ¹/₄ teaspoon salt, baking powder, baking soda and baking cocoa. Beat at low speed for 1 minute or until stiff dough forms. Shape into 1-inch balls. Place 2 inches apart on ungreased cookie sheet. Press cherry halfway into each ball. Heat chocolate chips, condensed milk, ¹/₄ teaspoon salt and cherry juice in saucepan until blended, stirring constantly. Drizzle 1 teaspoon chocolate mixture over each cherry. Reduce oven temperature to 350 degrees. Bake for 8 to 10 minutes or until light brown.

Approx Per Serving: Cal 96; Prot 1 g; Carbo 15 g; T Fat 4 g; 36% Calories from Fat; Chol 6 mg; Fiber 1 g; Sod 65 mg

Suzanne Gainer, Mon County HFH, Morgantown, WV

Chocolate Mint Dessert

Yield: 12 servings

1 cup flour
1 cup sugar
1/2 cup butter or margarine,
    softened
4 eggs
1 (16-ounce) can chocolate
    syrup

2 cups confectioners' sugar
1/2 cup butter, softened
1 tablespoon water
1/2 teaspoon mint extract
3 drops of green food coloring
6 tablespoons butter
1 cup semisweet chocolate chips

Combine flour, sugar, 1/2 cup butter, eggs and chocolate syrup in mixer bowl. Beat until smooth, scraping bowl occasionally. Spoon into greased 9x13-inch baking pan. Bake at 350 degrees for 25 to 30 minutes or until top springs back when lightly touched. Cool in pan. Combine confectioners' sugar, 1/2 cup butter, water, mint extract and food coloring in mixer bowl. Beat until smooth and of spreading consistency, scraping bowl occasionally. Spread evenly over baked layer. Chill, covered, in refrigerator. Heat 6 tablespoons butter and chocolate chips in saucepan until melted, stirring frequently. Remove from heat. Stir until smooth. Cool slightly. Drizzle over chilled layers. Chill, covered, for 1 hour or longer before slicing.

Approx Per Serving: Cal 541; Prot 5 g; Carbo 76 g; T Fat 27 g; 43% Calories from Fat; Chol 128 mg; Fiber 2 g; Sod 274 mg

Carol A. Hines, HFH of Butler County, Saxonburg, PA

White Chocolate Fruit Tart

Yield: 12 servings

3/4 cup butter, softened
1/2 cup confectioners' sugar
1 1/2 cups flour
10 ounces white chocolate or
    white chocolate chips
1/4 cup whipping cream
8 ounces cream cheese, softened

2 or 3 kiwifruit, sliced
1 1/2 cups blueberries
1 1/2 cups sliced strawberries
1/4 cup sugar
1 tablespoon cornstarch
1/2 cup pineapple juice
1 teaspoon lemon juice

Beat butter and confectioners' sugar in mixer bowl until light and fluffy. Add flour, mixing until easily handled dough forms. Press into 12-inch round baking pan sprayed with nonstick cooking spray. Bake at 300 degrees for 20 to 25 minutes or until light brown. Let stand until cool. Combine white chocolate and whipping cream in microwave-safe dish. Microwave for 2 to 3 minutes or until chocolate is soft. Add cream cheese, stirring until smooth. Spread evenly over baked layer. Arrange kiwifruit, blueberries and strawberries in decorative pattern over cream cheese mixture. Combine sugar and cornstarch in saucepan; mix well. Stir in pineapple juice and lemon juice. Cook over low heat until thickened, stirring constantly. Drizzle over fruit. Chill until serving time.

Approx Per Serving: Cal 440; Prot 5 g; Carbo 45 g; T Fat 28 g; 55% Calories from Fat; Chol 64 mg; Fiber 2 g; Sod 199 mg

Lois R. Carita, HFH of Greater Bucks County, Langhorne, PA

I was unemployed and feeling like I was contributing nothing to society. One sunny day, frustrated with my situation, I wrote to Habitat to see if they could use my help. They responded postively. Now I have a job but still try to volunteer whenever possible. Habitat gives all of us, those who give and those who receive, a chance to contribute in our own way to society.

LOIS R. CARITA
HFH OF GREATER BUCKS COUNTY

Cranberry Freeze

Yield: 10 servings

3 cups cranberries, ground or
  finely chopped
1¹/₂ cups sugar
1 (8-ounce) can crushed
  pineapple, drained

¹/₂ cup chopped walnuts
8 ounces cream cheese,
  softened
1 cup whipping cream, whipped

Combine cranberries and sugar in bowl; mix well. Stir in pineapple and walnuts. Add to cream cheese in bowl, stirring until mixed. Fold in whipped cream. Spoon into 6¹/₂-cup mold. Freeze until set. Let stand in refrigerator for 30 minutes before serving.

Approx Per Serving: Cal 342; Prot 3 g; Carbo 39 g; T Fat 21 g; 52% Calories from Fat; Chol 58 mg; Fiber 2 g; Sod 77 mg

Cathy Rupp, HFH of Whitley County, Columbia City, IN

Cranberry Pie

Yield: 6 servings

2 cups fresh cranberries
¹/₂ cup sugar
¹/₂ cup chopped walnuts
2 eggs, beaten

1 cup sugar
1 cup flour
¹/₂ cup melted margarine
¹/₂ cup melted shortening

Combine cranberries, ¹/₂ cup sugar and walnuts in bowl; mix well. Spread in greased 10-inch pie plate. Combine eggs and 1 cup sugar in mixer bowl. Beat until blended. Add flour alternately with margarine and shortening, beating well after each addition. Pour over cranberry mixture. Bake at 325 degrees for 1 hour.

Approx Per Serving: Cal 661; Prot 6 g; Carbo 72 g; T Fat 40 g; 54% Calories from Fat; Chol 71 mg; Fiber 2 g; Sod 202 mg

Beth Liberatore, Cayuga County HFH, Auburn, NY

Thank you for our beautiful house. We really love living in it. I have never ever in my whole life seen somebody doing something so beautiful and so fast without making one tinsey bitty tiny mistake. We really really really appreciate it. Thank you very very much.

Delicious Cranberry Pie

Yield: 8 servings

1 cup flour
1/2 cup sugar
1 1/2 teaspoons baking powder
1 egg, beaten
1/3 cup (or more) milk

1 cup fresh cranberries
1/4 cup butter
1/2 cup sugar
1/2 cup milk

Combine flour, 1/2 cup sugar and baking powder in bowl, stirring with fork until blended. Combine egg with 1/3 cup milk or more to measure 1/2 cup. Add to flour mixture; mix well. Fold in cranberries. Spoon into 8- or 9-inch glass pie plate. Bake at 350 degrees for 35 minutes. Heat butter, 1/2 cup sugar and 1/2 cup milk in saucepan just to the boiling point, stirring frequently. Drizzle over each pie slice just before serving.

Approx Per Serving: Cal 236; Prot 3 g; Carbo 40 g; T Fat 7 g; 28% Calories from Fat; Chol 46 mg; Fiber 1 g; Sod 141 mg

Carol Freeland, HFHI Board of Directors, Richardson, TX

Honey's Cranberry Pie

Yield: 8 servings

2 cups fresh cranberries
1/2 cup honey
1/2 cup finely chopped pecans
2 eggs, beaten
1 cup sugar

1 cup flour
1/2 cup melted butter or margarine
1/4 cup melted shortening

Spread cranberries evenly in 10-inch pie plate sprayed with butter-flavor nonstick cooking spray. Drizzle honey over cranberries; sprinkle with pecans. Beat eggs and sugar in mixer bowl until blended. Add flour, butter and shortening, beating until smooth. Pour over prepared layers. Bake at 325 degrees for 1 hour. Serve warm with ice cream.

Approx Per Serving: Cal 456; Prot 4 g; Carbo 59 g; T Fat 24 g; 47% Calories from Fat; Chol 84 mg; Fiber 2 g; Sod 135 mg

Debra J. Schrag, McPherson Area HFH, Moundridge, KS

Our affiliate in McPherson was born as a result of a dream of the McPherson College Campus Chapter. Students in the chapter raised the money for our first house. They were the organizers of the steering committee that started the affiliate, and then went on to build the house. We appreciate their work to put their dream into action.

DEBRA J. SCHRAG
MCPHERSON AREA HFH

Cranberry and Hazelnut Pie

Yield: 8 servings

4 ounces hazelnuts
1 unbaked (9-inch) deep-dish
   pie shell
8 ounces cranberries
3 eggs

1/8 teaspoon salt
1 cup packed dark brown sugar
1 cup light corn syrup
1/4 teaspoon vanilla extract
3 tablespoons melted butter

Sprinkle hazelnuts over bottom of pie shell. Top with cranberries. Beat eggs and salt in mixer bowl until eggs are lemon colored. Add brown sugar, corn syrup, vanilla and butter; mix well. Pour into prepared pie shell. Place pie plate on middle rack of oven. Bake at 450 degrees for 10 minutes. Reduce temperature to 350 degrees. Bake for 50 minutes longer or until set.

Approx Per Serving: Cal 494; Prot 6 g; Carbo 70 g; T Fat 23 g; 41% Calories from Fat; Chol 91 mg; Fiber 3 g; Sod 311 mg

Virginia Mattson, South Puget Sound HFH, Olympia, WA

New England Cranberry and Pear Pie

Yield: 6 servings

4 cups flour
1 tablespoon sugar
2 teaspoons salt
1 1/3 cups shortening
1 tablespoon vinegar
1/2 cup water
1 egg
2 cups sugar

1/4 teaspoon salt
3/4 cup water
3 cups whole fresh cranberries
1/4 cup cornstarch
2 tablespoons cold water
2 tablespoons margarine
1 tablespoon lemon juice
2 medium pears, peeled, chopped

Mix flour, 1 tablespoon sugar and 2 teaspoons salt in bowl. Cut in shortening with fork until crumbly. Beat vinegar, 1/2 cup water and egg in bowl until blended. Add to flour mixture, mixing with fork until mixture forms ball. Chill for 15 minutes or longer. Divide pastry into 5 portions. Roll 1 portion to fit 9-inch pie plate on lightly floured surface, reserving excess pastry. Fit into pie plate. Cut pear-shaped pieces out of reserved pastry for top. Freeze remaining 4 portions of dough for future use or store in refrigerator up to 3 days. Bring 2 cups sugar, 1/4 teaspoon salt and 3/4 cup water to a boil in saucepan, stirring occasionally. Stir in cranberries. Cook over low heat until cranberries pop, stirring occasionally. Stir in mixture of cornstarch and 2 tablespoons cold water. Cook until thickened and clear, stirring constantly. Remove from heat. Stir in margarine and lemon juice. Cool for 20 minutes. Stir in pears. Spoon into pastry-lined pie shell. Top with pear-shaped pastry. Bake at 425 degrees for 25 to 30 minutes or until brown and bubbly.

Nutritional information for this recipe is not available.

Bette MacDonald, Lakes Region HFH, Gilford, NH

Cranberry Orange Cake

Yield: 12 servings

1 cup fresh or frozen
  cranberries
1/4 cup sugar
2 tablespoons grated orange
  rind
1 1/2 cups oat bran
1/2 cup apple fiber

2 teaspoons baking powder
2 teaspoons vanilla extract
3/4 cup orange juice
2 tablespoons canola oil
1 cup water
3 egg whites
3/4 cup sugar

Process cranberries and 1/4 cup sugar in food processor until chopped. Stir in orange rind. Combine oat bran, apple fiber and baking powder in bowl; mix well. Stir in mixture of vanilla, orange juice, canola oil and water. Add the cranberry mixture; mix well. Beat egg whites in mixer bowl until soft peaks form. Add 3/4 cup sugar gradually, beating constantly until stiff peaks form. Fold egg whites 1/2 at a time into cranberry mixture. Spoon into 5x9-inch loaf pan sprayed with nonstick cooking spray. Bake at 350 degrees for 1 hour.

Approx Per Serving: Cal 130; Prot 3 g; Carbo 28 g; T Fat 3 g; 19% Calories from Fat; Chol 0 mg; Fiber 2 g; Sod 69 mg Nutritional information does not include apple fiber.

Cindy Riess, HFH of Oshkosh Inc., Oshkosh, WI

Crème de Menthe Squares

Yield: 36 servings

1/2 cup butter
1/2 cup baking cocoa
1/2 cup confectioners' sugar
1 egg, beaten
1 teaspoon vanilla extract
2 cups graham cracker crumbs
1/2 cup melted butter

1/3 cup crème de menthe
3 cups confectioners' sugar
1/4 cup butter
2 cups semisweet chocolate
  chips
1/2 cup chopped almonds

Combine 1/2 cup butter and baking cocoa in saucepan. Cook until blended, stirring constantly. Remove from heat. Add 1/2 cup confectioners' sugar, egg and vanilla; mix well. Stir in graham cracker crumbs. Press into bottom of ungreased 9x13-inch dish. Combine 1/2 cup melted butter and crème de menthe in mixer bowl; mix well. Beat in 3 cups confectioners' sugar at low speed until smooth. Spread over prepared layer. Chill for 30 minutes. Combine 1/4 cup butter and chocolate chips in saucepan. Cook over medium heat until blended, stirring constantly. Spread over chilled layers. Sprinkle with almonds. Chill for 1 to 2 hours or until set. Cut into squares. Store in refrigerator. May substitute 1/2 cup broken candy canes for almonds.

Approx Per Serving: Cal 200; Prot 2 g; Carbo 25 g; T Fat 11 g; 47% Calories from Fat; Chol 23 mg; Fiber 1 g; Sod 109 mg

Sandie Gray, HFH of Anderson County TN, Oak Ridge, TN

My dream, from the outset of the ministry of Habitat for Humanity, has been for our work to be a new frontier in Christian missions.

**MILLARD FULLER
PRESIDENT AND
CO-FOUNDER OF HFHI**

Gary Redenbacher's Crème Brûlée

Yield: 8 servings

Renae makes the custard, and Gary wields the propane torch when they prepare this recipe. He uses the same type of torch that a plumber uses to solder copper pipes together. Gary says he has seen propane torches used quite a bit in restaurants, but they are not a common fixture in the kitchen. The safest way to caramelize with a propane torch is to place the ramekins where nothing is flammable.

2¹/₂ cups whipping cream	**1 vanilla bean, split into**
1 cup milk	**halves lengthwise**
¹/₂ cup sugar	**9 egg yolks**
¹/₈ teaspoon salt	**8 teaspoons sugar**

Combine whipping cream, milk, ¹/₂ cup sugar, salt and vanilla bean in medium saucepan. Cook over medium heat until bubbles form around side of pan, stirring constantly. Remove from heat. Let stand for 10 minutes. Bring mixture to a gentle boil. Remove from heat; discard vanilla bean. Whisk egg yolks in bowl until blended. Stir small amount of hot mixture into egg yolks; stir egg yolks into hot mixture. Strain into 1-quart measuring cup. Pour into eight 6-ounce ramekins or custard cups. Place in roasting pan; add boiling water to reach ¹/₃ way up sides of ramekins. Place pan on center rack in oven. Bake at 325 degrees for 25 to 30 minutes or until edges are set and centers still quiver. Do not overbake; custards will set completely after chilling. Cool on wire rack for 30 minutes. Chill for 2 hours or longer. Place ramekins in high-sided roasting pan; surround with ice cubes and water. Sprinkle top of each custard with 1 teaspoon sugar. Using propane torch, caramelize top of each custard by heating sugar until it turns dark amber in color. Chill no longer than 10 minutes. Serve immediately. A more conventional method may be to caramelize custards using broiler. Place ramekins in high-sided roasting pan. Surround with ice cubes and water. Sprinkle each custard with 1¹/₂ tablespoons brown sugar; spray lightly with water to dampen brown sugar. Broil 1 to 2 minutes or until sugar turns dark amber in color. Chill no longer than 10 minutes. Serve immediately.

Approx Per Serving: Cal 407; Prot 6 g; Carbo 20 g; T Fat 34 g; 75% Calories from Fat; Chol 345 mg; Fiber 0 g; Sod 84 mg

Renae and Gary Redenbacher, Scotts Valley, CA

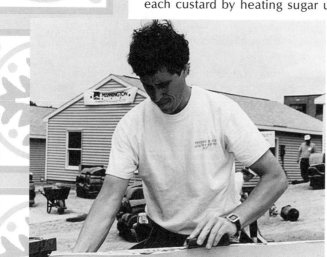

Photo by Don Hall

GARY REDENBACHER

Danish Puff

Yield: 16 servings

¹/₂ cup butter or margarine, softened
1 cup flour
2 tablespoons water
¹/₂ cup butter or margarine
1 cup water
1 teaspoon almond extract
1 cup flour
3 eggs
1¹/₂ cups confectioners' sugar
2 tablespoons water
1 teaspoon vanilla extract

Cut ¹/₂ cup butter into 1 cup flour in bowl until crumbly. Sprinkle with 2 tablespoons water; mix well. Shape into circle around edge of 12-inch round baking pan; circle should be approximately 4 inches wide. Combine ¹/₂ cup butter and 1 cup water in saucepan. Heat until butter melts, stirring occasionally. Remove from heat. Stir in almond extract and 1 cup flour. Cook over low heat until mixture forms ball, stirring constantly. Remove from heat. Add eggs 1 at a time, beating until glossy after each addition. Spread over top of circle. Bake at 350 degrees for 20 minutes. Drizzle with mixture of confectioners' sugar, 2 tablespoons water and vanilla. Decorate with red maraschino cherry halves and green maraschino cherry quarters arranged in shape of holly leaves. May frost with your favorite jelly or jam.

Approx Per Serving: Cal 216; Prot 3 g; Carbo 23 g; T Fat 13 g; 52% Calories from Fat; Chol 71 mg; Fiber <1 g; Sod 129 mg

Joan Pellnat, HFH of Buffalo, Buffalo, NY

Fruitcakes

Yield: 48 servings

2 pounds pitted dates, cut into halves
1 pound chopped pecans
8 ounces candied cherries, chopped
8 ounces candied pineapple, chopped
1 pound citrus peel
2 cups self-rising flour
2 cups sugar
8 eggs, beaten
¹/₄ cup vanilla extract

Combine dates, pecans, cherries, pineapple and citrus peel in bowl; mix well. Add mixture of flour and sugar to fruit, stirring gently to coat. Add mixture of eggs and vanilla gradually; mix well. Spoon into 4 loaf pans. Place pan of water on bottom shelf of oven for added moisture. Bake at 325 degrees for 1 hour. May substitute candied mixed fruit for citrus peel. May bake in 2 tube pans for 1¹/₂ hours or in 48 muffin cups for 30 minutes.

Approx Per Serving: Cal 243; Prot 3 g; Carbo 44 g; T Fat 7 g; 27% Calories from Fat; Chol 35 mg; Fiber 2 g; Sod 77 mg

Elizabeth A. Copeland, Satilla HFH, Waycross, GA

Fudgy Orange Cappuccino Torte

Yield: 16 servings

1 (21-ounce) package fudge brownie mix
$1/2$ cup vegetable oil
$1/4$ cup water
$1/4$ cup orange liqueur
2 eggs
1 teaspoon grated orange rind
4 ounces German's sweet chocolate, grated
1 cup sweetened condensed milk
6 ounces German's sweet chocolate
2 egg yolks, lightly beaten
2 tablespoons orange liqueur
$3/4$ cup finely chopped pecans
$1 1/2$ cups whipping cream
$3/4$ cup confectioners' sugar
2 tablespoons orange juice
1 teaspoon grated orange rind

Combine brownie mix, oil, water, $1/4$ cup orange liqueur, eggs and 1 teaspoon grated orange rind in bowl. Beat by hand 50 strokes. Stir in 4 ounces grated chocolate. Spoon into greased 9- or 10-inch springform pan. Bake at 350 degrees for 35 to 40 minutes or until center is set. Cool in pan. Combine condensed milk and 6 ounces German's sweet chocolate in saucepan. Cook over low heat until smooth, stirring constantly. Remove from heat. Stir 2 tablespoons hot mixture into egg yolks; stir egg yolks into hot mixture gradually. Cook over medium heat for 3 minutes, stirring constantly. Remove from heat. Stir in 2 tablespoons orange liqueur and pecans. Chill for 25 minutes or just until cooled. Spread over baked layer. Chill for 1 hour or until set. Loosen torte from side of pan with sharp knife; remove side of pan. Arrange chilled layers on serving platter. Beat whipping cream in mixer bowl until soft peaks form. Add confectioners' sugar, orange juice and 1 teaspoon orange rind gradually, beating constantly until stiff peaks form. Pipe or spread whipped cream mixture evenly over chilled layers. Garnish with twisted orange slices. Store in refrigerator. May substitute semisweet chocolate for German's sweet chocolate. May substitute orange juice for orange liqueur.

Approx Per Serving: Cal 500; Prot 6 g; Carbo 53 g; T Fat 30 g; 52% Calories from Fat; Chol 90 mg; Fiber 1 g; Sod 170 mg

Barbara J. Urbrock, HFH of Oshkosh Inc., Oshkosh, WI

Giant Ginger Cookies

Yield: 28 servings

4³/₄ cups sifted flour
1 tablespoon baking soda
¹/₂ teaspoon salt
2 teaspoons ginger
1 teaspoon ground cloves
1 teaspoon dry mustard
1 cup butter, softened

1 tablespoon brewed instant
  coffee
1 cup sugar
1 cup molasses
1 egg
³/₄ cup milk
1 (6-ounce) package currants

Position 2 oven racks to divide oven into thirds. Cut foil to fit cookie sheets. Sift flour, baking soda, salt, ginger, cloves and dry mustard together. Cream butter in mixer bowl until light and fluffy. Add coffee; mix well. Beat in sugar until blended. Add molasses, beating until smooth. Mix in egg; mixture will look curdled. Add the dry ingredients in 3 additions alternately with the milk in 2 additions, beating until smooth after each addition; scrape bowl as needed. Stir in currants. Drop by heaping tablespoonfuls 2¹/₂ to 3 inches apart onto foil; keep cookies as round as possible. Slide cookie sheet under foil. Bake at 350 degrees for 20 to 22 minutes or until tops of cookies spring back when lightly touched; reverse cookie sheet top to bottom and front to back several times to ensure even baking. Remove to wire rack to cool. Place wire rack on right-side-up cake pan or mixing bowl to prevent soggy cookie bottoms.

Approx Per Serving: Cal 212; Prot 3 g; Carbo 35 g; T Fat 7 g; 30% Calories from Fat; Chol 26 mg; Fiber 1 g; Sod 204 mg

Ann M. Felton, Central Oklahoma HFH, Oklahoma City, OK

Gingerbread Men

Yield: 36 servings

1 cup butter or margarine,
  softened
1 cup sugar
¹/₂ cup dark molasses
1 teaspoon cinnamon
1 teaspoon nutmeg

1 teaspoon ground cloves
1 teaspoon ginger
2 eggs, beaten
1 teaspoon vinegar
5 cups flour
1 teaspoon baking soda

Cream butter and sugar in mixer bowl until light and fluffy. Combine butter mixture with molasses, cinnamon, nutmeg, cloves and ginger in saucepan; mix well. Bring to a boil, stirring occasionally. Remove from heat. Let stand until lukewarm. Stir in eggs and vinegar. Add sifted mixture of flour and baking soda, stirring until soft dough forms. Chill for 2 to 10 hours. Divide dough into 6 portions. Roll each portion on lightly floured surface; cut with gingerbread-man cutter. Decorate with raisins for eyes and buttons and red hot cinnamon candies for mouths. Arrange on cookie sheet. Bake at 350 degrees for 8 to 10 minutes or until edges are crisp. Remove to wire rack to cool.

Approx Per Serving: Cal 146; Prot 2 g; Carbo 22 g; T Fat 6 g; 34% Calories from Fat; Chol 26 mg; Fiber <1 g; Sod 81 mg

Rosamond Fienning, Grayson County HFH, Sherman, TX

Grasshopper Cheesecake   *Yield: 12 servings*

**1¹/₂ cups finely crushed
   chocolate sandwich cookies**
**3 tablespoons melted butter or
   margarine**
**32 ounces cream cheese,
   softened**
**1 (14-ounce) can sweetened
   condensed milk**

4 eggs
3 tablespoons baking cocoa
2 teaspoons vanilla extract
3 tablespoons crème de menthe
2 tablespoons crème de cacao
**3 (1-ounce) squares semisweet
   chocolate**
¹/₃ cup whipping cream

Combine cookie crumbs and butter in bowl; mix well. Press over bottom of 9-inch springform pan. Beat cream cheese in mixer bowl until light and fluffy. Beat in condensed milk gradually. Add eggs; mix well. Divide beaten mixture into 2 portions. Beat baking cocoa and vanilla into 1 portion until blended. Spoon into prepared pan. Stir liqueurs into remaining portion. Spoon evenly over prepared layers. Bake at 300 degrees for 1 hour and 10 minutes or until set. Let stand in oven with door slightly ajar for 1 hour. Remove side of pan. Melt chocolate in double boiler over hot water, stirring until smooth. Add ¹/₃ cup whipping cream; mix well. Cook until blended, stirring constantly. Spread evenly over top of cheesecake. Garnish top with staggered ring of mint-chocolate after-dinner mints. Chill. Store in refrigerator.

Approx Per Serving: Cal 577; Prot 12 g; Carbo 39 g; T Fat 42 g; 63% Calories from Fat; Chol 182 mg; Fiber 1 g; Sod 410 mg

Colleen A. Breister, HFH of Oshkosh Inc., Oshkosh, WI

Holly Sprigs   *Yield: 30 servings*

Great dessert for children to make.

30 marshmallows
¹/₂ cup butter
1 teaspoon vanilla extract
2 teaspoons green food coloring

3¹/₂ cups cornflakes
**¹/₂ to ³/₄ cup red hot cinnamon
   candies**

Combine marshmallows, butter and vanilla in microwave-safe dish. Microwave until smooth, stirring occasionally. Stir in food coloring. Add cornflakes, stirring until coated. Drop by teaspoonfuls onto waxed paper. Decorate with candies. May shape into wreaths on waxed paper and decorate with red candied cherries and silver dragées.

Approx Per Serving: Cal 86; Prot <1 g; Carbo 14 g; T Fat 3 g; 32% Calories from Fat; Chol 8 mg; Fiber <1 g; Sod 66 mg

Judy Swanson, HFH of Horry County, Conway, SC

Kringles

Yield: 10 servings

1 cup water
¹/₂ cup margarine
1 cup flour

1 teaspoon almond or vanilla extract
3 eggs

Bring water and margarine to a boil in saucepan. Boil until margarine melts. Add flour quickly, stirring with wooden spoon until smooth and mixture leaves side of pan. Stir in almond flavoring. Add eggs 1 at a time, beating well after each addition. Spoon into circles on greased cookie sheet. Bake at 400 degrees for 45 minutes. Remove to wire rack to cool. May fill with whipped topping.

Approx Per Serving: Cal 149; Prot 3 g; Carbo 10 g; T Fat 11 g; 65% Calories from Fat; Chol 64 mg; Fiber <1 g; Sod 126 mg

Darla K. Burkett, South Puget Sound HFH, Olympia, WA

Lime Cheesecake

Yield: 12 servings

1¹/₄ cups graham cracker crumbs
2 tablespoons sugar
¹/₄ cup melted butter or margarine
1 teaspoon grated lime rind
24 ounces cream cheese, softened

³/₄ cup sugar
3 eggs
1 tablespoon grated lime rind
¹/₄ cup fresh lime juice
1 teaspoon vanilla extract
2 cups sour cream
3 tablespoons sugar

Combine graham cracker crumbs, 2 tablespoons sugar, butter and 1 teaspoon lime rind in bowl; mix well. Press evenly over bottom and side of 9-inch springform pan. Bake at 350 degrees for 5 to 6 minutes or until brown. Let stand until cool. Beat cream cheese in mixer bowl until light and fluffy. Add ³/₄ cup sugar gradually, beating until smooth. Add eggs 1 at a time, beating well after each addition. Stir in 1 tablespoon lime rind, lime juice and vanilla. Spoon over baked layer. Bake at 375 degrees for 45 minutes or until set. Combine sour cream and 3 tablespoons sugar in bowl; mix well. Spread evenly over hot cheesecake. Bake at 500 degrees for 5 minutes. Cool on wire rack to room temperature. Chill for 8 hours or longer. Remove side of pan. Garnish with strawberries and lime slices.

Approx Per Serving: Cal 456; Prot 8 g; Carbo 31 g; T Fat 34 g; 66% Calories from Fat; Chol 143 mg; Fiber <1 g; Sod 318 mg

Joyce Irmen, Cumberland County HFH, Kettle, KY

Our eight-member family was living in a two-bedroom house that had been condemned by the county. They were kindly waiting for us to move, because they knew we had no place to go. Praise God, He provided a nice four-bedroom home for us through Habitat for Humanity.

DARLA K. BURKETT
SOUTH PUGET SOUND HFH

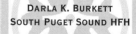

Macadamia Nut White Chocolate Chip Cookies

Yield: 36 servings

1/2 cup butter, softened
1/2 cup shortening
3/4 cup packed light brown sugar
2 tablespoons sugar
1 egg
1 1/2 teaspoons vanilla extract

2 cups flour
3/4 teaspoon baking soda
1/2 teaspoon baking powder
1/8 teaspoon salt
1 1/3 cups white chocolate chips
7 ounces salted whole macadamia nuts

Cream butter and shortening in mixer bowl until smooth, scraping bowl occasionally. Add brown sugar and sugar, beating until light and fluffy. Beat in egg and vanilla until blended. Add sifted mixture of flour, baking soda, baking powder and salt; mix well. Stir in white chocolate chips and macadamia nuts. Drop by rounded teaspoonfuls 2 1/2 inches apart onto greased cookie sheet; flatten slightly. Bake on middle shelf at 375 degrees for 8 to 9 minutes or until light brown; do not overbake. Cool in pan for 2 to 3 minutes. Remove to wire rack to cool completely. Store in airtight container.

Approx Per Serving: Cal 165; Prot 2 g; Carbo 14 g; T Fat 12 g; 62% Calories from Fat; Chol 14 mg; Fiber <1 g; Sod 78 mg

Sandy Hendershot, Greater Columbus HFH, Columbus, OH

The Habitat homes in Florida survived the hurricane because they were built on a solid foundation of love and the Rock of Christ Jesus.

JOYCE IRMEN
CUMBERLAND COUNTY HFH

Old English Cookies

Yield: 36 servings

1 teaspoon baking soda
1 cup strong coffee, chilled
1 cup shortening
2 cups packed brown sugar
1/2 cup sugar
3 eggs
1 teaspoon cinnamon
1 teaspoon ground cloves
1/4 teaspoon salt

1 cup plumped raisins, chilled
4 cups flour
1 teaspoon baking powder
2 cups sifted confectioners' sugar
3 tablespoons melted butter
1/2 teaspoon vanilla extract
1/4 cup light cream

Dissolve baking soda in coffee; mix well. Cream shortening, brown sugar, sugar, eggs, cinnamon, cloves and salt in mixer bowl. Add baking soda mixture and raisins; mix well. Stir in mixture of flour and baking powder. Spoon into greased and floured 10x15-inch baking pan. Bake at 350 degrees for 25 to 30 minutes or until edges pull from sides of pan. Beat confectioners' sugar, butter, vanilla and cream in mixer bowl until creamy. Spread over warm baked layer.

Approx Per Serving: Cal 198; Prot 2 g; Carbo 31 g; T Fat 8 g; 35% Calories from Fat; Chol 22 mg; Fiber <1 g; Sod 67 mg

Maizie Lanier, Marshall County HFH, Lacon, IL

Pumpkin Cake

Yield: 24 servings

1 cup vegetable oil
2 cups sugar
4 eggs
2 cups sifted flour
1 teaspoon salt
2 teaspoons cinnamon
1 teaspoon baking powder
2 teaspoons baking soda
1/2 teaspoon vanilla extract

1 (16-ounce) can pumpkin
4 ounces cream cheese,
    softened
1/4 cup butter or margarine,
    softened
1/2 (1-pound) package
    confectioners' sugar
1 teaspoon vanilla extract
1/2 cup chopped pecans

Cream oil and sugar in mixer bowl. Add eggs; mix well. Add mixture of flour, salt, cinnamon, baking powder and baking soda; mix well. Stir in 1/2 teaspoon vanilla and pumpkin. Spoon into greased 10x15-inch baking pan. Bake at 350 degrees for 40 to 50 minutes or until cake tests done. Let stand until cool. Beat cream cheese, butter, confectioners' sugar and 1 teaspoon vanilla in mixer bowl until of spreading consistency. Stir in pecans. Spread over baked layer.

Approx Per Serving: Cal 286; Prot 3 g; Carbo 36 g; T Fat 15 g; 47% Calories from Fat; Chol 46 mg; Fiber 1 g; Sod 216 mg

Eleanor Kruschke, Mesilla Valley HFH, Las Cruces, NM

Pumpkin Upside-Down Cake

Yield: 14 servings

3 eggs, lightly beaten
1 (29-ounce) can pumpkin
1 1/2 cups sugar
1 (12-ounce) can evaporated
    milk
2 teaspoons cinnamon

1 teaspoon nutmeg
1/2 teaspoon ginger
1 (2-layer) package yellow cake
    mix
3/4 cup melted margarine
1 cup chopped walnuts

Combine eggs, pumpkin, sugar, evaporated milk, cinnamon, nutmeg and ginger in bowl; mix well. Spoon into ungreased 9x13-inch cake pan. Sprinkle with cake mix; drizzle with melted margarine. Bake at 350 degrees for 30 minutes. Press walnuts gently into baked layer. Bake for 30 minutes longer or until brown. Let stand until cool. Serve with whipped cream.

Approx Per Serving: Cal 452; Prot 7 g; Carbo 59 g; T Fat 22 g; 43% Calories from Fat; Chol 53 mg; Fiber 3 g; Sod 398 mg

Beverly J. Anspaugh, Preble County HFH, New Madison, OH

Photo by Bill Sitterly

HABITAT PARTNERS IN PAPUA, NEW GUINEA

Pumpkin Praline Cake   *Yield: 12 servings*

1 cup packed brown sugar
1/2 cup margarine
1/4 cup whipping cream
3/4 cup chopped pecans
2 cups flour
2 teaspoons baking powder
2 teaspoons pumpkin pie spice
1 teaspoon baking soda
1 teaspoon salt

1 1/2 cups sugar
1 cup vegetable oil
4 eggs
2 cups canned pumpkin
1 3/4 cups whipping cream
1/4 cup confectioners' sugar,
**   sifted**
1/4 teaspoon vanilla extract

Combine brown sugar, margarine and 1/4 cup whipping cream in saucepan. Cook over low heat until sugar dissolves, stirring occasionally. Pour into two 9-inch round cake pans. Sprinkle with pecans. Combine flour, baking powder, pie spice, baking soda and salt in bowl; mix well. Beat sugar, oil and eggs in mixer bowl until blended. Add pumpkin and dry ingredients alternately, beating well after each addition. Spoon over pecans. Place pans on baking sheet. Bake at 350 degrees for 35 to 40 minutes or until layers test done. Cool in pans on wire rack for 5 minutes. Invert onto wire rack to cool. Spoon any topping that remains in pan over layers. Beat 1 3/4 cups whipping cream in mixer bowl until soft peaks form. Add confectioners' sugar and vanilla, beating constantly until stiff peaks form. Arrange 1 cake layer praline side up on serving platter. Spread with 3/4 of the whipped cream. Top with remaining cake layer praline side up. Dot top with remaining whipped cream. Chill until serving time.

Approx Per Serving: Cal 694; Prot 6 g; Carbo 64 g; T Fat 48 g; 60% Calories from Fat; Chol 125 mg; Fiber 2 g; Sod 435 mg

Cheri Timpel, Dane County HFH, Marshall, WI

Pumpkin Cake Roll

Yield: 8 servings

3 eggs
1 cup sugar
2/3 cup pumpkin
1 teaspoon lemon juice
3/4 cup flour
1 teaspoon baking powder
2 teaspoons cinnamon
1 teaspoon ginger

1/2 teaspoon salt
1/2 teaspoon nutmeg
1 cup finely chopped walnuts
1 cup confectioners' sugar
4 to 6 ounces cream cheese,
    softened
1/4 cup butter, softened
1/2 teaspoon vanilla extract

Beat eggs in mixer bowl at high speed for 5 minutes. Add sugar gradually, beating until blended. Stir in pumpkin and lemon juice. Fold in mixture of flour, baking powder, cinnamon, ginger, salt and nutmeg. Spoon into greased and floured 10x15-inch baking pan. Sprinkle with walnuts. Bake at 375 degrees for 15 minutes. Invert onto towel dusted with confectioners' sugar. Roll in towel as for jelly roll. Let stand until cool. Beat confectioners' sugar, cream cheese, butter and vanilla in mixer bowl until smooth. Unroll cake. Spread with cream cheese mixture; reroll. Chill until serving time. Garnish with whipped cream. May freeze for future use.

Approx Per Serving: Cal 455; Prot 8 g; Carbo 54 g; T Fat 25 g; 47% Calories from Fat; Chol 118 mg; Fiber 2 g; Sod 322 mg

Esther M. Bohlssen, HFH of Oshkosh Inc., Oshkosh, WI
Jan Russell, Washington County MD HFH, State Line, PA

Pumpkin Dip

Yield: 24 servings

8 ounces cream cheese
2 cups confectioners' sugar
1 (16-ounce) can pumpkin

1 teaspoon cinnamon
1/2 teaspoon ginger

Beat cream cheese in mixer bowl until light and fluffy. Add confectioners' sugar, pumpkin, cinnamon and ginger; mix well. Chill until serving time. Serve with apple slices, molasses cookies, gingersnap cookies or graham crackers.

Approx Per Serving: Cal 78; Prot 1 g; Carbo 12 g; T Fat 3 g; 37% Calories from Fat; Chol 10 mg; Fiber 1 g; Sod 29 mg

Mary Y. Cameron, Alpena Area HFH Inc., Ossineke, MI

"Sweat equity" is the unpaid labor invested by Habitat for Humanity homeowner partners in working on their own houses and/or those of others and are required hours for home ownership. Sweat equity also reduces the monetary cost of a house and increases the personal stake of each family member in their home.

Pumpkin Cheesecake   *Yield: 12 servings*

1²/₃ cups graham cracker crumbs
¹/₃ cup butter or margarine, softened
2 tablespoons light brown sugar
16 ounces cream cheese, softened
³/₄ cup packed light brown sugar
4 eggs
1 (16-ounce) can pumpkin

1 cup half-and-half
¹/₄ cup flour
2 teaspoons pumpkin pie spice
1 teaspoon vanilla extract
3 tablespoons graham cracker crumbs
2 tablespoons light brown sugar
1 tablespoon butter or margarine, softened
¹/₄ cup chopped walnuts

Combine 1²/₃ cups graham cracker crumbs, ¹/₃ cup butter and 2 tablespoons brown sugar in bowl, stirring with fork or pastry blender until crumbly. Press over bottom and 2 inches up side of 9-inch springform pan. Beat cream cheese in mixer bowl just until smooth. Add brown sugar gradually, beating just until light and fluffy. Add eggs 1 at a time, beating well after each addition. Beat in pumpkin, half-and-half, flour, pie spice and vanilla until blended. Spoon into prepared pan. Bake at 350 degrees for 60 to 70 minutes or until cheesecake tests done. Combine 3 tablespoons graham cracker crumbs, 2 tablespoons brown sugar and 1 tablespoon butter in bowl; mix well. Stir in walnuts. Spoon evenly over cheesecake. Turn off oven. Let cheesecake stand in oven with door slightly ajar for 1 hour. Remove to wire rack to cool completely. Chill for 4 to 10 hours before serving.

Approx Per Serving: Cal 408; Prot 8 g; Carbo 36 g; T Fat 27 g; 58% Calories from Fat; Chol 136 mg; Fiber 2 g; Sod 322 mg

Nancy Chance, Hamilton County HFH, Noblesville, IN

Habitat for Humanity is not a giveaway program, but is a joint venture in which those who benefit from this housing ministry are involved in the work at various levels along with those who desire to contribute their resources to make decent housing a reality.

Light Pumpkin Cheesecake

Yield: 16 servings

1¹/₂ cups graham cracker
  crumbs
2 tablespoons sugar
¹/₄ cup melted butter
24 ounces Neufchâtel cheese
³/₄ cup sugar
¹/₄ cup packed brown sugar
1 (16-ounce) can pumpkin

2 eggs
²/₃ cup evaporated skim milk
2 tablespoons cornstarch
1¹/₄ teaspoons cinnamon
¹/₂ teaspoon nutmeg
2 cups low-fat sour cream
¹/₄ cup sugar
1 teaspoon vanilla extract

Combine graham cracker crumbs, 2 tablespoons sugar and ¹/₄ cup butter in bowl; mix well. Pat over bottom and side of springform pan. Bake at 350 degrees for 6 to 8 minutes or until light brown. Let stand until cool. Beat Neufchâtel cheese, ³/₄ cup sugar and brown sugar in mixer bowl until light and fluffy. Beat in pumpkin, eggs and evaporated skim milk. Stir in cornstarch, cinnamon and nutmeg. Spread on baked layer. Bake at 350 degrees for 55 to 60 minutes or until cheesecake tests done. Combine sour cream, ¹/₄ cup sugar and vanilla in bowl; mix well. Spread over top of cheesecake. Bake for 5 minutes longer. Cool on wire rack. Remove side of pan. Chill until serving time.

Approx Per Serving: Cal 320; Prot 8 g; Carbo 32 g; T Fat 18 g; 51% Calories from Fat; Chol 79 mg; Fiber 1 g; Sod 302 mg

George Bready and Carrie Waters, Show-Me Central HFH
Columbia, MO

Pumpkin Mousse

Yield: 8 servings

1 tablespoon unflavored gelatin
¹/₂ cup dark rum
2 cups unsweetened pumpkin
1 teaspoon cinnamon
¹/₂ teaspoon salt
¹/₄ teaspoon ground cloves
4 egg yolks

¹/₂ cup packed brown sugar
¹/₂ cup sugar
¹/₄ cup unsalted butter
³/₄ cup whipping cream, stiffly
  beaten
4 egg whites
¹/₈ teaspoon cream of tartar

Soften gelatin in rum; mix well. Combine pumpkin, cinnamon, salt and cloves in bowl; mix well. Beat egg yolks in bowl until frothy. Add brown sugar and sugar, beating until thickened. Melt butter in double boiler. Stir in egg yolk mixture. Cook for 5 to 10 minutes or until thickened, stirring frequently. Add gelatin mixture, beating until smooth and shiny. Add to pumpkin mixture, stirring until blended. Let stand until room temperature. Fold in whipped cream. Beat egg whites with cream of tartar in mixer bowl until stiff peaks form. Fold into pumpkin mixture. Chill, covered with plastic wrap, for 2 to 10 hours. Spoon into 8 dessert bowls. Garnish with whipped cream and finely chopped candied ginger.

Approx Per Serving: Cal 304; Prot 5 g; Carbo 27 g; T Fat 17 g; 48% Calories from Fat; Chol 152 mg; Fiber 1 g; Sod 180 mg

Ann Marie McEntee, Jubilee HFH, Jacksonville, IL

Dark and Spicy Pumpkin Pie

Yield: 6 servings

2 eggs, beaten
1 cup packed dark brown sugar
1/2 teaspoon salt
1 tablespoon pumpkin pie spice
1 1/2 teaspoons cinnamon
3/4 teaspoon nutmeg

1 (16-ounce) can pumpkin
1 cup evaporated milk
1/2 cup maple syrup
1 unbaked (9-inch) deep-dish
   pie shell

Combine eggs, brown sugar, salt, pie spice, cinnamon, nutmeg, pumpkin, evaporated milk and maple syrup in bowl; mix well. Spoon into pie shell. Bake at 425 degrees for 15 minutes. Reduce oven temperature to 350 degrees. Bake for 30 minutes longer or until knife inserted halfway between center and edge comes out clean. Let stand until cool. Serve with whipped topping.

Approx Per Serving: Cal 458; Prot 8 g; Carbo 73 g; T Fat 16 g; 31% Calories from Fat; Chol 83 mg; Fiber 3 g; Sod 463 mg

Shawn S. Means, Mountaineer HFH, Charleston, WV

Homemade Pumpkin Pie

Yield: 6 servings

1 cup fresh strained cooked
   pumpkin
4 eggs, beaten
1 cup milk
1/2 teaspoon salt
3/4 cup sugar

1 teaspoon cinnamon
1 teaspoon nutmeg
1 teaspoon ginger
2 tablespoons cornstarch
1 recipe (1-crust) pie pastry

Combine pumpkin, eggs, milk and salt in bowl; mix well. Add mixture of sugar, cinnamon, nutmeg, ginger and cornstarch; mix well. Spoon into pastry-lined pie shell. Bake at 425 degrees for 15 minutes. Reduce oven temperature to 350 degrees. Bake for 50 minutes longer.

Approx Per Serving: Cal 348; Prot 8 g; Carbo 46 g; T Fat 15 g; 39% Calories from Fat; Chol 147 mg; Fiber 1 g; Sod 403 mg

Bob Tyrrel, Las Vegas NM HFH, Las Vegas, NM

Pumpkin Chiffon Pie

Yield: 6 servings

1 envelope unflavored gelatin
1/4 cup cold water
2/3 cup brown sugar
1/2 teaspoon salt
1/2 teaspoon cinnamon
1/2 teaspoon nutmeg
1/2 teaspoon ginger

11/4 cups mashed cooked
  pumpkin
3 egg yolks, beaten
1/2 cup milk
1 baked (9-inch) pie shell
3 egg whites
1/2 cup sugar

Soften gelatin in cold water; mix well. Bring gelatin, brown sugar, salt, cinnamon, nutmeg, ginger, pumpkin, egg yolks and milk to a boil in saucepan, stirring constantly. Remove from heat. Place saucepan in larger pan filled with cold water. Let stand until mixture mounds slightly when dropped from spoon. Beat egg whites in mixer bowl until soft peaks form. Add sugar gradually, beating constantly until stiff peaks form. Fold in pumpkin mixture. Spoon into pie shell. Chill for 2 hours or until set. Garnish with whipped cream.

Approx Per Serving: Cal 348; Prot 7 g; Carbo 50 g; T Fat 14 g; 35% Calories from Fat; Chol 109 mg; Fiber 1 g; Sod 390 mg

Marilyn C. Tilford, Foothills HFH, Grass Valley, CA

Sugar-Free Pumpkin Chiffon Dessert

Yield: 12 servings

2 envelopes unflavored gelatin
1/2 cup cold water
1 cup flour
1/2 cup chopped pecans
4 tablespoons melted margarine
6 egg yolks, beaten
2 (16-ounce) cans unsweetened
  pumpkin

2 teaspoons cinnamon
1 teaspoon nutmeg
2 teaspoons ginger
2 cups skim milk
6 egg whites, chilled
1/2 teaspoon cream of tartar
18 to 20 envelopes artificial
  sweetener

Soften gelatin in cold water; mix well. Combine flour, pecans and margarine in bowl; mix well. Press over bottom and 1/4 inch up side of 9-inch springform pan. Bake at 350 degrees for 15 minutes. Let stand until cool. Combine egg yolks, pumpkin, cinnamon, nutmeg, ginger and skim milk in saucepan; mix well. Cook over low heat until mixture comes to a boil, stirring constantly. Cook for 2 minutes longer, stirring constantly. Stir in gelatin. Cook until gelatin dissolves, stirring constantly. Let stand until cool. Beat egg whites in mixer bowl until soft peaks form. Add cream of tartar and artificial sweetener, beating constantly until stiff peaks form. Fold into pumpkin mixture. Spread over baked layer. Chill until set. Garnish with sugar-free whipped topping. May add 1 teaspoon salt to pumpkin mixture.

Approx Per Serving: Cal 211; Prot 8 g; Carbo 19 g; T Fat 12 g; 50% Calories from Fat; Chol 107 mg; Fiber 3 g; Sod 132 mg

Jody A. Brashear, Loudon County HFH Inc., Loudon, TN

Praline Pumpkin Pie

Yield: 6 servings

1/3 cup finely chopped pecans
1/3 cup packed brown sugar
3 tablespoons butter or
    margarine, softened
1 unbaked (9-inch) pie shell
3 eggs, lightly beaten
1/2 cup sugar
1/2 cup packed brown sugar
2 tablespoons flour

3/4 teaspoon salt
3/4 teaspoon cinnamon
1/2 teaspoon ginger
1/4 teaspoon ground cloves
1/4 teaspoon mace
11/2 cups drained cooked
    pumpkin
11/4 cups light cream, heated

Combine pecans, 1/3 cup brown sugar and butter in bowl; mix well. Press over bottom of pie shell. Prick side of pie shell. Bake at 450 degrees for 10 minutes. Cool for 2 minutes or longer. Combine eggs, sugar, 1/2 cup brown sugar, flour, salt, cinnamon, ginger, cloves, mace, pumpkin and cream in bowl; mix well. Pour over pecan mixture. Bake at 350 degrees for 50 to 60 minutes or until set. Let stand until cool. Garnish with whipped topping.

Approx Per Serving: Cal 617; Prot 7 g; Carbo 63 g; T Fat 39 g; 55% Calories from Fat; Chol 177 mg; Fiber 2 g; Sod 547 mg

Betty A. Woodell, Calcasieu Area HFH, Lake Charles, LA

Sherry Trifle

Yield: 16 servings

1 (4-ounce) package vanilla
    instant pudding mix
11/2 cups water
1 (14-ounce) can sweetened
    condensed milk
2 cups whipping cream,
    whipped

1 angel food cake, torn into
    bite-size pieces
1/2 cup sherry
1 (16-ounce) can peaches,
    drained, thinly sliced
1 (16-ounce) jar raspberry
    preserves

Combine pudding mix and water in bowl; mix well. Add condensed milk, beating until blended. Chill for 5 to 10 minutes. Fold in whipped cream. Chill for 5 to 10 minutes. Layer angel food cake pieces, sherry, peaches, preserves and pudding mixture 1/2 at a time in large serving bowl. Chill for 4 to 10 hours.

Approx Per Serving: Cal 396; Prot 5 g; Carbo 66 g; T Fat 13 g; 29% Calories from Fat; Chol 49 mg; Fiber 1 g; Sod 348 mg

Betty Jane Monsees, Flager HFH Inc., Palm Coast, IL

I did not remember to take a hat to our first work site, so I made a paper hat. Neighborhood children walking by asked, "Where did you get that hat?" I replied, "I made it." The children asked me to help them make hats. I showed them how to make the hats using newspapers. They in return helped me pick up trash on the lot and became Habitat Partners.

BETTY A. WOODELL
CALCASIEU AREA HFH

Mocha Shortbread with Raspberry Sauce

Yield: 6 servings

1/2 cup melted unsalted butter
1/3 cup confectioners' sugar
1/4 teaspoon salt
11 tablespoons flour
1/2 cup baking cocoa

1 teaspoon instant coffee granules
1/2 cup raspberry preserves
1 tablespoon raspberry liqueur

Combine butter, confectioners' sugar, salt, flour, baking cocoa and coffee granules in bowl; mix well. Press into ungreased 8- or 9-inch round baking dish. Score dough into 6 wedges. Bake at 350 degrees for 20 to 25 minutes or until shortbread tests done. Let stand until cool. Cut into wedges. Arrange shortbread on dessert plates; drizzle with mixture of preserves and liqueur. Garnish with fresh raspberries and fresh mint.

Approx Per Serving: Cal 305; Prot 3 g; Carbo 40 g; T Fat 17 g; 45% Calories from Fat; Chol 41 mg; Fiber 3 g; Sod 104 mg

Lynn Haviland-Samuelson, S.W. Iowa HFH, Shenandoah, IA

Granny's Spice Cookies

Yield: 48 servings

1 cup butter or margarine, softened
1 1/2 cups sugar
1 egg, lightly beaten
2 tablespoons light corn syrup
2 tablespoons grated orange rind

1 tablespoon cold water
3 1/4 cups flour
2 teaspoons baking soda
2 teaspoons cinnamon
1 teaspoon ginger
1/2 teaspoon ground cloves

Cream butter and sugar in mixer bowl until light and fluffy. Add egg, corn syrup, orange rind and cold water; mix well. Add mixture of flour, baking soda, cinnamon, ginger and cloves, mixing until blended. Chill for 1 hour or longer. Roll dough 1/8 inch thick on lightly floured surface; cut with cookie cutter. Place on greased cookie sheet. Decorate with candies of your choice. Bake at 375 degrees for 6 to 8 minutes or until light brown. Remove to wire rack to cool.

Approx Per Serving: Cal 93; Prot 1 g; Carbo 13 g; T Fat 4 g; 38% Calories from Fat; Chol 15 mg; Fiber <1 g; Sod 76 mg

Valerie Hudson, Cerro Gordo Area HFH, Mason City, IA

Strawberry Trifle

Yield: 12 servings

1 (2-layer) package yellow cake mix
2 (4-ounce) packages vanilla instant pudding mix, prepared
2 (10-ounce) packages frozen sliced strawberries, thawed
2 teaspoons vanilla extract
16 ounces whipped topping
2 cups sliced or whole strawberries
1/2 cup slivered almonds

Prepare and bake cake using package directions for two 8-inch round cake pans. Remove to wire rack to cool. Slice each layer horizontally into halves. Place 1 layer in glass serving bowl. Spread with 1/2 of the pudding and 1/2 of the undrained frozen strawberries in order listed. Loosen layers from side of bowl with sharp knife to allow strawberry juice to flow down side forming design. Arrange 2 cake layers over strawberries. Layer with remaining pudding and undrained strawberries. Top with remaining cake layer. Spread with mixture of vanilla and whipped topping. Top with 2 cups sliced or whole strawberries; sprinkle with almonds.

Approx Per Serving: Cal 507; Prot 8 g; Carbo 72 g; T Fat 21 g; 38% Calories from Fat; Chol 50 mg; Fiber 3 g; Sod 609 mg

Nola Bernstein, Henderson HFH, Henderson, KY

Tutti-Frutti Pudding Cake

Yield: 9 servings

1 egg, beaten
3/4 cup sugar
1 (16-ounce) can fruit cocktail, partially drained
1 cup flour
1/2 teaspoon cinnamon
1/4 teaspoon nutmeg
1/4 teaspoon ground cloves
1 teaspoon baking soda
3/4 cup packed brown sugar
1/2 teaspoon cinnamon
1/2 cup chopped walnuts

Combine egg, sugar and fruit cocktail in bowl; mix well. Add sifted mixture of flour, 1/2 teaspoon cinnamon, nutmeg, cloves and baking soda; mix well. Spoon into greased 9x9-inch baking pan. Sprinkle with mixture of brown sugar, 1/2 teaspoon cinnamon and walnuts. Bake at 325 degrees for 1 1/4 hours. Serve warm with whipped topping or ice cream. May substitute pecans for walnuts.

Approx Per Serving: Cal 260; Prot 3 g; Carbo 53 g; T Fat 5 g; 16% Calories from Fat; Chol 24 mg; Fiber 1 g; Sod 108 mg

Gloria B. Webster, HFH of Flagstaff, Flagstaff, AZ

INTERNATIONAL FAVORITES

"But the fruit of the Spirit is love, joy, peace, longsuffering, kindness, goodness, faithfulness, gentleness, self-control. Against such there is no law."

-Galatians 5:22-23

Amish Cookies

Yield: 90 servings

1 cup sugar
1 cup confectioners' sugar
1/2 cup margarine, softened
1/2 cup butter, softened
1 cup vegetable oil
2 eggs

2 teaspoons vanilla extract
4 1/2 cups flour
1 teaspoon baking soda
3/4 teaspoon cinnamon
1 teaspoon cream of tartar

Beat sugar, confectioners' sugar, margarine, butter, oil, eggs and vanilla in mixer bowl until smooth. Add flour, baking soda, cinnamon and cream of tartar, beating until blended. Shape into balls. Place on ungreased cookie sheet; flatten with fork. Bake at 350 degrees for 7 to 9 minutes or until light brown. Remove to wire rack to cool. May chill dough for 2 to 10 hours before baking.

Approx Per Serving: Cal 78; Prot 1 g; Carbo 8 g; T Fat 5 g; 53% Calories from Fat; Chol 7 mg; Fiber <1 g; Sod 33 mg

Carol Lowe, Callaway County HFH, Fulton, MO

Anise Cookies

Yield: 48 servings

3 eggs
1 cup sugar
1 cup milk
1 cup margarine, softened
1 tablespoon (rounded) shortening

1 (1-ounce) bottle anise extract
1 tablespoon (heaping) baking powder
5 cups (or more) flour

Combine eggs, sugar, milk, margarine, shortening, anise extract and baking powder in bowl, mixing until blended. Add flour, stirring until soft dough forms. Drop by teaspoonfuls onto cookie sheet. Bake at 375 degrees for 8 to 10 minutes; do not allow to brown. Cool completely on cookie sheet. May drizzle with confectioners' sugar glaze.

Approx Per Serving: Cal 110; Prot 2 g; Carbo 15 g; T Fat 5 g; 39% Calories from Fat; Chol 14 mg; Fiber <1 g; Sod 72 mg

Josephine Demidio, Wyoming Valley HFH, Wyoming, PA

Apricot Baklava

Yield: 24 servings

2 cups dried apricots
2 cups apricot juice
4 eggs
1 (16-ounce) package phyllo
   dough

1/2 cup melted butter
3 cups finely chopped toasted
   almonds
1 cup honey

Simmer apricots in juice in saucepan for 1 hour. Let stand until cool. Process apricot mixture and eggs in food processor until puréed. Layer 2 sheets phyllo dough on buttered baking sheet; cover remaining phyllo dough with damp cloth to prevent drying out. Brush with butter; sprinkle with almonds. Repeat process until 1/2 of the phyllo dough is used. Spread with apricot purée. Layer remaining phyllo, remaining butter and remaining almonds alternately over apricot layers until all ingredients are used, ending with almonds. Score top layers with sharp knife in diamond pattern. Bake at 350 degrees for 30 minutes. Cool for 20 minutes. Drizzle with honey.

Approx Per Serving: Cal 279; Prot 6 g; Carbo 35 g; T Fat 14 g; 44% Calories from Fat; Chol 46 mg; Fiber 3 g; Sod 145 mg

Nancy J. MacLeod, HFH of Green County WI, Monroe, WI

Brandied Bread Pudding

Yield: 8 servings

This recipe originated in Puerto Rico.

1 (16-ounce) loaf dry bread,
   crusts trimmed
4 cups milk
1 cup coconut cream
5 eggs, lightly beaten
1/2 teaspoon salt
1/4 cup sugar
1/2 teaspoon cinnamon
1/4 cup ground almonds

1/2 cup raisins
1/4 cup melted butter
1/2 cup butter, softened
3/4 cup sugar
2 tablespoons brandy
2 egg yolks
1/4 cup milk
2 egg whites

Tear bread into bite-size pieces in bowl. Pour 4 cups milk over bread. Let stand for 10 minutes. Mash until blended. Stir in coconut cream, eggs, salt, 1/4 cup sugar, cinnamon, almonds, raisins and 1/4 cup melted butter. Pour into greased 2 1/2-quart baking dish. Place in larger pan; add hot water to depth of 1 inch. Bake at 350 degrees for 1 1/2 hours. Let stand until cool. Cream 1/2 cup softened butter and 3/4 cup sugar in microwave-safe bowl until light and fluffy. Add brandy, egg yolks and 1/4 cup milk; mix well. Microwave until slightly thickened, stirring frequently. Let stand until cool. Beat egg whites in mixer bowl until frothy. Fold into brandy mixture. Pour over bread pudding.

Approx Per Serving: Cal 667; Prot 16 g; Carbo 71 g; T Fat 36 g; 48% Calories from Fat; Chol 250 mg; Fiber 2 g; Sod 734 mg

Denise L. Ruwe, West Chester/Mason HFH, West Chester, OH

Butter Kuchen

Yield: 12 servings

This recipe was translated to me by my husband, Wolfgang. It is a special "Kuchen" that his mother prepared for the family when he was a child growing up in Germany.

1 cup milk	1/4 cup melted butter, cooled
1 teaspoon sugar	1/2 teaspoon vanilla extract
1 envelope dry yeast	1/2 teaspoon almond extract
2 cups flour	1/4 cup melted butter
6 tablespoons sugar	1/4 cup butter, cut into 12 pieces
1/2 teaspoon almond extract	6 tablespoons sugar
1/4 teaspoon salt	1/3 cup sliced almonds

Scald milk in saucepan. Cool to 115 degrees. Combine 1/3 cup of the milk with 1 teaspoon sugar and yeast in bowl; mix well. Let stand for 5 to 10 minutes or until yeast dissolves and mixture bubbles. Place 1 1/2 cups of the flour in bowl; make well in center. Pour yeast mixture into well. Let stand for several minutes. Stir in remaining milk, 6 tablespoons sugar, 1/2 teaspoon almond extract, salt, 1/4 cup melted butter and enough remaining flour to make a soft dough. Let rise until doubled in bulk. Roll into 10x15-inch rectangle on lightly floured surface. Fit into buttered 10x15-inch pan; roll to edges. Brush with mixture of 1/2 teaspoon vanilla, 1/2 teaspoon almond extract and 1/4 cup melted butter. Press remaining 1/4 cup butter into dough. Sprinkle with 6 tablespoons sugar and almonds. Let rise until double in bulk. Bake at 350 degrees for 20 to 30 minutes or until brown. May double recipe and bake in two 10x15-inch baking pans.

Approx Per Serving: Cal 257; Prot 4 g; Carbo 30 g; T Fat 14 g; 48% Calories from Fat; Chol 34 mg; Fiber 1 g; Sod 173 mg

Kathleen Schmidt, Black Hills Area HFH, Nemo, SD

Date-Filled Oatmeal Cookies

Yield: 24 servings

This recipe originates from a Scotch-Irish immigrant family.

1/2 cup butter, softened
1/2 cup lard
1 cup packed brown sugar
2 cups rolled oats
2 cups flour
2 tablespoons baking powder
1 teaspoon salt
1/2 cup milk
8 ounces dates, chopped
1/4 cup packed brown sugar
1/2 cup water

Cream butter, lard and 1 cup brown sugar in mixer bowl until light and fluffy. Stir in oats. Add sifted mixture of flour, baking powder and salt; mix well. Stir in milk. Shape into balls. Place on greased cookie sheet; flatten with bottom of glass. Bake at 350 degrees just until edges turn brown. Remove to wire rack to cool. Combine dates, 1/4 cup brown sugar and water in saucepan; mix well. Simmer until of desired consistency, stirring frequently. Spread date filling on half the cookies; top with remaining cookies.

Approx Per Serving: Cal 202; Prot 3 g; Carbo 29 g; T Fat 9 g; 39% Calories from Fat; Chol 15 mg; Fiber 2 g; Sod 217 mg

Elizabeth H. Stewart, Flower City HFH, Rochester, NY

English Lemon Curd Tart

Yield: 8 servings

1/2 cup butter, softened
2 cups flour
1 egg yolk
1/4 cup confectioners' sugar
6 tablespoons water
4 egg yolks
1/2 cup sugar
2 ounces ground almonds
1/2 cup melted unsalted butter
5 ounces whipping cream
Juice of 2 lemons
Grated rind of 1 lemon

Cut 1/2 cup butter into flour in bowl until crumbly. Add 1 egg yolk, confectioners' sugar and water, mixing until mixture forms ball. Roll into circle to fit 10-inch flan pan on lightly floured surface. Line flan pan with pastry. Beat 4 egg yolks and sugar in mixer bowl until blended. Add almonds, 1/2 cup butter, whipping cream and lemon juice, beating until mixed. Fold in lemon rind. Spoon into prepared flan pan. Bake at 350 degrees for 40 minutes.

Approx Per Serving: Cal 523; Prot 7 g; Carbo 43 g; T Fat 37 g; 62% Calories from Fat; Chol 219 mg; Fiber 2 g; Sod 132 mg

Christine Hill, Sunderland, England

accomplishment the team felt, proudly displaying their day's work. But all of us "earth movers" had a good chuckle, seeing what seemed like such a small amount of dirt for a day's work. The leader expressed profound gratitude for our work. What a truly great organization—the camaraderie is inexpressible!

DENISE L. RUWE
WEST CHESTER/MASON HFH

Galettes
(French Waffle Cookies)

Yield: 48 servings

6 eggs
2 cups butter, softened
4 cups sugar
1/4 cup blackberry brandy
1 dash of cinnamon
1 dash of nutmeg
8 cups flour

Whisk eggs in bowl until blended. Combine butter and sugar in bowl; mix well. Add eggs; mix with whisk. Stir in brandy, cinnamon and nutmeg. Add flour; mix well. Shape into ball; dough will be sticky. Let stand, covered with towel, for 12 hours to 1 1/2 days. Turn dough. Let stand, covered with towel, for 12 hours longer. Shape dough into 1-inch balls. Place on cookie sheet. Bake using a galette iron according to manufacturer's directions. A galette iron is a cookie waffle iron with long handles. Cookies are baked by placing the iron on a heated burner and baking the cookies until brown on both sides, turning once.

Approx Per Serving: Cal 220; Prot 3 g; Carbo 33 g; T Fat 9 g; 35% Calories from Fat; Chol 47 mg; Fiber 1 g; Sod 87 mg

Veda Bafford, HFH of Iredell-Statesville, Statesville, NC

Houska
(Czech Holiday Bread)

Yield: 24 servings

2 cakes yeast
1 teaspoon sugar
2 cups milk, scalded, cooled to
    lukewarm
1/2 cup unsalted butter, softened
1 cup sugar
2 egg yolks
1 egg
1 teaspoon nutmeg
1 teaspoon salt
1 1/2 cup golden raisins
1/4 cup slivered almonds
6 cups sifted flour
2 egg whites, lightly beaten

Crumble yeast into bowl. Add 1 teaspoon sugar and 1/4 cup of the milk. Let stand for 5 minutes or until of sponge consistency. Cream butter in mixer bowl. Add 1 cup sugar, beating until light and fluffy. Beat in egg yolks and egg until smooth. Stir in nutmeg, salt, raisins, almonds and remaining milk. Add flour gradually, mixing until easily handled dough is formed. Knead until smooth and elastic; dough should be slightly sticky. Place in lightly greased bowl, turning to coat surface. Let rise for 2 hours or until doubled in bulk. Divide dough into 2 portions. Divide each portion into 4 large pieces, 3 medium pieces and 2 small pieces. Roll each piece into rope. Braid 4 large ropes; place in bottom of lightly greased loaf pan. Braid 3 medium ropes; place over prepared layer. Braid 2 small ropes; place on top. Repeat process with remaining dough portion. Let rise for 1 hour or until doubled in bulk. Brush with egg whites. Bake at 350 degrees for 50 minutes.

Approx Per Serving: Cal 235; Prot 5 g; Carbo 40 g; T Fat 6 g; 24% Calories from Fat; Chol 40 mg; Fiber 2 g; Sod 109 mg

George J. Kyncl, Morgan County HFH, Fort Morgan, CO

Hungarian Cookies

Yield: 24 servings

3¹/₂ cups flour
1 cup unsalted butter
3 eggs
1 cup sugar
4 teaspoons baking powder

¹/₂ cup milk
1 egg white, beaten until frothy
1 cup ground walnuts
1 cup sugar

Combine flour and butter in mixer bowl; mix well. Add eggs, 1 cup sugar, baking powder and milk. Beat at medium speed until smooth. Knead until easily handled dough forms. Shape into log; cut into 1-inch slices. Dip 1 side of each slice in egg white; dip in mixture of walnuts and 1 cup sugar. Place sugar side up 1 inch apart on greased cookie sheet. Bake at 325 degrees for 20 to 30 minutes or until light brown.

Approx Per Serving: Cal 233; Prot 4 g; Carbo 31 g; T Fat 11 g; 40% Calories from Fat; Chol 48 mg; Fiber 1 g; Sod 69 mg

Joyce M. Hales, HFH Venice Area Inc., Sarasota, FL

Mexican Flan

Yield: 6 servings

¹/₃ cup sugar
4 eggs
²/₃ cup sugar

2 cups milk
1 (1¹/₂-inch) cinnamon stick
³/₄ teaspoon vanilla extract

Heat ¹/₃ cup sugar in heavy skillet over medium heat until sugar melts; do not stir. Cook 3 to 4 minutes longer or until golden brown. Pour into 1¹/₂- to 2-quart dish, swirling to coat side and bottom. Let stand until cool. Beat eggs in mixer bowl. Add ²/₃ cup sugar gradually, beating constantly until blended. Heat milk and cinnamon stick in saucepan until mixture bubbles. Discard cinnamon stick. Cool slightly. Pour into egg mixture gradually, stirring constantly until blended. Stir in vanilla. Pour into prepared dish. Place in larger baking pan; add hot water to depth of 1 inch. Bake at 325 degrees for 40 minutes or until knife inserted in center comes out clean. Let stand until cool. Chill until serving time. Invert onto serving platter. Garnish with fresh fruit.

Approx Per Serving: Cal 232; Prot 7 g; Carbo 39 g; T Fat 6 g; 23% Calories from Fat; Chol 152 mg; Fiber 0 g; Sod 82 mg

Faye Cook, HFH of East King County, Carnation, WA

After serving as President of the United States, Rosalynn and I believed it was important for us to continue to make a meaningful contribution to people's lives. And we have, with Habitat for Humanity. We believe in Habitat's integrity, effectiveness and tremendous vision. With Habitat, we build more than houses. We build families, communities and hope.

FORMER PRESIDENT JIMMY CARTER HFH VOLUNTEER

Norwegian Chocolate Cake

Yield: 15 servings

2 cups packed brown sugar
1/2 cup butter, softened
1/2 cup sour milk
2 teaspoons baking soda
2 cups flour
1 cup boiling water
2 (1-ounce) squares chocolate, chopped

2 eggs
4 1/2 tablespoons sugar
2 tablespoons water
2/3 cup shortening
2 1/2 cups confectioners' sugar
1 egg
1 tablespoon vanilla extract

Cream brown sugar and butter in mixer bowl until light and fluffy. Add sour milk and sifted mixture of baking soda and flour. Add 1/2 cup of the boiling water. Beat for 2 minutes, scraping bowl occasionally. Add chocolate, 2 eggs and remaining boiling water. Beat for 2 minutes, scraping bowl occasionally. Spoon into cake pan. Bake at 350 degrees for 40 minutes. Bring sugar and 2 tablespoons water to a boil in saucepan. Boil until of syrupy consistency, stirring frequently. Remove from heat. Cream shortening, confectioners' sugar, 1 egg and vanilla in mixer bowl until light and fluffy. Add syrup gradually, beating constantly until blended. Spread evenly over cake.

Approx Per Serving: Cal 421; Prot 4 g; Carbo 62 g; T Fat 19 g; 39% Calories from Fat; Chol 60 mg; Fiber 1 g; Sod 199 mg

Betty Rude, HFH of Missoula, Missoula, MT

Pennsylvania Dutch Shoofly Pies

Yield: 12 servings

1 teaspoon (heaping) baking soda
1/2 teaspoon vinegar
1 cup molasses
1 cup boiling water

2 unbaked (9-inch) pie shells
3 cups flour
1 cup packed brown sugar
1/4 teaspoon salt
1/2 cup butter, softened

Dissolve baking soda in vinegar; mix well. Combine molasses and boiling water in bowl; mix well. Stir in baking soda mixture. Pour into pie shells. Combine flour, brown sugar and salt in bowl; mix well. Cut in butter until crumbly. Sprinkle over pie fillings. Bake at 350 degrees for 30 minutes.

Approx Per Serving: Cal 469; Prot 5 g; Carbo 72 g; T Fat 18 g; 35% Calories from Fat; Chol 21 mg; Fiber 1 g; Sod 370 mg

Betsy Levin, HFH of the Lehigh Valley, Allentown, PA

Potica
(Slovenian Nut Roll)

Yield: 60 servings

Potica is an essential part of any celebration in a Slovenian family.

2 envelopes dry yeast	1/2 cup butter or margarine
1 tablespoon sugar	1 1/2 cups half-and-half
1/2 cup lukewarm water	2 cups sugar
1 1/2 cups milk	1/2 cup honey
1/2 cup butter	1 tablespoon vanilla extract
5 egg yolks	2 pounds walnuts, finely ground
3/4 cup sugar	5 egg whites, stiffly beaten
2 teaspoons salt	2 cups dark raisins
1 tablespoon vanilla extract	2 cups golden raisins
7 to 8 cups flour, sifted	

Sprinkle yeast and 1 tablespoon sugar over water; mix well. Let stand in warm place for 10 minutes or until foamy. Scald milk in saucepan. Add butter, stirring until blended. Cool to lukewarm. Beat egg yolks, 3/4 cup sugar, salt and 1 tablespoon vanilla in mixer bowl until blended. Add yeast mixture and egg mixture to milk mixture; mix well. Add flour gradually, beating with wooden spoon until easily handled dough is formed. Knead on floured surface for 15 minutes or until smooth and elastic. Place in greased bowl, turning to coat surface. Let rise, covered with towel, in warm place for 2 hours or until doubled in bulk. Heat 1/2 cup butter in saucepan until melted. Stir in half-and-half, 2 cups sugar, honey and 1 tablespoon vanilla. Bring to a rolling boil. Pour over walnuts in bowl; mix well. Let stand until cool. Fold in egg whites. Roll dough into 3x4 foot rectangle on floured surface. Spread with walnut mixture; sprinkle with raisins. Roll as for jelly roll; cut into 5 loaves. Place loaves seam side down in five 5x9-inch loaf pans. Let rise for 1 hour. Bake at 325 degrees for 1 hour. Invert onto wire rack to cool.

Approx Per Serving: Cal 283; Prot 5 g; Carbo 37 g; T Fat 14 g; 43% Calories from Fat; Chol 29 mg; Fiber 2 g; Sod 116 mg

Juanell Boyd and Barbara Van Dewoestine, Southeastern Steuben County HFH, Horseheads, NY

Pfefferneusse (Pepper Nuts)

Yield: 270 servings

This recipe has been in our family for many generations and has been improved by my mother until the cookies are simply perfect!

1 cup molasses
1 cup light corn syrup
1 cup plus 2 tablespoons
   packed brown sugar
1/2 cup butter or margarine
1/2 cup shortening
1/2 to 3/4 teaspoon pepper
1/2 teaspoon ground cloves
1/2 teaspoon allspice

1 teaspoon cinnamon
1 1/4 teaspoons ground anise
1/4 teaspoon ginger
1/4 teaspoon salt
2 eggs, beaten
8 cups flour
1 teaspoon baking powder
1/2 teaspoon baking soda

Combine molasses, corn syrup, brown sugar, butter and shortening in saucepan. Cook until blended, stirring frequently. Cool slightly. Combine with pepper, cloves, allspice, cinnamon, anise, ginger and salt in bowl; mix well. Add eggs; mix well. Stir in mixture of flour, baking powder and baking soda. Let stand, covered, for 8 to 10 hours. Shape into 1-inch balls. Place on greased cookie sheet. Bake at 325 degrees for 10 to 15 minutes or until light brown. Store in airtight container in cool dark place for 2 weeks before serving. May freeze for future use. May add chopped nuts.

Approx Per Serving: Cal 30; Prot <1 g; Carbo 5 g; T Fat 1 g; 24% Calories from Fat; Chol 2 mg; Fiber <1 g; Sod 11 mg

Mary Sue Weston, HFH of St. Joseph County, Constantine, MI

Sailor Duff

Yield: 8 servings

1 teaspoon baking soda
2 tablespoons (or more) warm
   water
1 egg
2 tablespoons sugar
1/2 cup molasses
2 tablespoons melted butter

1 1/2 cups cake flour
1/2 cup boiling water
2 egg yolks, beaten
1 cup confectioners' sugar
1 teaspoon vanilla extract
1 cup whipped cream

Dissolve baking soda in warm water in bowl; mix well. Beat egg and sugar in mixer bowl until smooth. Add molasses, beating until blended. Beat in butter until smooth. Add baking soda mixture; mix well. Add cake flour; mix well. Stir in boiling water. Steam in steamer for 45 minutes. Beat egg yolks, confectioners sugar and vanilla in mixer bowl until of desired consistency. Fold in whipped cream just before serving. Spoon over warm pudding.

Approx Per Serving: Cal 299; Prot 3 g; Carbo 44 g; T Fat 13 g; 38% Calories from Fat; Chol 108 mg; Fiber <1 g; Sod 222 mg

Catharine P. Engle, Barry County HFH, Hastings, MI

Scandinavian Sweet Soup

Yield: 8 servings

1/2 cup minute tapioca
2 1/2 cups boiling water
1 cup sugar
1 cinnamon stick
1 cup raisins
1 cup prunes
1 cup dried apricots
1 cup chopped apple
1 tablespoon vinegar
1 cup grape juice

Stir tapioca into boiling water in saucepan. Add sugar, cinnamon stick, raisins, prunes, apricots, apple and vinegar; mix well. Bring to a boil; reduce heat. Simmer until fruit is tender, stirring occasionally. Stir in grape juice. Discard cinnamon stick. Serve hot.

Approx Per Serving: Cal 306; Prot 2 g; Carbo 79 g; T Fat <1 g; 1% Calories from Fat; Chol 0 mg; Fiber 4 g; Sod 6 mg

Barb Sanderson, Itasca County HFH, Grand Rapids, MN

Scottish Shortbread

Yield: 20 servings

1 cup butter, softened
1/2 cup sugar
1/4 teaspoon salt
2 cups flour

Cream butter, sugar and salt in mixer bowl until light and fluffy. Add flour, mixing until blended. Press into 9x9-inch baking pan or spring-form pan. Prick lines with fork into dough. Bake at 325 degrees for 25 to 30 minutes or just until edges turn golden brown. Cut into squares while warm. May cool and break along pierced lines. May add vanilla and ground lemon rind to dough. May substitute 1 cup whole wheat flour for 1 cup of the all-purpose flour.

Approx Per Serving: Cal 146; Prot 1 g; Carbo 15 g; T Fat 9 g; 57% Calories from Fat; Chol 25 mg; Fiber <1 g; Sod 121 mg

Elizabeth H. Stewart

Grandma Nixon's Scotch Shortbread

Yield: 8 servings

1 cup packed brown sugar
5 cups flour
2 cups butter, softened

Sift brown sugar and flour into bowl; mix well. Cut in butter until crumbly. Roll 3/4 inch thick on lightly floured surface; cut with 4-inch cutter. Place on baking sheet. Prick in design of choice with fork. Bake at 275 degrees for 1 hour. Remove to wire rack to cool. Wrap in foil. Store in airtight container for several weeks.

Approx Per Serving: Cal 776; Prot 9 g; Carbo 82 g; T Fat 47 g; 54% Calories from Fat; Chol 124 mg; Fiber 2 g; Sod 479 mg

Judy O'Brien, Blue Spruce HFH, Evergreen, CO

When one six-year-old was told that Christmas would be slim, he said, "It doesn't matter. I have my house."

CATHARINE P. ENGLE
BARRY COUNTY HFH

Skeakagor (Swedish Dessert Sand Cookies)

Yield: 48 servings

This is a traditional southern Swedish recipe given to me by my sister-in-law. It was given to her by her mother.

14 tablespoons butter	**1/2 teaspoon hjorthornsalt**
1 cup sugar	**1 tablespoon vanilla sugar**
2 cups plus 2 tablespoons flour	

Heat butter in saucepan until light brown, stirring frequently. Let stand until the next day. Stir butter until white in color. Add sugar; mix well. Stir in mixture of flour and hjorthornsalt. Add vanilla sugar; mix well. Flatten dough in bowl. Scoop with teaspoon; cup with other hand to form into walnut-shaped cookie. Place on cookie sheet. Bake at 260 degrees for 30 minutes or at 300 degrees for 22 minutes. Order hjorthornsalt through Anderson Butik, a Swedish import store, at 120 West Lincoln, P.O.Box 151, Lindsborg, Kansas 67456 or call 1-(913) 227-2183.

Approx Per Serving: Cal 67; Prot 1 g; Carbo 9 g; T Fat 3 g; 45% Calories from Fat; Chol 9 mg; Fiber <1 g; Sod 57 mg

Veda Bafford, HFH of Iredell-Statesville, Statesville, NC

Swedish Cardamom Cakes

Yield: 84 servings

1 cup butter, softened	**2 teaspoons baking powder**
2 cups sugar	**1/2 teaspoon salt**
2 eggs	**1 cup chopped almonds**
1 cup sour cream	**1 teaspoon ground cardamom**
3 1/2 cups flour	

Cream butter and sugar in mixer bowl until light and fluffy. Add eggs; mix well. Stir in sour cream. Add mixture of flour, baking powder and salt; mix well. Stir in almonds and cardamom. Spread batter in greased foil-lined 9x13-inch baking pan. Bake at 350 degrees for 45 to 50 minutes or until wooden pick inserted in center comes out clean. Cool in pan for 15 minutes. Invert onto wire rack to cool completely. Cut horizontally into 3 strips. Chill for several hours. Cut into 1/2-inch slices. Place on ungreased baking sheet. Bake at 300 degrees for 20 minutes; turn slices. Bake for 10 minutes longer. Remove to wire rack to cool. Store in airtight container.

Approx Per Serving: Cal 74; Prot 1 g; Carbo 9 g; T Fat 4 g; 45% Calories from Fat; Chol 12 mg; Fiber <1 g; Sod 46 mg

Jennifer Gregg, Marshall County HFH, Washburn, IL

One of my favorite stories involves one of our homeowners who agreed to move into a rather bad neighborhood. He and his family have stood firm in the face of danger, confronting drug dealers and taking them to court on every opportunity. Because of their courageous stand, the neighborhood has improved greatly and is well on its way to becoming a neighborhood geared to more wholesome families.

**VEDA BAFFORD
HFH OF IREDELL-STATESVILLE**

Tart Cherry Soup

Yield: 4 servings

1 cup flour
1 teaspoon baking powder
1 tablespoon sugar
1/8 teaspoon salt
2 eggs, beaten
1 tablespoon butter, softened
1/4 cup milk

3 cups tart cherries
3 cups water
2 cinnamon sticks, broken into
   1-inch pieces
1 tablespoon butter
1/2 cup (or more) sugar

Combine flour, baking powder, 1 tablespoon sugar and salt in bowl; mix well. Stir in eggs, 1 tablespoon butter and milk until blended. Combine cherries and water in saucepan. Add cinnamon pieces, 1 tablespoon butter and 1/2 cup sugar; mix well. Bring mixture to a boil, stirring occasionally. Drop flour mixture 1 teaspoon at a time into boiling cherry mixture. Cook for 4 to 5 minutes or until dumplings are firm. Discard cinnamon pieces.

Approx Per Serving: Cal 379; Prot 8 g; Carbo 67 g; T Fat 9 g; 22% Calories from Fat; Chol 124 mg; Fiber 2 g; Sod 251 mg

Dennis R. Hameister, Tri-County HFH, Centre Hall, PA

Tiramisù

Yield: 8 servings

5 egg yolks
1/2 cup sugar
8 ounces mascarpone cheese
1 tablespoon brandy
5 egg whites

1 tablespoon sugar
2/3 cup espresso or strong coffee
1 tablespoon brandy
24 ladyfingers
2 tablespoons baking cocoa

Beat egg yolks and 1/2 cup sugar in mixer bowl for 1 minute or until thick and lemon colored. Spoon into double boiler over boiling water; reduce heat. Cook over low heat for 8 to 10 minutes or until of desired consistency, stirring constantly. Remove from heat. Stir in mascarpone cheese and 1 tablespoon brandy. Beat egg whites in mixer bowl until soft peaks form. Add 1 tablespoon sugar, beating constantly until stiff peaks form. Fold in mascarpone mixture. Combine espresso and 1 tablespoon brandy in shallow dish; mix well. Dip 1 side of ladyfingers into brandy mixture. Layer ladyfingers, mascarpone cheese mixture and baking cocoa 1/2 at a time in 3-quart dish. Chill for 1 hour. May substitute creamed mixture of 8 ounces cream cheese, 1/4 cup sour cream and 2 tablespoons whipping cream for mascarpone cheese.

Approx Per Serving: Cal 333; Prot 10 g; Carbo 36 g; T Fat 16 g; 44% Calories from Fat; Chol 284 mg; Fiber 1 g; Sod 172 mg

Bonnie McManus, Mercer County HFH, Adamsville, PA

Très Léches

Yield: 15 servings

6 egg whites
2 cups sugar
6 egg yolks
2 cups flour
1 tablespoon baking powder
1/2 cup milk
1 tablespoon vanilla extract
11/2 (14-ounce) cans sweetened condensed milk

11/2 (12-ounce) cans evaporated milk
11/2 cups whipping cream
3 egg yolks, beaten
3 egg whites
3 tablespoons sugar

Beat 6 egg whites in mixer bowl until stiff peaks form. Add 2 cups sugar sugar, 6 egg yolks, flour, baking powder, milk and vanilla in order listed gradually; mix well. Spoon into ungreased 9x13-inch cake pan. Bake at 350 degrees for 30 minutes. Loosen cake from side of pan with sharp knife. Invert onto wire rack. Cool for 1 hour. Pierce cake with fork. Return to cake pan or appropriate container. Pour mixture of condensed milk, evaporated milk, whipping cream and 3 egg yolks over cake. Beat 3 egg whites in mixer bowl until soft peaks form. Add 3 tablespoons sugar gradually, beating constantly until stiff peaks form. Spread over cake; garnish with cherries. May substitute 1 cup honey for 3 tablespoons sugar in meringue.

Approx Per Serving:
Cal 483; Prot 12 g;
Carbo 69 g; T Fat 18 g;
34% Calories from Fat;
Chol 184 mg; Fiber <1 g;
Sod 203 mg

Jeanne Ahrend,
Mon County HFH,
Morgantown, WV

Photo by HFHI

A NEW HABITAT HOUSE GOES UP IN INDIA

AMARETTO
Amaretto Almond Cheesecake, 106
Chocolate Amaretto
    Cheesecake, 106

AMBROSIA
Ambrosia, 158
Ambrosia Cake, 34
Fruit Delight, 165
Mother's Ambrosia, 158

APPLE
All-Season Sweet Bread, 158
Apple and Pear Cheese Crisp, 93
Apple Cake, 34
Apple Cookies, 12
Apple Crisp, 92
Apple Crumb Pie, 75
Apple Dumplings, 91
Apple Nut Cake, 35
Apple Pudding, 97
Apple Supreme, 130
Apple Turnovers, 159
Baked Apple Pudding, 98
Baked Apple Rolls, 92
Cocoa Apple Cake, 36
Delicious Apple Pie Cake, 36
Divine Apple Crisp, 93
Easy Apple Crisp, 93
Easy Apple Macaroon, 94
Frosted Apple Cake, 35
Good Old Brown Betty, 162
Hal Ketchum's Maple-Glazed
    Apple Tart, 90
Homemade Apple Pie, 74
Knobby Apple Cake, 37
No-Added-Sugar Apple Pie, 159
No-Crust Apple Pie, 75
Old-Fashioned Apple Dumplings, 91
Quick Apple Cake, 37
Rich Apple Cake, 38
Roman Apple Cake, 38
Sugar-Free Apple Pie, 76
Winesap Apple Cake, 39

APPLESAUCE
Applesauce Cake, 39
Chocolate Applesauce Cake, 131
Granny's Applesauce Cake, 40

APRICOT
Apricot Baklava, 221
Apricot Cake, 40
Apricot Pies, 177
Bonbon Cake, 42
Do-Ahead Apricot Dessert, 98
No-Flour Chocolate Cake, 164
Scandinavian Sweet Soup, 229

BANANA
All-Season Sweet Bread, 158
Banana Muffins, 160
Banana Pudding, 99
Banana Raisin Date Bread, 161
Banana Snack Cake, 160

Banana Split Cake, 177
Banana Split Ice Cream, 116
Chocolate Banana Pecan Pie, 80
Creamy Banana Pudding, 99
Hummingbird Cake, 52

BLACKBERRY
Blackberry Pie, 76
Busy Day Jam Cake, 53
Galettes (French Waffle
    Cookies), 224

BLUEBERRY
Berry Torte, 161
Blueberry Buckle, 94
Blueberry Cobbler, 95
Blueberry Delight, 178
Blueberry Kuchen, 95
Blueberry 'n Cheese Pie, 77
Fruit Sheet Pie, 142
Newman's Very Own Lemon
    Blueberry Cake, 54

Brandy Alexander Soufflé, 194

BROWNIES
Brownies, 22
Butterscotch Brownies, 22
Chocolate Nut Brownies, 133
Different Brownie Cookies, 13
Favorite Brownies, 23
Frosted Brownies, 23
Low-Fat Brownies, 162
Old-Fashioned Brownies, 24
Simply Delicious Brownies, 24
Zucchini Brownies, 155

BUTTERSCOTCH. See also Caramel
Butterscotch Brownies, 22
Chocolate Scotcheroos, 135
Seven-Layer Bars, 31

CAKES. See also Cakes, Pound;
    Cupcakes
Ambrosia Cake, 34
Apple Cake, 34
Apple Nut Cake, 35
Applesauce Cake, 39
Apricot Cake, 40
Banana Snack Cake, 160
Basic Layer Cake, 41
Bishop's Cake, 41
Bonbon Cake, 42
Busy Day Jam Cake, 53
Candy Bar Cake, 42
Caramel Chocolate Cake, 43
Carrot Cake, 43
Carrot Cake with Cream Cheese
    Frosting, 44
Carrot Zucchini Cake, 45
Celebration Cake, 46
Chocolate Applesauce Cake, 131
Chocolate Chip Cake, 47
Chocolate Cocoa Cake, 163
Chocolate Sheet Cake, 47

Chocolate Sheet Cake with Pecan
    Fudge Frosting, 135
Coca-Cola Cake, 48
Cocoa Apple Cake, 36
Coconut Cake, 50
Coke Cake, 49
Cola Cake, 49
Cranberry Orange Cake, 201
Crazy Cake, 165
Cream of Coconut Cake, 50
Date Nut Loaf, 51
Death by Chocolate, 72
Delicious Apple Pie Cake, 36
Divine Carrot Cake, 44
Fabulous Carrot Cake, 45
Frosted Apple Cake, 35
Fruitcakes, 185, 203
Fruit Cocktail Cake, 51
Funny Cake, 52
Granny's Applesauce Cake, 40
Heavenly Light Dessert, 167
Hummingbird Cake, 52
Knobby Apple Cake, 37
Lazy Man's Cake, 53
Lemon Cake Squares, 143
Lemon Pudding Cake, 55
Lemony Pudding Cake, 55
Mandarin Orange Cake, 57
Mississippi Mud Cake, 56
Moist Chocolate Cake, 46
Murder by Chocolate, 136
Newman's Very Own Lemon
    Blueberry Cake, 54
No-Flour Chocolate Cake, 164
Norwegian Chocolate Cake, 226
Only-Four-Steps Cake, 56
Orange Scotch Cake, 146
Orange Slice Cake, 57
Plum Cake, 58
Poor Man's Cake, 58
Poppy Seed Cake, 59
Prune Cake, 64
Pumpkin Cake, 209
Pumpkin Cake Roll, 211
Pumpkin Gingerbread, 151
Pumpkin Praline Cake, 210
Pumpkin Upside-Down Cake, 209
Quick Apple Cake, 37
Raisin Loaf Cake, 65
Rich Apple Cake, 38
Roman Apple Cake, 38
Rompin' Rutabaga Cake, 65
Scripture Cake, 66
Snackin' Cake, 66
Sponge Cake, 174
Swedish Cardamom Cakes, 230
Swedish Walnut Cake, 68
Texas Sheet Cake, 67
Tomato Soup Cake, 67
Tres Leches, 232
Turtle Cake, 68
Tutti-Frutti Pudding Cake, 218
White Chocolate Cake, 48
Winesap Apple Cake, 39
Zucchini Chocolate Cake, 69

CAKES, POUND
Black Walnut Coconut Pound
  Cake, 60
Buttermilk Pound Cakes, 61
Butter Pound Cake, 61
Caramel Nut Pound Cake, 62
Chocolate Pound Cake, 61
Company Sour Cream Pound
  Cake, 63
Easy Pound Cake, 62
Lemony Sour Cream Pound
  Cake, 64
Pound Cake, 60
Sour Cream Pound Cake, 63

CANDY
Almond Roca, 8
Amy Grant's Iced Pecan Halves, 11
Best-Ever Pralines, 11
Buckeye Balls, 179
Caramel Corn Pops, 130
Chocolate Marshmallow Church
  Windows, 9
Date Balls, 183
Fudge Delight, 9
Incredible Caramels, 8
Lemon Fudge, 9
Microwave Peanut Brittle, 10
Peanut Butter Balls, 147
Praline Graham Yummies, 150
Smith College Fudge, 10
Super Pralines, 12

CARAMEL. *See also* Butterscotch
Caramel Chocolate Cake, 43
Caramel Cookies, 14
Caramel Corn Pops, 130
Caramel Nut Pound Cake, 62
Caramel Pies, 77
Chocolate Nut Brownies, 133
German Chocolate Caramel
  Bars, 132
Incredible Caramels, 8
Turtle Cake, 68

CARROT
Carrot Cake, 43
Carrot Cake with Cream Cheese
  Frosting, 44
Carrot Zucchini Cake, 45
Divine Carrot Cake, 44
Fabulous Carrot Cake, 45

CHEESECAKES
Amaretto Almond Cheesecake, 106
Chocolate Amaretto
  Cheesecake, 106
Chocolate Tofu Cheesecake, 163
Company Cheesecake, 107
Easy Cheesecake, 107
Easy Praline Cheesecake, 110
Grasshopper Cheesecake, 206
Individual Lime Cheesecakes, 169
Jessica's Cheesecake, 108
Lee's Praline Cheesecake, 111

Lemon Cheesecake, 108
Light Pumpkin Cheesecake, 213
Lime Cheesecake, 207
Mini Cheesecakes, 109
No-Bake Lemon Cheesecake, 109
Peanut Butter Cheesecake, 147
Praline Cheesecake, 110
Pumpkin Cheesecake, 212
Secret Cheesecake, 111

CHERRY
Almond and Cherry Butter
  Cookies, 194
Angel Cake Dessert, 176
Baked Chocolate-Covered
  Cherries, 196
Banana Split Ice Cream, 116
Best-in-Town Cherry Pie, 78
Cherries-in-the-Snow, 179
Cherries-on-Snow, 126
Cherry Cobbler, 96
Cherry Delight, 96
Cherry Fantasy, 131
Cherry Pudding, 101
Cherry Surprise, 78
Cherry Walnut Christmas
  Bars, 196
Chocolate Cherry Bars, 25
Chocolate Fruit Cookie Bars, 26
Easy Cheesecake, 107
Fruitcakes, 185, 203
Fruit Pizza, 141
Fruit Squares, 29
Ladyfinger Delight, 186
Layered Fruit Fluff, 140
Pineapple and Cherry Dump
  Cake, 149
Punch Bowl Cake, 151
Tart Cherry Soup, 231

CHOCOLATE
Almond Roca, 8
Any-Occasion Chocolate Pie, 79
Baked Chocolate-Covered
  Cherries, 196
Bittersweet Chocolate Torte, 136
Black Bottom Cupcakes, 69
Blender Mousse, 125
Bonbon Cake, 42
Brownies, 22
Buckeye Balls, 179
Buster Bar Dessert, 117
Candy Bar Cake, 42
Caramel Chocolate Cake, 43
Celebration Cake, 46
Chocolate Amaretto
  Cheesecake, 106
Chocolate Applesauce Cake, 131
Chocolate Caramel Nut
  Bars, 132
Chocolate Cherry Bars, 25
Chocolate Chip Cake, 47
Chocolate Cocoa Cake, 163
Chocolate Coffee Cupcakes, 70
Chocolate Cookies, 180

Chocolate Cream Pie, 180
Chocolate Dessert, 102
Chocolate Eclair Cake, 181
Chocolate Eclair Torte, 112
Chocolate Fudge
  Upside-Down Dessert, 102
Chocolate Layer Dessert, 133
Chocolate Marshmallow Church
  Windows, 9
Chocolate Mint Cream, 118
Chocolate Mint Dessert, 197
Chocolate Mint Snaps, 134
Chocolate Nut Brownies, 133
Chocolate Pie, 79
Chocolate Pound Cake, 61
Chocolate Satin Pie, 180
Chocolate Scotcheroos, 135
Chocolate Sheet Cake, 47
Chocolate Sheet Cake with Pecan
  Fudge Frosting, 135
Chocolate Streusel Bars, 27
Chocolate Tofu Cheesecake, 163
Chocolate Truffle Mousse, 126
Chocolate Walnut Bread
  Pudding, 100
Coca-Cola Cake, 48
Cocoa Apple Cake, 36
Cocoa Cheese Sandwich
  Cookies, 16
Coffee Ice Cream Dessert, 117
Coke Cake, 49
Cola Cake, 49
Cookie Whip, 181
Crazy Cake, 165
Crème de Menthe Squares, 201
Death by Chocolate, 72
Delightful Ice Cream Pie, 119
Different Brownie Cookies, 13
Dirt Cake, 183
Dirt Dessert, 184
Drumstick Dessert, 103
Easy-as-Pie, 81
Favorite Brownies, 23
French Silk Chocolate Pie, 80
Frosted Brownies, 23
Frozen Yummy Dessert, 125
Fudge Delight, 9
Fudge Squares, 30
Fudgy Orange Cappuccino
  Torte, 204
Funny Cake, 52
German Chocolate Caramel
  Bars, 132
Gobs, 18
Grasshopper Cheesecake, 206
Ho-Ho Bars, 30
Hot Fudge Pudding Cake, 103
Kahlúa Punch Bowl Cake, 152
Lazy Man's Cake, 53
Low-Fat Brownies, 162
Mississippi Mud Cake, 56
Mocha Fudge Pie, 82
Moist Chocolate Cake, 46
Murder by Chocolate, 136
No-Flour Chocolate Cake, 164

Norwegian Chocolate Cake, 226
Old-Fashioned Brownies, 24
Peanut Butter Balls, 147
Peanut Chocolate Dessert, 148
People Chow, 190
Rocky Road Bars, 192
Simply Delicious Brownies, 24
Smith College Fudge, 10
Texas Sheet Cake, 67
Truly Different Cupcakes, 71
Turtle Cake, 68
Yummy Dessert, 192
Zucchini Chocolate Cake, 69

CHOCOLATE CHIP
Black Bottom Cupcakes, 69
Brownies, 22
Caramel Cookies, 14
Celebration Cake, 46
Chocolate Banana Pecan
    Pie, 80
Chocolate Caramel Nut Bars, 132
Chocolate Chip Cake, 47
Chocolate Chip Cookies, 14
Chocolate Chip Pie, 81
Chocolate Fruit Cookie Bars, 26
Chocolate Nut Brownies, 133
Chocolate Peanut Butter Surprise
    Bars, 26
Chocolate Pecan Bars, 27
Chocolate Streusel Bars, 27
Cocoa Apple Cake, 36
Coconut Chocolate Chip Tea
    Cakes, 16
Cookie Brittle, 139
Cowboy Cookies, 17
German Chocolate Caramel
    Bars, 132
Hillary Clinton's Chocolate Chip
    Cookies, 15
Lentil Oatmeal Cookies, 168
Pots de Crème, 191
Rich Chocolate Chip Cookies, 134
Seven-Layer Bars, 31
Surprise Pudding, 104
Take-a-Break Chocolate Chip
    Cookies, 15
Toll House Pie, 88
Turtle Cake, 68
Zucchini Brownies, 155
Zucchini Cookies, 156

COBBLERS
Blueberry Buckle, 94
Blueberry Cobbler, 95
Blueberry Kuchen, 95
Cherry Cobbler, 96
Cherry Delight, 96
Divine Peach Cobbler, 146
Peach Cobbler, 97

COCONUT
Ambrosia, 158
Banana Split Cake, 177
Banana Split Ice Cream, 116

Black Walnut Coconut Pound
    Cake, 60
Brandied Bread Pudding, 221
Caramel Pies, 77
Carrot Cake, 43
Carrot Cake with Cream Cheese
    Frosting, 44
Celebration Cake, 46
Chocolate Cookies, 180
Coconut Cake, 50
Coconut Chocolate Chip Tea
    Cakes, 16
Cookie-Jar Specials, 17
Cream of Coconut Cake, 50
Date Balls, 183
Delight Dessert, 140
Flaky Golden Angel Pie, 74
Japanese Fruit Pie, 82
Mandarin Orange Cake, 57
Mississippi Mud Cake, 56
Mother's Ambrosia, 158
Oatmeal Cookies, 20
Oatmeal Pie, 84
Orange Slice Cake, 57
Seven-Layer Bars, 31
Snackin' Cake, 66
Zucchini Chocolate Cake, 69

COFFEE
Chocolate Coffee Cupcakes, 70
Coffee Ice Cream Dessert, 117
Delightful Ice Cream Pie, 119
Mocha Fudge Pie, 82
Old English Cookies, 208
Texas Sheet Cake, 67
Tiramisù, 231

COOKIES. See also Cookies, Bar
Almond and Cherry Butter
    Cookies, 194
Amish Cookies, 220
Anise Cookies, 220
Apple Cookies, 12
Baked Chocolate-Covered
    Cherries, 196
Black Hearts (Spice Cookies), 13
Cheese Crisps, 195
Chocolate Chip Cookies, 14
Chocolate Cookies, 180
Chocolate Mint Snaps, 134
Cocoa Cheese Sandwich
    Cookies, 16
Coconut Chocolate Chip Tea
    Cakes, 16
Cookie Brittle, 139
Cookie-Jar Specials, 17
Cowboy Cookies, 17
Cream Cheese Cookies, 17
Crunchy Cookies, 182
Date-Filled Oatmeal Cookies, 223
Different Brownie Cookies, 13
Galettes (French Waffle
    Cookies), 224
Giant Ginger Cookies, 205
Gingerbread Men, 205

Gobs, 18
Grandma's Molasses Cookies, 145
Granny's Spice Cookies, 217
Granola Cereal Cookies, 18
Guess-Again Cookies, 19
Hillary Clinton's Chocolate Chip
    Cookies, 15
Holly Sprigs, 206
Hungarian Cookies, 225
Icebox Cookies, 142
Iced Lemon Cookies, 143
Kringles, 207
Lemon Cookies, 19
Lentil Oatmeal Cookies, 168
Macadamia Nut White Chocolate
    Chip Cookies, 208
Meringue Puffs, 169
Oatmeal Cookies, 20
Old English Cookies, 208
Old-Fashioned Sugar Cookies, 153
Pfefferneusse or Pepper Nuts, 228
Rich Chocolate Chip Cookies, 134
Rosalynn Carter's Raisin Oatmeal
    Cookies, 172
Skeakagor (Swedish Dessert Sand
    Cookies), 230
Snickerdoodles, 20
Sugar Cookies, 21
Take-a-Break Chocolate Chip
    Cookies, 15
Texas Crunch Cookies, 21
Zucchini Cookies, 156

COOKIES, BAR
Brownies, 22
Butterscotch Brownies, 22
Butterscotch Grahams, 195
Caramel Cookies, 14
Cheesecake Bars, 25
Cherry Walnut Christmas Bars, 196
Chewy Cream Cheese Bars, 28
Chocolate Caramel Nut Bars, 132
Chocolate Cherry Bars, 25
Chocolate Fruit Cookie Bars, 26
Chocolate Nut Brownies, 133
Chocolate Peanut Butter Surprise
    Bars, 26
Chocolate Pecan Bars, 27
Chocolate Scotcheroos, 135
Chocolate Streusel Bars, 27
Crème de Menthe Squares, 201
Crispy Rice Bars, 182
Date and Nut Squares, 29
Date Nut Bars, 28
Favorite Brownies, 23
Frosted Brownies, 23
Frosty Strawberry Squares, 32
Fruit Squares, 29
Fudge Squares, 30
German Chocolate Caramel
    Bars, 132
Graham Cracker Cake Squares, 186
Ho-Ho Bars, 30
Low-Fat Brownies, 162
Old-Fashioned Brownies, 24

Peanut Butter Swirls, 31
Pecan Pie Bars, 149
Rocky Road Bars, 192
Santa Ynez Valley Toffee Bars, 154
Seven-Layer Bars, 31
Simply Delicious Brownies, 24
Tipper Gore's Tennessee Treats, 32
Zucchini Brownies, 155

CRANBERRY
Cranberry and Hazelnut Pie, 200
Cranberry Freeze, 198
Cranberry Orange Cake, 201
Cranberry Pie, 198
Delicious Cranberry Pie, 199
Honey's Cranberry Pie, 199
New England Cranberry and Pear
    Pie, 200

CRISPS
Apple and Pear Cheese Crisp, 93
Apple Crisp, 92
Divine Apple Crisp, 93
Easy Apple Crisp, 93
Easy Apple Macaroon, 94
Good Old Brown Betty, 162

CUPCAKES
Black Bottom Cupcakes, 69
Castle Cakes with Cream Sauce, 70
Chocolate Coffee Cupcakes, 70
Truly Different Cupcakes, 71

DATES
Banana Raisin Date Bread, 161
Carrot Cake with Cream Cheese
    Frosting, 44
Chocolate Fruit Cookie Bars, 26
Date and Nut Squares, 29
Date Balls, 183
Date-Filled Oatmeal Cookies, 223
Date Nut Bars, 28
Date Nut Loaf, 51
Fruitcakes, 185, 203
Granny's Applesauce Cake, 40
Orange Slice Cake, 57
Scripture Cake, 66
Tipper Gore's Tennessee Treats, 32

DUMPLINGS
Apple Dumplings, 91
Apple Turnovers, 159
Baked Apple Rolls, 92
Old-Fashioned Apple Dumplings, 91

FROSTINGS. See also Individual Cakes
Carrot Cake with Cream Cheese
    Frosting, 44
Chocolate Sheet Cake with Pecan
    Fudge Frosting, 135
Ersatz Whipped Cream Frosting, 71

FROZEN DESSERTS
Buster Bar Dessert, 117
Chocolate Mint Cream, 118

Coffee Ice Cream Dessert, 117
Cranberry Freeze, 198
Crème de Menthe Pie, 118
Daiquiri Delight, 119
Delightful Ice Cream Pie, 119
Frozen Fresh Peaches in Orange
    Juice, 171
Frozen Lemon Dessert, 144
Frozen Peanut Butter Pies, 122
Frozen Yummy Dessert, 125
Ice Cream Cake, 120
Key Lime Pie, 121
Lemon Custard, 121
Oreo Ice Cream Pies, 122
Peanut Butter Yogurt Pie, 123
Pear Ice Cream Dessert with
    Raspberry Sauce, 123
Pumpkin Squares, 124
Rainbow Dessert, 124
Three-In-One Sherbet, 173

FRUIT COCKTAIL
Angel Fluff, 176
Fruit Cocktail Cake, 51
Mixed Fruit Dessert, 166
Tutti-Frutti Pudding Cake, 218

GRAPE
Blueberry Delight, 178
Company Fruit Pizza, 141
Fruit Parfait, 166
Fruit Pizza, 141
Grapes Juanita, 167

Houska (Czech Holiday Bread), 224

ICE CREAM
Banana Split Ice Cream, 116
Buster Bar Dessert, 117
Coffee Ice Cream Dessert, 117
Delightful Ice Cream Pie, 119
Frozen Yummy Dessert, 125
Ice Cream and Chocolate Chip
    Cookie with Java, 120
Ice Cream Cake, 120
Old-Fashioned Homemade Ice
    Cream, 116
Orange Juice Ice Cream, 170
Oreo Ice Cream Pies, 122
Pear Ice Cream Dessert with
    Raspberry Sauce, 123
Pumpkin Squares, 124
Rainbow Dessert, 124

LEMON
Bob Hope's Favorite Lemon Pie, 83
Different Brownie Cookies, 13
English Lemon Curd Tart, 223
Frozen Lemon Dessert, 144
Iced Lemon Cookies, 143
Lemon Cake Squares, 143
Lemon Cheesecake, 108
Lemon Cookies, 19
Lemon Cream Angel Cake, 187
Lemon Custard, 121

Lemon Delight, 187
Lemon Dessert, 144
Lemon Fudge, 9
Lemon Mousse, 128
Lemon Pecan Tarts, 145
Lemon Pudding Cake, 55
Lemon Snow, 168
Lemon Sponge Pie, 83
Lemony Pudding Cake, 55
Lemony Sour Cream Pound
    Cake, 64
Mock Pineapple Cheese Pie, 171
Newman's Very Own Lemon
    Blueberry Cake, 54
No-Bake Lemon Cheesecake, 109
Rainbow Dessert, 124

LIME
Hawaiian Pineapple Dessert, 171
Ice Cream Cake, 120
Individual Lime Cheesecakes, 169
Key Lime Pie, 121
Lime Cheesecake, 207
Lime Pie, 84
Lime Swirl, 188
Northern Key Lime Pie, 84

MINT
Chocolate Mint Cream, 118
Chocolate Mint Dessert, 197
Chocolate Mint Snaps, 134
Crème de Menthe Pie, 118
Crème de Menthe Squares, 201
Grasshopper Cheesecake, 206

MOUSSES
Blender Mousse, 125
Cherries-on-Snow, 126
Chocolate Truffle Mousse, 126
Gone-with-the-Wind, 127
Lemon Mousse, 128
Pumpkin Mousse, 213
Raspberry Mousse, 128
White Chocolate Mousse, 127

MUFFINS
Banana Muffins, 160
Low-Fat Cinnamon and Oatmeal
    Muffins, 164

OATMEAL
Chocolate Cookies, 180
Cowboy Cookies, 17
Date-Filled Oatmeal Cookies, 223
Lentil Oatmeal Cookies, 168
Low-Fat Cinnamon and Oatmeal
    Muffins, 164
Oatmeal Cookies, 20
Oatmeal Pie, 84
Rosalynn Carter's Raisin Oatmeal
    Cookies, 172
Snackin' Cake, 66

ORANGE
Ambrosia, 158

Ambrosia Cake, 34
Cranberry Orange Cake, 201
Creamy Orange Dessert, 170
Easy Fruit Dessert, 185
Frozen Fresh Peaches in Orange
    Juice, 171
Fruit Delight, 165
Fudgy Orange Cappuccino
    Torte, 204
Ice Cream Cake, 120
Mandarin Orange Cake, 57
Mixed Fruit Dessert, 166
Mother's Ambrosia, 158
Orange Juice Ice Cream, 170
Orange Scotch Cake, 146
Orange Slice Cake, 57

PASTRIES. *See also* Pies; Tarts
Apricot Baklava, 221
Butter Kuchen, 222
Coffee Cake, 138
Danish Puff, 203
Easy Pastry, 89
Mom's Best Cinnamon Rolls, 137
Nut Rolls, 138
Philadelphia Danish, 139
Pie Pastry, 89
Potica (Slovenian Nut Roll), 227

PEACH
Amazing Peach Pudding, 104
Divine Peach Cobbler, 146
Frozen Fresh Peaches in Orange
    Juice, 171
Heavenly Light Dessert, 167
Peach Cobbler, 97
Peach Cream Pie, 85
Peach Custard Pie, 85
Rainbow Dessert, 124
Sherry Trifle, 216

PEANUT
Apple Supreme, 130
Buster Bar Dessert, 117
Chocolate Peanut Butter Surprise
    Bars, 26
Chocolate Scotcheroos, 135
Company Peanut Butter Pie, 189
Creamy Peanut Butter Pie, 188
Drumstick Dessert, 103
Frozen Peanut Butter Pies, 122
Microwave Peanut Brittle, 10
Peanut Butter Balls, 147
Peanut Butter Cheesecake, 147
Peanut Butter Cream Pie, 190
Peanut Butter Crisps, 148
Peanut Butter Pie, 85
Peanut Butter Swirls, 31
Peanut Butter Yogurt Pie, 123
Peanut Chocolate Dessert, 148
People Chow, 190
Rich Peanut Butter Pie, 189

PECAN
Amy Grant's Iced Pecan Halves, 11

Best-Ever Pralines, 11
Caramel Nut Pound Cake, 62
Chocolate Banana Pecan Pie, 80
Chocolate Pecan Bars, 27
Chocolate Sheet Cake with Pecan
    Fudge Frosting, 135
Fruitcakes, 185, 203
Lemon Pecan Tarts, 145
Nut Rolls, 138
Pecan Pie Bars, 149
Super Pralines, 12

PIES. *See also* Tarts
Any-Occasion Chocolate Pie, 79
Apple Crumb Pie, 75
Apricot Pies, 177
Best-in-Town Cherry Pie, 78
Blackberry Pie, 76
Blueberry 'n Cheese Pie, 77
Bob Hope's Favorite Lemon Pie, 83
Caramel Pies, 77
Cherry Surprise, 78
Chess Pie, 78
Chocolate Banana Pecan Pie, 80
Chocolate Chip Pie, 81
Chocolate Cream Pie, 180
Chocolate Pie, 79
Chocolate Satin Pie, 180
Company Peanut Butter Pie, 189
Cranberry and Hazelnut Pie, 200
Cranberry Pie, 198
Creamy Peanut Butter Pie, 188
Crème de Menthe Pie, 118
Dark and Spicy Pumpkin Pie, 214
Delicious Cranberry Pie, 199
Delightful Ice Cream Pie, 119
Easy-as-Pie, 81
Flaky Golden Angel Pie, 74
French Silk Chocolate Pie, 80
Frozen Peanut Butter Pies, 122
Fruit Sheet Pie, 142
Homemade Apple Pie, 74
Homemade Pumpkin Pie, 214
Honey's Cranberry Pie, 199
Japanese Fruit Pie, 82
Key Lime Pie, 121
Lemon Sponge Pie, 83
Lime Pie, 84
Mocha Fudge Pie, 82
Mock Pineapple Cheese Pie, 171
Mom's Sugar Pies, 88
New England Cranberry and Pear
    Pie, 200
No-Added-Sugar Apple Pie, 159
No-Crust Apple Pie, 75
Northern Key Lime Pie, 84
Oatmeal Pie, 84
Oreo Ice Cream Pies, 122
Peach Cream Pie, 85
Peach Custard Pie, 85
Peanut Butter Cream Pie, 190
Peanut Butter Pie, 85
Peanut Butter Yogurt Pie, 123
Pennsylvania Dutch Shoofly
    Pies, 226

Praline Pumpkin Pie, 216
Pudding Pie, 191
Pumpkin Chiffon Pie, 215
Pumpkin Pie, 172
Raisin Cream Pie, 86
Raspberry Cream Pie, 87
Raspberry Pie, 87
Rich Peanut Butter Pie, 189
Sour Cream Raisin Pie, 86
Strawberry Pie, 88
Sugar-Free Apple Pie, 76
Toll House Pie, 88

PINEAPPLE
All-Season Sweet Bread, 158
Ambrosia Cake, 34
Apple Supreme, 130
Apricot Pies, 177
Banana Split Cake, 177
Banana Split Ice Cream, 116
Blueberry Delight, 178
Carrot Cake, 43
Carrot Cake with Cream Cheese
    Frosting, 44
Company Fruit Pizza, 141
Company Punch Bowl
    Cake, 152
Cranberry Freeze, 198
Creamy Orange Dessert, 170
Daiquiri Delight, 119
Easy Fruit Dessert, 185
Fruitcakes, 203
Fruit Delight, 165
Fruit Pizza, 141
Gone-with-the-Wind, 127
Great Pineapple Dessert, 150
Hawaiian Pineapple Dessert, 171
Hummingbird Cake, 52
Japanese Fruit Pie, 82
Mixed Fruit Dessert, 166
Mother's Ambrosia, 158
Pavlova, 113
Pineapple and Cherry Dump
    Cake, 149
Punch Bowl Cake, 151
Swedish Walnut Cake, 68

PIZZA
Company Fruit Pizza, 141
Fruit Pizza, 141

Play Dough, 156

PRALINE
Best-Ever Pralines, 11
Easy Praline Cheesecake, 110
Lee's Praline Cheesecake, 111
Praline Cheesecake, 110
Praline Graham Yummies, 150
Praline Pumpkin Pie, 216
Pumpkin Praline Cake, 210
Super Pralines, 12

PRUNE
Chocolate Cocoa Cake, 163

Prune Cake, 64
Scandinavian Sweet Soup, 229

PUDDINGS
Amazing Peach Pudding, 104
Apple Pudding, 97
Apple Supreme, 130
Baked Apple Pudding, 98
Banana Pudding, 99
Berry Delight, 178
Brandied Bread Pudding, 221
Bread Pudding with Rum
    Sauce, 100
Cherry Pudding, 101
Chocolate Dessert, 102
Chocolate Fudge Upside-Down
    Dessert, 102
Chocolate Walnut Bread
    Pudding, 100
Creamy Banana Pudding, 99
Do-Ahead Apricot Dessert, 98
Drumstick Dessert, 103
French Pudding, 184
Gary Redenbacher's Créme
    Brûlée, 202
Great-Grandmother's Bread
    Pudding, 101
Hot Fudge Pudding Cake, 103
Mexican Flan, 225
Old-Fashioned Rice Pudding, 173
Ozark Pudding, 104
Pots de Crème, 191
Pudding Pie, 191
Sailor Duff, 228
Surprise Pudding, 104
Tapioca Pudding, 174

PUMPKIN
Dark and Spicy Pumpkin Pie, 214
Homemade Pumpkin Pie, 214
Light Pumpkin Cheesecake, 213
Praline Pumpkin Pie, 216
Pumpkin Cake, 209
Pumpkin Cake Roll, 211
Pumpkin Cheesecake, 212
Pumpkin Chiffon Pie, 215
Pumpkin Dip, 211
Pumpkin Gingerbread, 151
Pumpkin Mousse, 213
Pumpkin Pie, 172
Pumpkin Praline Cake, 210
Pumpkin Squares, 124
Pumpkin Upside-Down Cake, 209
Sugar-Free Pumpkin Chiffon
    Dessert, 215

RAISIN
Banana Raisin Date Bread, 161
Fruitcakes, 185
Icebox Cookies, 142

Lemon Pecan Tarts, 145
Old English Cookies, 208
Orange Scotch Cake, 146
Poor Man's Cake, 58
Potica (Slovenian Nut Roll), 227
Raisin Cream Pie, 86
Raisin Loaf Cake, 65
Rompin' Rutabaga Cake, 65
Rosalynn Carter's Raisin Oatmeal
    Cookies, 172
Scripture Cake, 66
Sour Cream Raisin Pie, 86

RASPBERRY
Berry Torte, 161
Bittersweet Chocolate Torte, 136
Chocolate Truffle Mousse, 126
Fruit Squares, 29
Ice Cream Cake, 120
Lemon Mousse, 128
Mocha Shortbread with Raspberry
    Sauce, 217
Pear Ice Cream Dessert with
    Raspberry Sauce, 123
Rainbow Dessert, 124
Raspberry Cream Pie, 87
Raspberry Mousse, 128
Raspberry Pie, 87
Schaum Tortes, 114
Sherry Trifle, 216

SHORTBREAD
Grandma Nixon's Scotch
    Shortbread, 229
Mocha Shortbread with Raspberry
    Sauce, 217
Scottish Shortbread, 229

STRAWBERRY
Berry Torte, 161
Company Fruit Pizza, 141
Company Punch Bowl Cake, 152
Frosty Strawberry Squares, 32
Pavlova, 113
Strawberry Delight, 153
Strawberry Pie, 88
Strawberry Trifle, 218
White Chocolate Fruit Tart, 197

TARTS
Butter Tarts, 90
English Lemon Curd Tart, 223
Hal Ketchum's Maple-Glazed Apple
    Tart, 90
Lemon Pecan Tarts, 145
White Chocolate Fruit Tart, 197

TORTES
Berry Torte, 161
Bittersweet Chocolate Torte, 136

Chocolate Eclair Torte, 112
Company Schaum Torte, 114
Fudgy Orange Cappuccino
    Torte, 204
Graham Cracker Torte, 112
Pavlova, 113
Schaum Tortes, 114

TRIFLES
Cherries-in-the-Snow, 179
Company Punch Bowl Cake, 152
Kahlúa Punch Bowl Cake, 152
Ladyfinger Delight, 186
Lemon Cream Angel Cake, 187
Punch Bowl Cake, 151
Sherry Trifle, 216
Strawberry Trifle, 218
Tiramisù, 231

WALNUT
Apple Cake, 34
Black Walnut Coconut Pound
    Cake, 60
Busy Day Jam Cake, 53
Carrot Cake, 43
Carrot Zucchini Cake, 45
Cherry Walnut Christmas Bars, 196
Chocolate Caramel Nut Bars, 132
Chocolate Walnut Bread
    Pudding, 100
Date and Nut Squares, 29
Date Nut Loaf, 51
Divine Carrot Cake, 44
Frosted Apple Cake, 35
Fudge Squares, 30
Hungarian Cookies, 225
Ice Cream Cake, 120
Lentil Oatmeal Cookies, 168
Potica (Slovenian Nut Roll), 227
Praline Cheesecake, 110
Pumpkin Upside-Down Cake, 209
Scripture Cake, 66
Swedish Walnut Cake, 68

WHITE CHOCOLATE
Fruit Pizza, 141
Macadamia Nut White Chocolate
    Chip Cookies, 208
White Chocolate Cake, 48
White Chocolate Fruit Tart, 197
White Chocolate Mousse, 127

ZUCCHINI
Best-Ever Zucchini Bread, 155
Carrot Zucchini Cake, 45
Zucchini Bread, 154
Zucchini Brownies, 155
Zucchini Chocolate Cake, 69
Zucchini Cookies, 156

To order additional copies of this cookbook, please contact your local Habitat for Humanity affiliate or campus chapter. If the cookbook is not available locally, you may order copies from Habitat for Humanity International.

❏ *From Our House to Yours* cookbook(s), #1410   Qty. _____   x $12.95   = _____
                                                      (6 or more: $10.95)

❏ *Home Sweet Habitat* cookbook(s), #1414   Qty. _____   x $12.95   = _____
                                                      (6 or more: $10.95)

❏ *From Our House to Yours* and *Home Sweet Habitat*   Qty. _____   x $23.95   = _____
    cookbook set(s), #1415   (3 or more: $21.90)

                         Postage and Handling (see chart below) $ _____

                                      Total Amount $ _____

Name _____

Address _____

City _____ State _____ Zip _____

Method of Payment (no cash):

❏ Check   ❏ Money Order   ❏ VISA   ❏ MasterCard   Card Number_____

Expires_____ Phone (_____)_____ Signature _____

Postage and Handling (USA only):

Order Total:	Charges:
$10.00 or less	$ 2.00
$10.00–$19.99	$ 2.75
$20.00–$49.99	$ 5.00
$50.00–$99.99	$ 7.00
$100.00 or more	$11.00

Mail order and payment to:
Habitat for Humanity International
121 Habitat Street
Americus, Georgia 31709-3498

To order by phone: 1 (800) 422-5914
or **Fax** (912) 924-5730

Thank you for your order.

To order additional copies of this cookbook, please contact your local Habitat for Humanity affiliate or campus chapter. If the cookbook is not available locally, you may order copies from Habitat for Humanity International.

❏ *From Our House to Yours* cookbook(s), #1410   Qty. _____   x $12.95   = _____
                                                      (6 or more: $10.95)

❏ *Home Sweet Habitat* cookbook(s), #1414   Qty. _____   x $12.95   = _____
                                                      (6 or more: $10.95)

❏ *From Our House to Yours* and *Home Sweet Habitat*   Qty. _____   x $23.95   = _____
    cookbook set(s), #1415   (3 or more: $21.90)

                         Postage and Handling (see chart below) $ _____

                                      Total Amount $ _____

Name _____

Address _____

City _____ State _____ Zip _____

Method of Payment (no cash):

❏ Check   ❏ Money Order   ❏ VISA   ❏ MasterCard   Card Number_____

Expires_____ Phone (_____)_____ Signature _____

Postage and Handling (USA only):

Order Total:	Charges:
$10.00 or less	$ 2.00
$10.00–$19.99	$ 2.75
$20.00–$49.99	$ 5.00
$50.00–$99.99	$ 7.00
$100.00 or more	$11.00

Mail order and payment to:
Habitat for Humanity International
121 Habitat Street
Americus, Georgia 31709-3498

To order by phone: 1 (800) 422-5914
or **Fax** (912) 924-5730

Thank you for your order.